CONTESTED TAIWAN

TAIWAN AND THE WORLD

William Lavely, Madeleine Yue Dong, James Lin

Series Editors

Lev Nachman

CONTESTED TAIWAN

Sovereignty, Social Movements, and Party Formation

UNIVERSITY OF WASHINGTON PRESS SEATTLE

Contested Taiwan was made possible in part by funding from the Taiwan Studies Program, a division of the Henry M. Jackson School of International Studies at the University of Washington.

Additional support for this publication was provided by the Chiang Ching-kuo Foundation for International Scholarly Exchange.

This book will be made open access within three years of publication thanks to Path to Open, a program developed to bring about equitable access and impact for the entire scholarly community, including authors, researchers, libraries, and university presses around the world. Learn more at https://about.jstor.org/path-to-open/.

Design by Mindy Basinger Hill / Composed in Adobe Garamond Pro

UNIVERSITY OF WASHINGTON PRESS *uwapress.uw.edu*

Library of Congress Cataloging-in-Publication Data
Names: Nachman, Lev author
Title: Contested Taiwan : sovereignty, social movements, and party formation / Lev Nachman.
Other titles: Sovereignty, social movements, and party formation
Description: Seattle : University of Washington Press, 2025. | Series: Taiwan and the world | Includes bibliographical references and index.
Identifiers: LCCN 2025007201 (print) | LCCN 2025007202 (ebook) | ISBN 9780295753911 hardcover | ISBN 9780295753928 paperback | ISBN 9780295753935 ebook
Subjects: LCSH: Taiwan—Politics and government—2000- | Political parties—Taiwan—History—21st century | Sunflower Movement, Taiwan, 2014 | Protest movements—Taiwan—History—21st century | National characteristics, Taiwan
Classification: LCC JQ1539.A45 N33 2025 (print) | LCC JQ1539.A45 (ebook) | DDC 324.251249—dc23/eng/20250410
LC record available at https://lccn.loc.gov/2025007201
LC ebook record available at https://lccn.loc.gov/2025007202

∞ This paper meets the requirements of ANSI/NISO Z39.48-1992 (Permanence of Paper).

CONTENTS

For my first academic role models,

Marty and Ben Nachman

ACKNOWLEDGMENTS

I know it is a cliché for an academic to start off a book with "it takes a village," but my goodness, it is so true! I have been blessed with villages all around the world, in Omaha, Nebraska, Tacoma, Washington, Irvine, California, Nanjing, China, and, most important, in Taichung and Taipei, Taiwan. With the release of this book, the culmination of over ten years of research and work, it is hard not to reflect back to a time in my life when I had zero academic passion. I struggled in high school and had little affection for learning. In no way would the sixteen-year-old Lev think he would end up with an advanced degree in political science, working as a university professor, publishing books on Taiwanese politics. I am only here because of my villages, who for the last thirty-two years have collectively nurtured, challenged, and cultivated me into the person I am today. Of the many privileges I have in my life, my friends, mentors, and family—my villages—are the most precious. I am sincerely grateful for you all.

I must begin by expressing my deepest gratitude to my mentors at the University of California, Irvine. Their guidance has been crucial to my academic success; no number of words could express how grateful I am to them. Thank you to my advisor, Jeffrey Kopstein, for teaching me how to ask a question like a proper social scientist, and to Yang Su for teaching me how to answer a question like one. I am thankful to Samantha Vortherms for being a source of wisdom and support, especially during fieldwork. Thank you to Sara Goodman, who taught me how to navigate the world of academia and grow as a graduate student. I am grateful to Jeffrey Wasserstrom for his unending enthusiasm and encouragement, and for teaching me how to be an engaged public intellectual.

I am also grateful to those academic mentors whose guidance and encouragement prompted me to pursuit a PhD. Thank you to Karl Fields and Lotus Perry at the University of Puget Sound, who were the first to encourage me to study abroad in Taiwan and planted the idea that Taiwanese politics could be a long-term research agenda. Thank you to Professor Hua Tao, my advisor at the Hopkins Nanjing Center and one of my most influential teachers, who supported and advocated for my research on the Sunflower Movement and Taiwanese politics, despite being based in the People's Republic of China. I am also thankful to Roda Mushkat, Adam Webb, Cornelius Kubler, and David Arase for their guidance and encouragement when I was applying to PhD programs.

My year as the Hou Family Postdoctoral Fellow in Taiwan Studies at the Harvard Fairbank Center was a transformative experience, without which this book may have never seen the light of day. I am thankful to Michael Szonyi for teaching me how to write a book proposal and pitch to editors and for graciously helping me prepare for the job market during the COVID pandemic. I am indebted to Steve Goldstein and the Hou family for championing Taiwan studies at the Fairbank Center and supporting my research for so many years. I am especially grateful to my many academic colleagues in Boston, all of whom were sources of sanity, inspiration, and friendship during an especially turbulent time for recent graduates: Shane Lin, Yi-Tang Lin, Kevin Luo, James Evans, Lilly Lee, Ching-Shin Huang, Wei-Ting Chen, Aaron Glasserman, Chagai Weiss, and Joshua Friedman.

I am grateful to my amazing support network from UC Irvine and Fulbright, without whom I never would have completed my studies: Nathan Chan, Amanda McQuade, Benjamin Hoyt, Shauna Gillooly, Benjamin Raynor, Brian Spivey, Phoebe Moon, John Mok, Hannah Kim, Timothy Hartshorn, Lawrence Vulis, Eric Layman, Mathew Wild, Eliana Ritz, Mike Thompson-Brusstar, and Katharin Tai.

Thank you to Ming-sho Ho and the National Taiwan University Department of Sociology, my incredibly generous and supportive hosts during my two years of fieldwork in Taiwan. The Fulbright program sponsored my time abroad and served as an organizational home during my time in the field. I am grateful to Randall Nadeau for making Fulbright a supportive safe haven for scholars in Taiwan.

I also want to thank the Taiwan studies community—especially the Taiwan political science clique—who have been nothing but warm, welcoming, and encouraging ever since I showed up as a young graduate student. In the often-toxic world of academia, the Taiwan studies community is nothing but supportive to anyone who wants to study Taiwan in any way. I am especially grateful to Shelley Rigger, who has gone from being an academic idol to a colleague and coauthor. I must also give special thanks to Maggie Lewis, who has been a friend and mentor to me in ways I aspire to be for other junior scholars. I am grateful to Thomas Gold, Nathan Batto, Sara Newland, Wei-Ting Yen, Kharis Templeman, Jacques deLisle, Dafydd Fell, Timothy Rich, Joseph Wong, Austin Wang, Ian Rowen, Kerim Friedman, Evan Dawley, James Lin, Ian Chong, Chiaoning Su, Derek Sheridan, Liu Wen, and so many other brilliant scholars, who all have been invaluable sources of guidance and friendship in and out of the academy.

I am grateful to my fellow professors at National Taiwan University and National Chengchi University, who welcomed me into Taiwanese academia with open arms. I am honored to have started my academic career in Taiwan, and my enthusiasm remains high because of my excellent colleagues here. Thank you to Yilin Chiang, Jack Neubauer, Ou Tzu-Chi, Fabricio Fernández, Fanny Guinot, Hungying Chen, Shirley Lin, Harry Harding, and Torrent Pien for their support during my time at NCCU. Thank you to Adrien Rauchfleisch, Chelsea Chou, Hans Tung, Ijin Hong, Sarah Liu, Jiun-Da Lin, and my new colleagues at the Graduate Institute of National Development for giving me such a warm welcome to NTU.

I am forever thankful for my friends in Taiwan, many of whom I have known since 2012 and who have since become family to me. They deserve special thanks for patiently listening to me ramble about social movements and political parties nonstop for over a decade: Kenny Chen, Ryan Hsieh, Tingwei Chen, Noah Tien, Chris Chao, Kuan-Ting Lin, Yenyu Lin, Meikey Lai, Ryan Liu, Angie Hong, Zoe Lan, Eric Liao, Youhao Lin, Emily Lin, David Huang, Louie Wu, Orange Kuo, Dorris Lin, Denis Chen, William Yang, Emily Haver, Kit Lee, Thompson Chau, Rosalyn Shih, Ryan Ho Kilpatrick, Mary Pye, Eathan Lai, Sophie Yu, Yang Kang, Erin Hale, Sally Jensen, Rita Chiang, Edee Chen, Man-Man Chao, Ai-Men Lau, Mario Armira, Tomás Swinburne, Mark Popplewell, Sidney Niu, Chris Horton, Michael Fahey, Jessica Drun, Meg Lin, Joyu Wang, and many others, who I am certainly forgetting to name here (please forgive me).

I am especially grateful to four friends who deserve special mention in regard to this book. First is Brian Hioe, my longtime collaborator and confidant, who graciously read all of my work on Taiwanese social movements and political parties and provided extensive feedback on this book over the years. Next is Kevin Luo, who was the first person to read this book as a cohesive manuscript and whose friendship and mentorship has only made me a stronger political scientist. I am grateful to Oleksandr Shyn for our inspirational discussions on comparing Ukraine and Taiwan and for his thoughtful feedback on the chapter on Ukraine. Finally, I am thankful for Chason Dailey, one of my closest friends in Taiwan, who helped edit this entire book for language and grammar. His aptitude and patience for proofreading my writing over the years, from tweets to journal articles, is truly invaluable.

Thank you to my friends who are not in Taiwan but who have supported me from afar for decades, especially Alan Smith, Ian Fox, and Kat Gilbert.

I am thankful to my Uncle Dale and Aunt Patty, who have treated me like their own son and welcomed me into the Nachman/Pan clan in Taiwan. It has been such a joy to get to know this side of our family, and my time in Taiwan would not be half of what it has been without the support they have offered, especially Auntie Jade and Cousin Jun-Jun. I am especially grateful for my cousin Shaina, who beyond being the big sister I never had, has become one of my best friends and biggest cheerleaders.

Most important, I am thankful to my parents and brothers for their unending support. I know I used to stress out my parents by skipping school and getting Cs in math class. Although I have come a long way, I unfortunately now stress them out by living far away, in a place that CNN tells them is dangerous and war-prone. I am grateful they love and support me regardless. I truly would never have made it this far in life without them. Thank you Gary and Sheila, and shoutout to Beth.

Thank you to the University of Washington Press, especially Caitlin Tyler-Richards and Lorri Hagman. I am also grateful to the anonymous reviewers whose feedback strengthened this book immensely.

Finally, thank you to all the activists, politicians, organizers, and volunteers in Taiwan who spent hundreds of hours talking with me for this book's research. When I began my fieldwork, I truly did not know whether I, an overly eager white American graduate student, would be taken seriously. I will always be grateful that my contacts in Taiwan thought my research was exciting and worth their time to assist. I would be nowhere without their knowledge.

Some material in chapters 2 and 5 comes from a previously published chapter, "From Sunflowers to Suits: How Spatial Openings Affect Movement Party Formation," in *Sunflowers and Umbrellas: Social Movements, Expressive Practices, and Political Culture in Taiwan and Hong Kong*, edited by Sebastian Veg and Thomas Gold, China Research Monograph 76 (Berkeley, CA: Institute of East Asian Studies, 2020).

Some interview data from chapter 4 first appeared in "Misalignment between Social Movements and Political Parties in Taiwan's 2016 Election: Not All Grass Roots Are Green," *Asian Survey* 58, no. 5 (2018): 874–97.

PREFACE

We have set a new standard for relations between Taiwan and China. We have made it known to the government that the future of Taiwan belongs to Taiwan's 23 million people and that Taiwan's future should be decided by us.
—Lin Fei-fan / Sunflower Movement student leader, March 30, 2014

At around 9:00 p.m. on March 18, 2014, activists stormed Taiwan's Legislative Yuan and began a twenty-four-day occupation of the parliamentary building, in protest of the Cross-Strait Service Trade Agreement (CSSTA), which had passed the day prior. This was the start of what became known as the Sunflower Movement. After months of debate, fear had spread across civil society over the nature of the CSSTA, a trade bill that had the potential to redefine the most fundamental and all-defining issue in Taiwanese politics: relations between Taiwan and China. The controversial bill, the movement that opposed it, and the political parties that formed as a result of it changed Taiwan forever.

The CSSTA was controversial for two main reasons.[1] First, the contents of the bill were perceived to heavily favor China's interests over Taiwan's, giving China exclusive access to much of Taiwan's service sector, which at the time made up nearly 65 percent of Taiwan's gross domestic product (GDP). Second, the nature of the bill's negotiations was controversial, as they took place in China behind closed doors by representatives of the Chinese Communist Party (CCP) and the Chinese Nationalist Party (KMT), leading to the primary scandal surrounding the passage of the bill.[2] The bill was passed by the KMT without proper legislative review and formally discussed on the parliamentary floor for only thirty seconds, a moment that became known as the "30-Second Incident."[3] Word began to spread about how the bill was passed and people began paying attention to both the bill's contents and the context under which it had been negotiated. Outrage ensued over the "black box" that the bill put Taiwan in, the KMT's complicit role, and the questionable method of the bill's passage.

Angered by the bill and its surrounding contentions, social movement organizations called for an emergency mobilization of as many nongovernment organizations (NGOs) and activists as possible the day prior to the bill's passage, culminating in hundreds gathering outside the Legislative Yuan building. Activists had begun protesting by the afternoon of March 18, a day mostly comprised of speeches, performances, and demonstrations. That evening, a group of around fifty activists charged the Legislative Yuan in a planned effort to raise the stakes of the protest, successfully gaining access to the government building.

Word of the protests and the occupation of the Legislative Yuan began to spread throughout Taiwan. After seeing the high level of commitment activists were willing to undertake to protest the bill, everyday people began to mobilize and join the protests. Soon demonstrations and protests broke out all around Taiwan. The Sunflower Movement had fully bloomed.[4]

The Sunflower Movement grew like wildfire. Over the following three weeks, what had started as a contentious protest scene quickly became a microcosm of civil society in the form of a protest village. Outside the Legislative Yuan, activists set up areas where they could sleep, eat, shower, and engage with other protesters and organizers.[5] Despite the framing of the Sunflower Movement as a "student movement," the scene inside and outside the Legislative Yuan included far more than just college-age protesters. At its peak, as many as five hundred thousand Taiwanese citizens of all ages participated in the protests. Inside the Legislative Yuan were groups of social activists and organizers who had spent years preparing for this moment of serious opposition to China and the KMT.

Relations between protesters and police remained tense throughout the occupation. Clashes with law enforcement eventually climaxed when protesters also tried to occupy the Executive Yuan, resulting in a police crackdown. Hundreds were injured and over sixty activists were arrested.[6] Police use of batons and water cannons led to accusations of brutality and further escalated national support for the protest.[7] What began as a domestic protest soon began to gather international support as well, especially from Taiwanese diasporic communities. The rest of the protestors remained cautiously peaceful. Organizers and politicians—including some from the Democratic Progressive Party (DPP)—tried their best to keep the peace, despite high tensions between various political actors.[8]

The Sunflower Movement had one clear demand: that the KMT withdraw the bill and set up a formal mechanism for close review of all current and future trade deals with China. The path the protesters took to achieve this demand was fraught and difficult. Civil society leaders and politicians across Taiwan's political spectrum sought to capitalize on the protests for their own gain. Parties and organizations at different times wanted to co-opt the movement or be seen as closely associated with the protesters. Meanwhile, protesters and movement leaders were weary and skeptical of political assistance, trying their best to stick to their demands.[9]

On April 10, 2014, after weeks of protests, the activists succeeded: the government shelved the CSSTA, handing the KMT a bitter defeat and making Sunflower one of the most successful protests in Taiwan's history. Following their victory, the activists withdrew from the Legislative Yuan and student leaders turned themselves in to the authorities for having violated the law during the previous months.

The Sunflower Movement may have been catalyzed by a trade bill, but it was not a protest about trade. Economic policy, monetary practices, and good business were not at the forefront of protesters' minds. In contested states like Taiwan, something as seemingly apolitical as an economic trade bill is often not just about the subject matter at hand. The Sunflower Movement formed out of concern for the quality of Taiwanese democracy, identity, resistance against China, and how the Taiwanese people saw their future.

One of the most peculiar outcomes of the Sunflower Movement was what became of many of the social movement organizers and activists who participated. For the next several years, dozens of Sunflower activists entered formal politics. Some joined the DPP, some remained independent, and some founded a new cohort of *movement parties*.[10] The two biggest movement parties that became serious electoral contenders after the Sunflower Movement were founded and staffed by Sunflower activists: the New Power Party (NPP) and the Social Democratic Party (SDP). The NPP and SDP both formed as pro-Taiwanese independence and anti-CCP and anti-KMT parties.[11]

Despite years of advocating for Taiwanese independence, of protesting the KMT, and of denouncing the CCP, this cohort of activists had never formed their own political party or parties. Previously they had strictly adhered to informal modes of political participation like protest and activism to express their dissent about the formal political systems that hindered Taiwanese independence. Something about 2014 was different. Something in the nature of the Sunflower Movement changed the calculus for the activists. Instead of simply returning to activism, they felt the need to radically change their approach to politics and do something that social movement activists typically do not do: they entered formal politics, created new social movement based political parties, and ran in elections.

The Sunflower Movement—steeped in issues of contested identity and territory—led to the peculiar outcome of movement party formation and political party relations in a contested state. The case of movement parties in Taiwan demands scholarly attention. First, the political and historical context in which they formed shows the critical importance of *contestation* as a mode of international influence on domestic politics. Second, and of crucial importance for the current study: the formation of movement parties remains an important puzzle for social science inquiry. The key variables for movement parties' rise cannot be explained by existing logics of party formation alone. Instead, a new understanding of movement parties and how they operate in contested states such as Taiwan is required. This is the task to which we now turn.

CONTESTED TAIWAN

INTRODUCTION

I first met Ah-T, a pro-independence activist from Taichung, Taiwan, when I was an undergraduate at Tunghai University in 2012. Ah-T was one of the first Taiwanese contacts to introduce me to Taiwan's world of social activism, protest, and the giant existential questions of Taiwan's identity and sovereignty. In 2015, during the aftermath of the Sunflower Movement, I began conducting formal interviews with him and other activists who had participated in the movement. It was only then that I began to fully understand the motivation behind his activism and what he wanted for his home's future.

Our first interview took place outside a music festival, where his thrash metal band was playing a gig. He sported a "Keep Angry and Fuck the KMT" T-shirt that exposed his double-sleeve black tattoos and his guitar was plastered with Taiwanese independence stickers. He said, "We Taiwanese currently have no options. On one hand, we have to deal with China, and at the same time, we also have to deal with the KMT. Inside, outside, how can we become an independent Taiwan for Taiwanese people when we are called the so-called Republic of China but also have the 'People's Republic of China' attacking us?"[1]

At the beginning of my fieldwork, I did not fully appreciate just how ubiquitous questions of identity and territory were for Taiwanese people. There was seemingly nothing I could talk about with activists that did not come back to two topics: what it meant to be Taiwanese and what Taiwan's future ought to be. Ah-T taught me that these seemingly simple questions—Who are we? and Where are we?—are far more fraught in Taiwan than in most parts of the world. For some, Taiwan should simply be called Taiwan; it is home to Taiwanese people. For others it should be called the Republic of China (ROC) as it is home to Taiwanese *and* Chinese people. For still others, such as the people outside of Taiwan and particularly people in China, Taiwan is part of the People's Republic of China (PRC) as it is home to Chinese people.

The reality is that Taiwan is stuck in a gray zone. A place called Taiwan certainly exists, but what exactly Taiwan *is* is, surprisingly, more difficult to answer. Taiwan is not the only state that maintains some sovereignty over its borders while simultaneously being claimed by a neighboring state. Palestine,

Ukraine, Nagorno Karabakh, Somaliland, and many others like Taiwan fall into this category of *contested state*.

A contested state is one that maintains de facto sovereignty over its borders but is unrecognized by the international order and is claimed by another *contesting* state. What makes a contested state particularly unique, however, is that its *political spectrum* is defined by its contested status. While non-contested states define their politics along traditional left-right issues, the politics of contested states are based on questions of identity and territory. Contested states blend international relations and local issues of identity, which results in intricate and difficult questions about *who* its people are and *where* it exists. Contested states do not define their political spectrums along progressive-conservative lines, tax redistribution, or the reach of state institutions. Instead, a contested state frames its political spectrum on one of identity and support for independence versus unification with its contesting state. This has wide-ranging implications for academic understanding of several issues, from how people in contested states self-identify, how they vote, how they see citizenship, to which political or policy issues they care about and when and why they protest and enter the formal political arena. Contested states thus pose a significant, if largely unremarked upon, challenge to social science theories.

After the Sunflower Movement subsided, Ah-T went on to become an ardent supporter of a newly formed political party called the New Power Party (NPP). The NPP's platform was pro-independence and anti-China, and it offered a new political vehicle for young activists interested in working within the formal political system for the first time, setting it apart from the established pro-independence–leaning Democratic Progressive Party (DPP) and the authoritarian-turned-democratic KMT. The NPP was also separate from other small pro-independence parties, such as Taiwan Solidarity Union or Green Party Taiwan. Regardless of existing political parties, in the wake of the Sunflower Movement, activists decided to take matters into their own hands and form their own political parties. In the years following, movement parties like the NPP not only formed, but ran in—and won—elections and activists went from protesting in the streets for Taiwanese independence to giving speeches in parliament about reforms needed to address Taiwan's sovereignty.

When social and political scientists study movement party formation, we rely on long-studied theoretical explanations. We turn to established arguments, such as new cleavage formation, which posits that as new issues arise and space forms within a political spectrum, new parties form to fill that space.[2] Or, we look to existing party systems as a way to study incentives or barriers to entry for new party formation.[3] We may also think of political opportunity structure theory and consider whether and how the social movement in question sees its political context as open to new party formation.[4]

My time with Taiwanese activists has shown me there is something missing from the established social movement and political party theories I learned as a political science graduate student.[5] Existing theories about why social movements become political parties do not explain what the world witnessed in Taiwan after the Sunflower Movement. Political issues like Taiwanese independence are not new to political discourse, nor are new parties like the NPP filling a spatial opening within Taiwan's political spectrum. Historically, barriers to Taiwan's electoral system have been low and the ability of social movements to produce political parties was possible long before 2014. Indeed, the political context of 2014 was not more open or conducive to party formation than it had been in the past. From many an activist's perspective, political opportunities had actually become more closed off.

Why, then, did parties like the NPP form out of the Sunflower Movement? What pushed activists like Ah-T, who otherwise hated political parties, to suddenly change their entire political mode of operation and support formal political organizations? I discovered there is something qualitatively different about Taiwan for which the existing repertoire of theories could not fully account. What is it about Taiwan's social movements and political parties that is seemingly different? It is Taiwan's contestation.

Movement parties in contested states form differently than movement parties in non-contested states. In a contested state, movement party formation is not about the identification of new issues, the established electoral system, or political opportunities. Instead, it is about two different, understudied variables related to contestation: threats from the contesting state (China, in Taiwan's case) and activist relations with existing pro-independence parties (such as the DPP). High levels of threat from the contesting state and poor movement party relations are two necessary conditions for movement party formation in contested states. How contested states are qualitatively different is revealed by tracing the processes of movement party formation in Taiwan in the aftermath of the 2014 Sunflower Movement.

When a state like Taiwan is contested, its questions of identity and territory are unresolved. It is unable to fully answer two questions that every state must know: Who are we? and Where are we? Taiwan's political cleavage is not defined by the traditional left-right divide, but instead by questions of sovereignty and connection it encounters in its relations with the contesting state that claims it, the People's Republic of China. How do politics in contested states operate outside the norm in places like Taiwan, which have this unique underlying political cleavage of contestation?

Typically, scholarship sees "contested" as a demarcation in only the international realm and surrounding issues of recognition. International issues of contestation are indeed fundamental to any study of contested states in general and Taiwan in particular, but what is missing is how issues of contestation affect domestic politics and civil society within contested states. A necessary feature to understand about contested statehood—beyond the international factors—is how contestation defines the domestic politics of a place. Along with international features, a state is contested when its domestic politics is defined by questions of *who* and *where*. Contestation is not a single, international dimension. Rather, places like Taiwan face dual levels of contestation, that is, at both the international *and* the domestic levels. How these different dimensions of contestation are formed and how they influence international politics varies, but together they fundamentally define how politics function in contested places like Taiwan.

The case of the 2014 Sunflower Movement is a particularly worthy puzzle for political scientists, sociologists, and especially long-time scholars of Taiwan. Social movements and protests are fundamental parts of Taiwan's history, especially since Taiwan's democratization. Whether the Wild Lily Movement, the environmental protests of the 1990s, Indigenous rights protests of the 2010s, the Red Shirts Movement, the Wild Strawberry Movement, the Anti–Media Monopoly Movement, or the innumerable other protests that have occurred, social movements have produced core memories for Taiwan's democratic development.

With so many social movements mobilizing since Taiwan's democratization, one may think that movement parties must be a frequent occurrence for Taiwanese politics. Yet they are not. Despite the countless social movements that have arisen in Taiwan over the last thirty years, none of them produced a movement party, except for the 2014 Sunflower Movement.[6] The Sunflower Movement was special, in no small part because it was the first time that activists chose to switch their strategy from informal street protest to an established party organization active in formal politics.

Why Contested States Matter

Contested states represent the majority of critical geopolitical flashpoints in today's world. War and regional instability are increasingly related to the status of contested states. Taiwan is among the best-known of the world's contested states because its unresolved status is ubiquitous in the contemporary discourse surrounding China. While political scientists and policymakers may be trying to understand how to best navigate today's complex geopolitical tensions around contested states, there is dire need for a better theoretical understanding of how domestic and international factors drive political participation *within* contested states. This analysis provides a theoretical grounding and empirically robust framework for understanding how and why people in contested states participate in formal and informal politics. Ever since the 2014 Sunflower Movement—Taiwan's history-defining mass protest mobilized over issues of contestation—a whole cohort of new movement parties have formed and found electoral success. These pro-independence parties have awakened a generation who have the potential to change Taiwan's status and East Asia's regional order. Anyone who wants to predict the future of cross-strait politics must understand not just how these movement parties came into power but how the fundamental question of Taiwan's contestation penetrates all aspects of both international and domestic politics.

Why Movement Parties Matter

Movement parties have the potential to be the most radically transformative organizations in formal politics, especially in contested states. Their social movement origins set up their political agenda to be more outspoken and aggressive. In the context of contested states like Taiwan, this means that movement parties are more likely to strongly advocate for either independence or unification in ways that established parties either cannot or will not do. Movement activists usually seek to challenge a contested state's domestic status quo through social protest, as well as potentially challenging the state's international status quo by successfully entering the formal political structure. If a movement party can enter formal politics, it gains access to the political arena in a way that allows it to meaningfully influence if and how a contested state addresses its fundamental questions of who and where.[7]

Why a social movement becomes a political party is a classic question for social scientists, but the current examination intervenes in a different way, asking the same question but using a case that does not fit our current understanding of social movement–political party relations. Most research and understanding of movement parties comes from empirical studies based in Western Europe and Latin America, and most explanations focus on the emergence of new issues, established systems, or social movement structure. However, today's most consequential flashpoints—Taiwan and Ukraine—cannot be explained through these lenses alone because the two are contested states. Existing literature does not consider how typical forms of political participation, such as social movement mobilization or political party formation, change when a state's political context exists in an existential crisis state of being. Taiwan is novel not just because of its geopolitical position within East Asia, an underrepresented region in the movement party literature, but because of the many movement parties that formed out of the Sunflower Movement, making it a particularly powerful case study.

Movement party operations are one of the most apropos ways to examine domestic drivers in contested states because they combine both formal and informal channels of political participation. However, very few movement parties emanated out of social movements and movement parties are themselves an empirically rare phenomenon. They typically arise from a social movements attempting to transform their strategy, from the informal arena of protest to the formal arena of political engagement. They are "coalitions of political activists who emanate from social movements and try to apply the organizational and strategic practices of social movements in the arena of party competition . . . One day, legislators of movement parties may debate bills in parliamentary committees, but the next day, they participate in disruptive demonstrations or the non-violent occupation of government sites."[8] Not all social movements become, or even want to become, political parties. Political party formation is a specific strategy a social movement chooses to undertake only in extreme cases and under certain conditions.[9] Movement parties are one of the "main political consequences of social movements at the structural level."[10] Movement parties may be rare, but they can be of national and international importance. A movement that mobilizes around the issue of a contested state's sovereignty and that creates a political party to change the direction of the formal political approach has the potential to shape or reshape a regional political order.

Why Taiwan Matters

Comparing Taiwan to other contested states such as Somaliland, Nagorno Karabakh, or Ukraine may seem unusual. All these states are in different stages of development, exist in different political contexts, and do not share strong relations among themselves. However, they all share some critical features: they define their fundamental political questions around territory and identity and they struggle and strive to become legitimate entities in the eyes of the international order. They exist in limbo together and share many of the same political struggles, despite variations in their specific situations.

Taiwan itself is special. Among many contested states, Taiwan is the gold standard of what can be achieved within the bounded gray zone of contestation. It is diplomatically unrecognized and yet a fundamental part of the global economy. Major powers like the United States and China are heavily invested in Taiwan's role in today's global supply chain, and they have a strong interest in its continued existence, even if as a contested state. Taiwan is also an advanced democracy that holds free and fair elections and is one of the most free and equal countries in the Asia Pacific. It enjoys a level of development beyond most other contested states. Given all this, what does Taiwan have to say about contested status more broadly?

It is precisely because Taiwan is so ahead of most other contested states that it is worth studying. Taiwan's democratic advancement, economic development, and political importance today have not resolved any of its fundamental questions of identity or territory. Its existence is just as contested as its fellow contested states, despite all its successes.

The Argument

Why do some social movements in contested states like Taiwan become political parties while others do not? How does Taiwan's existential status as a contested state change the way we typically understand how and why social movements mobilize and political parties form? I propose two necessary conditions for movement party formation that are unique to contested states: a dire level of threat from the neighboring state that claims it and an irreconcilable clash between pro-independence activists and existing pro-independence–leaning parties. By theorizing on and contextualizing these two conditions, I aim to show when and how movements and parties have the potential to alter a contested state's domestic and international political standing. Taiwan's history as a contested state and a survey of the different contested claims over Taiwan made by multiple states over time help explain how contestation defines Taiwanese politics today.

Any explanation for movement party creation in Taiwan begins with acknowledgment of the first necessary condition: a critical level of threat from China. Different types of threats affect social movement mobilization differently, and when certain kinds of threats are felt at certain thresholds, activists are likely to feel a sense of urgency to enter formal politics. A comparative historical analysis of two critical moments of Chinese threats demonstrates this effect: the Third Taiwan Strait Crisis and the Sunflower Movement.

The second necessary condition is a matter of the relationship between social movements and existing political parties. When pro-independence activists (who seek formal de jure sovereignty) see pro-independence parties as incapable or corrupt, they feel compelled to take matters into their own hands by forming a new pro-independence party. This complex relationship can be seen in the dynamics between Taiwan's Democratic Progressive Party and the 2014 Sunflower Movement and also in how the DPP's pro-independence politics have varied over time. The Sunflower Movement served as the mechanism through which two movement parties, the New Power

FIGURE 1. Explanation of the Argument

	CONTESTING STATE THREAT LOW	CONTESTING STATE THREAT HIGH
Social movement–established party relations weak	No mobilization, no party formation	Mobilization, movement party formation
Social movement–established party relations strong	No mobilization, no party formation	No mobilization, no party formation

Party and the Social Democratic Party, formed out of the protests and how the Chinese threat and perceptions of the DPP were necessary conditions for their formation.

Data and Methods

Research for this book is based on more than five years of fieldwork conducted between 2015 and 2021 and more than 150 in-depth, semi-structured interviews with social activists, movement organizers, party staff workers, and politicians. Interviews were conducted in offices, coffee shops, parks, and libraries; all were audio-recorded with the subject's permission. Interview times ranged from thirty minutes to more than two hours. Many subjects were interviewed multiple times.

Some interviewed activists were directly involved with the movement as leaders and organizers, while others were general participants. This variety demonstrated a wide range of perspectives from within the movement and data from the interviews was central to the resulting analysis and conclusion. I found many of the activists willing to sit for interviews through personal connections I had within activist circles and by word-of-mouth. I then used snowball sampling to reach other activists. Many times an interview subject would recommend other people for me to approach.

To qualify for consideration as a movement party member, a subject must have joined one of the new movement parties formed after the Sunflower Movement. Movement party members were also found using a snowball sampling method. The interview data is supplemented with official primary sources, including newspaper articles from the five decades that preceded the Sunflower Movement, personal writings by state elites, party statements, secondary sources by historians who have studied contemporary Taiwanese history, and official Chinese Communist Party speeches discussing Taiwan.

The qualitative methods that were used include process tracing and comparative historical analysis to determine the different pathways and constraints faced by activists as they navigated the journey from movement to party. Process tracing, particularly regarding threat and moderation, takes a longue durée approach, both for the sake of a comprehensive trace but also to eliminate alternative explanations.

In Sum

Two key conditions are necessary for movement parties to form in contested states: a critical level of threat and a loss of faith in established parties' ability to effect change. Movements and parties nevertheless have the potential to alter a contested state's domestic politics and international political standing and different types of threat affect social movement mobilization differently. When certain kinds of threats are felt at certain thresholds, activists are likely to feel a sense of urgency that leads them to enter formal politics. When those seeking formal recognized sovereignty see pro-independence parties as no longer viable party vehicles, it pushes them to take matters into their own hands by forming new parties. Although I focus on the novel East Asian case of Taiwan, this theory of movement parties can speak widely to conditions in other contested states around the world, including Ukraine. Like Taiwan, Ukraine's fundamental political questions are defined by contested identity, territory, and integration with Russia.

By reconstructing how we view places like Taiwan using prevailing models of social movement mobilization and political party formation, we are better able to answer the questions of the "who" and the "where" in the everyday lives of citizens in contested states. By centering the agency of Taiwanese citizens, we can articulate the strategic decisions and motivations that must be made regarding political participation. "Contestation" is not simply an international demarcation used to identify states that are unwelcomed in the international order or that only maintain de facto independence. Contestation is simultaneously the fundamental driver for domestic politics.

ONE

Conceptualizing Contestation

Before delving into the complex puzzle of Taiwan's movement parties' creation, let us first establish conceptual boundaries about what is meant by "state," "contested state," "contesting state," and "movement party." What is a state? At the most basic political science conceptualization level, a state is a bundle of institutions that maintains both internal and external sovereignty over a given people and territory. A sovereign state can pass and enforce laws, uphold rights, and resolve disputes. A sovereign state can also create security, be recognized by and interact with other sovereign states, and maintain a monopoly over education and the legitimate use of force. Legal understandings of statehood and sovereignty have varied over time, but contemporary definitions are rooted in the 1933 Montevideo Convention on the Rights and Duties of States.[1] Four criteria named in the convention together became known as *traditional declaration theory* and have served as a baseline for describing statehood through the post-1945 world: a permanent population, a defined territory, an operational government, and the capacity to conduct relations with other states. During the 1960s and 1970s, however, mass decolonization occurred throughout the world and the rules for who could claim statehood changed.[2] Initially the intention of the United Nations (UN) was to offer independence to former colonies that sought self-determination. The wording of the 1970 Declaration on the Granting of Independence to Colonial Countries and Peoples declares that power must be transferred to the people of non-self-governing and dependent territories: "The establishment of a sovereign and independent state, the free association or integration with an independent state or the emergence into any other political status freely determined by a people constitute modes of implementing the right of self-determination by that people."[3]

A second major wave of new state formation came following the end of the Cold War.[4] Former Soviet states, with the endorsement of the UN, began to establish themselves in Eastern and Central Europe. By the end of the 1990s the majority of the world had largely been carved into sovereign nation-states. The states that had suffered under empire had had their days in court and made their cases for independence. The global order had obliged their desire for self-determination and, despite a few imperfect borders, the world map was settled.

But not everyone who desired statehood had the opportunity to make their case. More than a handful of former colonial states were never given a hearing, nor the option of self-determination. Some former Soviet states were instead lumped together with a new state that had made its case first.[5] When a group or territory sought independence during a time outside these two waves of state formation, it was almost always met with resistance and typically failed. Outside of these two eras, any new state seeking formal acceptance and recognition was seen as troublesome or its case was viewed as a domestic political issue for a preexisting state to settle internally. The rules of state formation became, and are still, particularly restrictive, favoring maintenance of the international status quo over allowing a new state to form, regardless of how legitimate a potential new state's claim may be.

High barriers to entry into the international order, however, have not stopped new states from forming. New states still form in ways and places most formal states may not expect, let alone approve of, such as through military conflict or unrecognized secession. The international order typically does not acknowledge or recognize such new states. As a result, in today's world dozens of states exist that are functional and de facto sovereign, unrecognized, and contested states by the countries they claim to be independent from.[6]

What Is a Contested State?

The concept of a contested state, unsurprisingly, is itself contested. Though contested states vary in their formation and capacity, they share several key similarities that make them, for all intents and purposes, similar. First, like a non-contested state, a contested state is a bundle of institutions that enforces laws, upholds rights, and maintains a monopoly over education and the legitimate use of force over a given territory. Contested states maintain de facto independence, meaning they exert sovereignty over their territories and peoples, but theirs is a sovereignty that is contested by one or more contesting states. In addition, contested states lack de jure independence, meaning they are not recognized as states by the international order, they are denied access to international organizations and institutions, they lack diplomatic relations with most countries in the world, and they have no agency or say in most global matters.[7] As Scott Pegg describes, a contested state is "a functioning reality that is denied legitimacy by the rest of international society."[8] Pegg's formal definition focuses on states having all the same features as non-contested states: "They are a political movement that possesses substantial control over a specific territory and population but lacks recognition of its sovereignty by the international community." Raul Toomla uses a simpler definition, defining contested states as "entities that fulfill the Montevideo criteria for statehood but lack international recognition."[9] Based on existing scholarship on contested statehood by such writers as Nina Caspersen, Pegg, and Toomla, these features must be present for a state to be considered contested:

1. De facto independence, gained following warfare or conflict.
2. Control of two-thirds of the defined territory, including the capital and main cities.
3. Failure to achieve widespread international recognition.
4. Demonstrated staying power (at least two years of territorial control).
5. Attributes of statehood, but not part of the exclusive group of international de jure states.
6. A continuing claim of contestation, with the outbreak of warfare a distinct possibility.
7. Leaders who demonstrate the state's legitimacy and seek to build state institutions.
8. Claimed by a contesting state that coercively incentivizes unification from both the contested state and the international order.
9. Defines its domestic political spectrum by issues of contested international recognition, territory, and identity, not by traditional left-right politics.[10]

These criteria importantly exclude small territorial rebellions, separatist movements, political organizations that lack meaningful control over their territories and/or state institutions, or that have existed for less than two years. These exclusions are not meant to deem potential contested states as unimportant or uninteresting, but simply to instead give parameters for the current analysis.

What Is a Contesting State?

Lack of recognition from the international order is not the biggest challenge faced by a contested state. Rather, the biggest challenge is lack of recognition from just one country that acts as the biggest roadblock for gaining de jure statehood: the contesting state.[11] Ned Dobos rightly points out that the combination of both international recognition and contesting country consent is ultimately required for a contested state to fully cast off its contested status.[12] Although a contested state does not hold full agency for determining when it is no longer contested, recognition from the contesting state is still a necessary condition for full de jure statehood. So long as the contesting state both refuses to recognize a contested state and articulates its intent to unify, the ultimate conditions of contestation cannot be resolved. Despite the term's ubiquitous usage regarding contested and unrecognized states, clear conceptualization of what exactly a contesting state is and does remains underexplained. Specifically, a contesting state:

1. Considers its contested states to be in violation of its territorial integrity;
2. Does not recognize the contested state's territorial claims;
3. Does not recognize the contested state's national identity or ethnic identity as valid or legitimate;
4. Maintains a colonialist power dynamic with the contested state;
5. Signals its intentions or threatens to integrate the contested state through force or by other means;
6. Discourages the international system from engaging with the contested state; and
7. Does not wield sovereignty over the contested state, despite not recognizing its own lack of sovereignty or the contested state's de facto sovereignty.

Not all contesting states threaten the contested state with imminent war, but unification is the desired eventual goal. In other words, the contesting state does not "like" the contested state and does not want the contested state to exist. What exactly contesting states do to solve this "dislike" varies. Historically, contested states often were simply absorbed into the states that claimed them. At other times, special privileges were created for territories within the confines of the contesting state's territory, such as the experience of Quebec in Canada. For most contesting states, however, military action is the most common course of action. Yet most contested states do not seek military conflict with their contesting states, especially if they have achieved de facto sovereignty. As Caspersen and Pegg both note, contested states typically form out of military conflict. And, as Charles Tilly established decades ago, war can often be the cause of state formation, but what makes contested states unique is that their statehood and sovereignty go unresolved long after military conflicts end.

Contested states are widely regarded as potential flash points for conflict. Although this may be the reality for many contested states, it is important to interrogate why contested states are flash points. The power dynamic that exists between contesting and contested states is typically overlooked as the cause, since contested states are typically seen as troublemakers and contesting states as responsible countries trying to protect their borders. However, a power differential exists between the two: contesting states often have the backing of the international system, which almost always supports their efforts to suppress new state formation. As Caspersen describes, "The international system of sovereign states is rigged to ensure that the [contesting] state prevails."[13] If military action does arise, the conflict is typically initiated by the contesting state to protect its territorial integrity. This does not mean that contested states do not engage in violent or military tactics when trying to establish or maintain their de facto sovereignty. However, the impetus for military violence is often initiated by the contesting state but framed as the fault of the contested state. It is rarely the contested state that threatens the contesting state with violent takeover.

The connection between political violence and contested statehood should not be discounted. Most contested states are formed out of violence and continue to either perpetrate or be victims of violence after their formation. Unlike other types of states, which might be prone to war or violence because of weak institutions or a lack of strong civil society (conditions that many contested states also face), contested states are predisposed to violence because of the contesting state's known intentions to unify and pull it back into its territory. What makes a contested state particularly prone to violence is the distinct possibility that a larger, more powerful state will one day invade it.

The final and most important element of the contested-contesting state dynamic is sovereignty. A key feature of a contested state is its de facto sovereignty over its territory, which usually means a contesting state does not have actual control over its land. Although contesting states often rhetorically refer to contested states as their own territories, contested states function as separate entities. Exactly how much power a contesting state does exert over a contested state can vary. Some contested states are established and have enough capacity to resist international influence, including influence from their contesting states. Others, particularly newer contested states, are weaker and prone to influence by the contesting states. This emphasis may seem like a truism, but it is worth highlighting, that a contested state's domestic politics and political institutions, citizenship, and control of the military are not decided nor run by the contesting state. Instead, contested states set up their own political systems with their own political goals and purposes, and the daily life of politics is qualitatively separate and distinct from that of the contesting states.

What Do Contested States Want?

Contested states do not want to be contested. It is an unconventional, unsatisfactory, and ultimately dangerous status. However, a contested state often must accept its contested status and operate within the status quo of the contested-contesting dynamic, either because attempting to change its status would lead to war with the state that claims it or because it does not have the domestic or international means to change its status. Ideally, a contested state wants to gain de jure independence. Not only is recognition by other states a necessary condition for full statehood; it also grants a contested state access to international organizations, opens pathways for formal diplomatic relations, and ultimately normalizes it into the international order. As Pegg notes, no matter how strong, robust, or powerful a contested state becomes, its organizational structure and fundamental existence will not be seen as legitimate so long as it remains unrecognized. Recognition has long been seen by political scientists as a fundamental condition for formal statehood, making it a clear and necessary condition for the resolution of a contested state's status.

Recognition, however, is not the end-all for a contested state. If the goal for a contested state is to resolve its status and become fully normalized into the international order, then recognition by other states is only one piece of the puzzle. There is another fundamental desire that a contested state wants that often goes undiscussed and undertheorized in the literature: a desire for the contesting state to drop its claims. It does not only matter that the world recognizes a contested state; it also matters that the major actor in the world that has deemed the state contested in the first place abandons its hope for unification. As long as the contesting state maintains its position that the contesting state is illegitimate, even if the rest of the world recognizes the contesting state's legitimacy, the issue of contestation will remain open. A powerful state that does not drop its contesting claim will continue to deeply influence and affect the contested state's domestic and international situation, even if the contested state gains recognition by the international order. Thus "recognition," while a necessary condition for full statehood, is not in itself a sufficient condition because it does not account for the continued claims by the contesting state.

Contested versus Unrecognized

Previous writers have overwhelmingly focused on international recognition (and/or the lack of it) as the key underlying descriptor for the type of state in question.[14] Caspersen highlights just how important recognition is and the paradox it brings to contested states: "Unrecognized states suffer simultaneously from a lack of international attention and from too much international attention."[15] The importance of the concept of "recognition" has become so pervasive that full volumes of the political science literature have overwhelmingly defined the kind of state in question as "unrecognized" instead of contested.[16] But gaining international recognition, despite being a necessary condition for resolving a contested state's status, solves only half of the dilemma. The other half is the contesting state's claims over the state.

So long as the contesting state continues to claim the contested state as its own, regardless of international recognition, the question of contestation cannot be fully resolved. Recognition is an important but often overstated part of the concerns of contested states.[17]

For example, if the world were to unambiguously recognize the People's Republic of China's claim over Taiwan or Russia's claim over Ukraine, a sense of closure to those advocating for either the sovereignty or unity of these states would not suddenly appear. Taiwanese would not suddenly identify as Chinese and Ukrainians would not suddenly identify as Russian. Or, if the world decided to recognize Taiwan as an independent country, China would not suddenly abandon its claims. Perhaps the most evident case is that of Ukraine: Ukraine's de jure international status, gained after the breakup of the Soviet Union, has not stopped Russia from claiming it. Recognition cannot fully resolve a state's issue of contestation. Instead, resolution first requires domestic decisions over questions of who and where. Second, resolution requires the contesting state to drop its claims over the contested state. Even when a state's right to self-determination is legitimate and the rest of the world recognizes this legitimacy, this is not enough to settle the question of contestation. So long as the contesting state makes claims to the contested state, the question of formal status cannot be fully resolved. Though recognition might be a necessary condition for statehood and for resolving a contested state's status, it alone is not sufficient for resolving its contested status.

Since contestation defines the political cleavage structure of these kinds of states, we must turn our attention to domestic politics, institutions, and civil society to properly understand exactly how contestation matters. Contestation is as much a domestic question, one in constant discussion and negotiation within a society, as it is an international question debated between states. When we focus on recognition as the key description of contested or de facto states, we lose sight of a critical relationship: between the contested state and the contesting state, not between the contested state and the international system. To put it simply, recognition alone is an unsatisfactory word for describing why a state is contested. As Deon Geldenhuys puts it, recognition "is a matter of political discretion, not a legal or moral duty. If we really want to understand how contested states function, we must look beyond recognition as our fundamental framework of analysis."[18]

Domestic Politics in Contested States

The domestic political questions that drive Taiwan's everyday politics are defined by contestation, as can be seen in the workings of two of the most important types of political organizations: social movements and political parties. Why focus on seemingly small domestic organizations like movements and parties in a book on contested states? Because those who participate in mass protest movements or join pro-independence political parties in contested states are the actors with the most agency over a changing political status. When social activists with strong pro-independence viewpoints form their own parties and get elected, they gain the potential to directly influence a state's contested status. If we truly want to understand how contestation matters in domestic contexts, we must turn our attention to protests and parties.

I learned just how fundamental these two types of political organizations are by spending time with movement party activists in Taiwan. Activists like Ah-T make their everyday political decisions based on how they feel about their own individual identity and their relationship to the state and to the neighboring state that claims their state as its own. Indeed, past political science scholarship and decades of public opinion data show that most people in Taiwan are like Ah-T and now, more and more people in Taiwan have begun to identify as Taiwanese exclusively, not as Chinese or as Taiwanese *and* Chinese. Everyday political participation—such as whether to vote and protest, which parties to support, or what issues to care about during elections—are filtered through an understanding of Taiwan's contestation.[19] As soon as one begins to investigate how politics function in Taiwan, it quickly becomes apparent that contestation runs wide and deep.

As in most contested states, the dominant left-right spectrum in Taiwan is not defined by wealth, ideas for redistribution, or social issues, but rather by contestation. This is not to say that other issues are not salient, but they are often politicized along the independence-unification divide. This is true of social issues like environmentalism and, more pertinent to this discussion, economic issues such as a trade bill regulating Taiwan's service sector. All political issues are connected to Taiwan's contested status. Even topics that may seem to be unrelated to China are linked to Taiwan's foundational questions of identity and territory.

Two parties have defined Taiwanese politics since its democratization: the Chinese Nationalist Party and the Democratic Progressive Party. Traditionally, the KMT is seen as the pro-unification–leaning party on one end of Taiwan's political spectrum and the DPP is seen as the pro-independence–leaning party on the other. The KMT and the DPP, however, are not the only political parties in Taiwan. In part due to Taiwan's hybrid electoral system, the country's political institutions allow for small parties to hold a certain amount of political power.[20] Pro-independence parties like the New Power Party (NPP) have found success, due to Taiwan's combination of first-past-the-post and proportional-representation electoral systems. Taiwan arrived at this sophisticated democratic system through decades of regime change mapped onto a canvas of varying colonialisms and foreign rule. The history of how Taiwan became contested and yet prevailed as a democracy with open elections is fundamental to understanding any other political question about it.

How Contestation Functions

Data gleaned from extensive public opinion and electoral surveys shows that the most salient issue in Taiwanese politics is the independence-unification divide (often called "the China factor").[21] Although environmental and economic issues like wealth distribution play a major role in most advanced democracies, "Taiwan is not such a case . . . as parties and politicians raised these issues, they sometimes caught the public's attention, but these issues did not form political cleavages."[22] When other issues do become salient, they are often politicized in the context of independence versus unification. For example, the anti–nuclear power issue, a popular social issue in Taiwan, is often coded as a pro-independence issue.[23] While other issues are sometimes more salient in certain elections, they never are as decisive as the independence-unification question. Voters almost always use the lens of independence-unification to decide how to vote during national elections, held every four years. No other issues have successfully formed cleavages that last beyond one or two electoral cycles.[24]

Issues that typically define the left-right spectrum in other countries do not neatly map onto Taiwan. Social issues such as LGBTQ rights and labor reform do not correlate with being pro-independence or pro-unification, and neither the DPP nor the KMT make a habit of promoting housing reform, labor rights, or other progressive policies. In fact, contrary to what many would expect from a party with the word "progressive" in its name, many DPP social policies lean conservative. Despite recently passing same-sex marriage legislation, some of the harshest critics of legalizing LGBTQ rights have come from the DPP side of Taiwan's political spectrum. As the joke among Taiwan studies political scientists goes, "What do a pterodactyl and the DPP have in common? The first 'p' is silent."

Conceptualizing Independence

Words like *independence*, *status quo*, and *unification* are frequently used without acknowledging that these are not fixed positions and are only general points on a continuum on which multiple interpretations or advocacy positions exist.[25]

One of the most complicated yet crucial dynamics within Taiwanese politics is what it means for Taiwan to be independent. For some, "Taiwanese independence" means independence as the Republic of China, also known as ROC independence, or *hua du* in standard Chinese (Mandarin). This type of independence accepts the ROC framework that exists today and seeks to make Taiwan formally independent as a "second China." For others, "Taiwanese independence" means independence from the PRC *and* from the ROC through the formation of the Republic of Taiwan, which is called *tai du* in standard Chinese. For independence activists, Taiwanese independence necessitates abandonment of the entire ROC framework that has shaped politics on the island since 1945 and instituting an entirely new constitution and government in its place. To these activists, ROC independence is not real independence because it still centers their country's sovereignty around China. Often, advocacy for independence is concerned with independence from the ROC, since it is the actual Chinese framework that governs Taiwan. Taiwanese independence activists, of course, also want independence from the PRC, but independence advocacy is often more about independence from the ROC which actual governs Taiwan, rather than the PRC that claims Taiwan from a distance. Which country people are fighting for in Taiwan—the Republic of China or the Republic of Taiwan—is itself a fundamentally contested question that straddles the line between state-building and nation-building. Conceptualizing independence becomes even more complicated when Indigenous autonomy is brought into the mix. For centuries, Indigenous Taiwanese groups have been excluded from decisions about Taiwan's future. In recent years activists have stepped up efforts to incorporate Indigenous perspectives into defining Taiwanese independence.

Similarly, the meaning of "unification" as a concept varies. Although it may seem simple to say that someone who supports unification supports wanting to be part of China, *which* China they mean and under what style of government can vary. There are major qualitative differences between advocating for unification and democracy under the ROC versus advocating for unification and authoritarianism under the PRC. The difference between these conceptualizations of unification is worth noting, even if the ideas are grouped together along the unification spectrum and lack broad support.

Finally, "status quo" is itself a hotly debated term within Taiwanese politics. While all major parties define themselves as being pro–status quo, what they and the Taiwanese electorate understand as the status quo varies widely. Because little data exists on how voters conceptualize the status quo, its definition is often left to be delimited by the parties or political pundits. Some claim that being pro–status quo is synonymous with supporting de facto independence, while others consider the status quo an endorsement of the ROC. Still others see the status quo as an ambiguous yet pragmatic means of buying time and avoiding war or as a means to *not* take a particular stance on Taiwan's sovereignty. Thus it would be a mistake to assume that Taiwanese voters across the political spectrum who advocate for the status quo all want the same thing. What we can posit, nevertheless, is that being pro–status quo means not wanting a change in Taiwan's current status, at least for now, thereby avoiding formal de jure independence (which would lead to war with the PRC) or unification (which would lead to the end of democratic Taiwan). To be pro–status quo, then, is to advocate for accepting Taiwan's contested status, not because it is ideal but because it allows Taiwan to continue to exist in an imperfect peace.

TWO

How Taiwan Became Contested

There are two unequal sides to every contested state. There are the contesting state's claims, which includes its grievances against the state trying to fully separate from it and its own claims to legitimacy over its sociocultural identity. There are also the contested state's claims, which includes its grievances against the state trying to annex it and its own stake in legitimatizing their citizens' own sociocultural identity. These two sides are unequal because the contesting state will always have more power over the contested state. International order is primed to side with the status quo, meaning that the contesting state's claims are always seen as the more legitimate.[1] Power lies almost always with the contesting state, because it knows it will likely have the backing of the international community. Even when a contested state has a strong moral claim, such as a demand for the right to self-determination, or an economic or political claim that is beneficial to the international order, the path of least resistance—one that will cause the least amount of instability or risk to the world order—is to side with the contesting state over the contested state.

To understand how a state becomes contested, these dynamics must be understood from two different dimensions: the international and the domestic. A state is contested when its international recognition is disputed and also when issues of territory and identity define its domestic politics. These two dimensions are closely related in both their development and how one influences the other. The case of Taiwan is no different. How Taiwan became contested is a multidimensional question that must be approached from both domestic and international perspectives. China's claims over Taiwan have pushed Taiwan, as the Republic of China, out of the international order. Even if the world does not necessarily accept China's claims over Taiwan, other states often acknowledge China's claims and legitimate them by not formally recognizing Taiwan as a de jure independent state, not treating Taiwan as part of the international community. At the same time, Taiwan domestically wrestles with who and where it exists: are the people who live there Taiwanese, Chinese, or both? Is it the ROC, Taiwan, or some combination of the two?

It is important to provide context that establishes how these questions came to define Taiwanese politics. Historical retellings of Taiwan's or China's histories cannot provide definitive answers to either Taiwan or China's claims. Historical context is, however, necessary to highlight key events and factors that shaped Taiwan into the unrecognized democracy it is today.

China's Claims to Taiwan

Any speech by a PRC leader today will almost always include the infamous line, "Since ancient times, Taiwan has been an inseparable part of China."[2] While China makes claims to Taiwan that are ancient in nature, its actual claims over Taiwan are a relatively modern invention.[3] PRC representatives use a combination of ancient arguments and internationally accepted language of "territorial integrity" and "legality" to justify its claims. The sources and citations for these arguments primarily come from key moments in Chinese/Taiwanese history: the Zheng pirate family's control over Taiwan and, subsequently, the Qing Dynasty's limited control over the island.[4]

It is critical to note that Taiwanese history does not begin with China. Long before any Chinese, Japanese, or European person ever laid a foot on Taiwan, the islands were teeming with cultures and peoples whose histories now long been lost.[5] Before Taiwan became the center of geopolitical contention, Indigenous Taiwanese populated the island for more than six thousand years. Many argue that Austronesian peoples in Southeast Asia originated in Taiwan.[6] Indigenous Taiwanese, however, have long been written out of much of Taiwan's history by scholars of both China and Taiwan, despite their ever-long presence and role in Taiwan's contested state formation process. Indeed, of role Indigenous Taiwanese is critical to understanding how China claimed and saw Taiwan during its imperial era.

Ironically, before Taiwan was claimed by China, it was already a contested state. It had been colonized by the Dutch and Spanish empires and was a home to populations from modern-day China, Japan, Malaysia, the Philippines, and beyond. Pirates also made Taiwan their home. Its geographic location made it a key port for seafarers carrying out both legitimate and illegitimate means of trade and livelihood. And, of course, it was home to a large Indigenous population, who lived all over the island.

All these groups laid claims to Taiwan. None, however, had full control of the island. For example, even though the 1600s are referred to as the Dutch colonial period, it is an overstatement to say the Dutch had sovereignty over all of Taiwan and more accurate to portray the Dutch as having built specific colonies along the west coast over which they had authority, particularly in southern Taiwan. Even Indigenous tribes lived separately from each other and their cultures and lifestyles varied widely. To this day they are not a monolithic group.

The story of Zheng Cheng-gong, known posthumously as Koxinga, is the quintessential historical story known in Taiwan, in China, and even in Japan.[7] Koxinga was a Ming dynasty loyalist and son of the infamous pirate warlord Zheng Zhi-long.[8] Koxinga was born into his father's world of pirating and his Japanese mother's in Nagasaki, Japan. Despite his father's endeavors, Koxinga became a scholar and eventually moved up the ranks in the Ming dynasty.

As the Ming era was coming to an end, the Manchurian Qing were quickly taking power. Koxinga, relying partially on his father's naval power, tried to defeat the Qing, but lost. He was the first major power fleeing to Taiwan after being defeated in a Chinese civil war; the second was the KMT. At the time, the Dutch were largely in control of Taiwan's southern territory.[9] Koxinga, who had a good relationship with the Dutch through his father, attacked them anyway, driving the Dutch out. Koxinga, in fleeing to Taiwan, also brought tens of thousands of Han to the island, marking it as one of the first major eras of settler colonialism in Taiwan.[10] By arriving in Taiwan, Koxinga, who is revered as a Chinese hero for fighting against the barbaric Qing and foreign Dutch, claimed Taiwan as part of China. The Zheng regime lasted in Taiwan for only twenty years before the Qing defeated the regime, claiming Taiwan for its own.

In 1684 the Qing dynasty, the last dynasty of Imperial China, brought Taiwan into its borders. It is important to emphasize this point: before the late 1600s, Taiwan was not formally integrated into the Chinese empire, even during the conquering Mongolian Yuan dynasty. It would be another two hundred years, in 1887, before Taiwan was first designated a province.

The Qing's Claims to Taiwan

Seventeenth-century records from the Qing Kangxi emperor infamously describe Taiwan as "no bigger than a ball of mud."[11] Qing travelers to Taiwan viewed the island as inhospitable and not worth investing resources in, and the Qing dynasty came close to letting Taiwan go. But one former Koxinga naval officer convinced the dynastic rulers that Taiwan was of geopolitical importance and to keep control of the island.[12] The Qing continued to control Taiwan, but their authority over the island was largely weak. Many Indigenous populations resisted Qing rule, leading the Qing to struggle and eventually give up on trying to gain full control of the island.

Dutch, Japanese, and other European colonizing powers still saw the geopolitical and economic importance of Taiwan. The most famous case of an attempt to grow influence on Taiwan came from a Japanese expedition in the late 1800s.[13] With no colonizing authority on the eastern side of Taiwan, the Japanese tried to carve out their own sphere of influence there. Ultimately their expedition failed, but it was enough of a push for the Qing to realize they had to reestablish within East Asia their authority and legitimacy as the rulers of Taiwan.

For two hundred years Taiwan was ruled as a prefecture under the province of Fujian. Only in 1887 did the Qing designate Taiwan as a province. The Qing then began a new policy program of "opening the mountains and pacifying the savages," a final attempt at gaining full control of the island and the Indigenous population who, based off their own wording, were constantly seen in an overwhelmingly pejorative light.[14] This moment is important because it marked the first time Taiwan was considered a province of China. Eight years later, though, the Qing lost the Sino-Japanese War, signed the Treaty of Shimonoseki, and ceded Taiwan to Japanese rule. Simply put, Taiwan was only a province of China for eight years.[15]

Are China's Claims Legitimate?

Legal scholars and historians have debated for centuries over the authoritative nature of China's claims over Taiwan and, more broadly, over the South China Sea.[16] Are its claims based in fact? Is it accurate for China to say that Taiwan has been an inalienable part of China since ancient times? Is Taiwan's contested status just a question of legality?

Ultimately it does not matter how legally binding or historically accurate China's claims over Taiwan are. From China's perspective, Taiwan is part of its mythic history and state-building origin story. Taiwan and the imperial origins of China's claim have been written into the book of contemporary Chinese nationalism and therefore are not bound to legal assertions. What matters is that China continues to claim Taiwan along these primordial lines and places extremely heavy value on the claims. So long as the PRC continues to do this, China's claims over Taiwan will matter, regardless of their technical accuracy. No legal argument or factual proof of Taiwan's status or China's claims will resolve Taiwan's contested status.

Proto-Taiwanese Identity

Despite people living on Taiwan for centuries, the birth of a Taiwanese identity is a relatively modern invention. There was no cohesive Taiwanese identity during the Qing dynasty, when Han people slowly became the majority in Taiwan's population. Nor was there a strong Chinese identity, especially since Qing rule was relatively weak over the island. Qing and Chinese identity are also not inherently synonymous. Most importantly, our understanding of "Chinese" and "Taiwanese" identity are modern terms, despite early signs of identity formation.[17]

The earliest iterations of contemporary Taiwanese identity can be traced to the Japanese colonial era.[18] When Taiwan became a Japanese colony, it faced harsh violence and crackdowns, especially toward Taiwan's Indigenous population. Those living in Taiwan became second-class citizens to the newly arrived Japanese nationals. However, unlike colonies such as Korea and Manchuria, where domestic populations faced ongoing violence for the duration of Japan's colonial reign, life in Taiwan was relatively peaceful. There were, however, clear social stratifications between Japanese, Han, and Indigenous Taiwanese, with the Indigenous receiving particularly harsh treatment during Japanese rule. Taiwanese elites who were able to learn Japanese were also treated better than most Han, who only spoke Hokkien.[19] Japan's colonial era is responsible for a number of critical state-building aspects of contemporary Taiwan, including land reform, education reform, and the creation of domestic infrastructure like railways and roads.[20] Taiwan became so successful that it was considered Japan's "model colony," both because of how the local population was incorporated as colonial subjects into Japanese empire and because of how Japan was able to modernize Taiwan.

One of the most important developments of Japan's colonial era was the rise of Taiwanese consciousness. The first groups to begin thinking and writing about "Taiwan for the Taiwanese" were student movements based in Taiwan, Japan, and even China.[21] Taiwanese elites, despite still being seen as second-class citizens to Japanese, were nevertheless able to secure high levels of education for their children, sending them abroad to Tokyo and even to China to study.

There were two distinct groups of proto-Taiwanese identity movements: reformers and radicals. While both groups advocated for the idea of Taiwan for the Taiwanese, their tactics and understanding of what it meant to be Taiwanese varied.[22] Reformers were ultimately concerned with trying to improve life for the Taiwanese under Japanese colonial rule. For example, the New People's Society's main goal was to abolish the key colonial law that established Taiwanese citizens as secondary to Japanese citizens and legalized discriminatory practices against Taiwanese people.[23] This movement eventually grew to the point where it advocated for an entirely Taiwanese parliament to govern Taiwan's political system. For reformers, Taiwanese identity was as a part of the Han nation, and their time in Tokyo led to them interpreting their Taiwanese identity as "backward," even when compared to Han living in China. As part of the Taiwanese elite, reformers saw most Taiwanese as needing "cultural enlightenment." They focused on trying to educate Taiwanese back home by growing civil society and performing public speeches, seminars, and artistic productions.

More radical groups advocating for Taiwanese identity were heavily influenced by socialism and Marxist thought. They saw most Taiwanese as "unenlightened" and part of a "weak and small nation," but also saw Taiwan as separate from the Chinese nation. They considered their movement for Taiwanese emancipation part of "the global liberation movement of oppressed peoples." These groups were even critical of the New People's Society in Tokyo, which they saw as too reformist-minded and too compromising because of their attempts to reform the Taiwanese people's status within Japan's colonial system, rather than working to abolish the colonial system entirely. These groups appealed strongly to China for help, believing their connection to China provided the rationale for requesting assistance and also that their common enemy was Japan.

The different histories of reformers and radicals show that the concept of Taiwanese identity has long been a matter of contestation, one that echoes in the same questions present in Taiwan today. Some saw Taiwanese identity as connected to China and Chinese identity, while others saw it as a separate identity. For some Taiwanese there was a tension between wanting to identify with a nostalgic and imagined sense of China, versus identifying with the Japanese cultural context in which they lived. This anxiety of identity and lack of feeling of belonging is what set the social foundation for the creation of a third *Taiwanese* identity.

As Leo Ching writes, the Taiwanese living during the Japanese colonial era were stuck between senses of belonging to either Japan or to China, but never truly belonging to either.[24] This third "consciousness" is what created space for Taiwanese to see a new sense of self. As 1900s literatus and advocate of Taiwanese identity and culture Huang Shi-hui wrote: "Taiwan is a peculiar world. Politically, Chinese common language is not allowable. Nationally (in terms of historical experience), Japanese common language is not desirable. Therefore, I suggest that we create an independent Taiwanese culture in order to adjust ourselves to the reality in Taiwan."[25] Student movements were not the only avenues through which Taiwanese resisted Japanese rule. Even elites who gained status among the Japanese used their limited power to create space for Taiwanese agency within their colonial constraints.[26] The 1920s student movement marked the beginning of Taiwanese self-determination and Taiwanese identity as well as the longstanding and deep tradition of student protest and social movements in Taiwan. Almost every major moment of political transition in Taiwan has been accompanied by social protest, often forged by university students.[27]

Meanwhile, in China

During the time Taiwan was colonized by Japan, China was domestically going through one of its most difficult and dynamic moments in history.

In 1911 the Xinhai Revolution marked the end of both the Qing dynasty and Imperial China. In 1912 Sun Yat-sen and his Chinese Nationalist Party founded the Republic of China, then competed for the next decade with numerous other "warlords" over who was going to become the legitimate and authoritative governing body of China.[28] After a complex military and political struggle, the KMT came out on top and the ROC was recognized as the official government of China, both domestically and internationally. Sun died in 1925 and, after a bloody internal skirmish among KMT elite, Generalissimo Chiang Kai-shek became the next leader of the KMT and the ROC.

From 1912 to 1949 the ROC ruled the Chinese mainland.[29] But as a country, the ROC was rife with corruption, run with weak institutions, and, most important, busy dealing with two different wars: the Chinese civil war with the Communist Party of China and the Japanese War of Aggression.[30] Despite the difficult position in which the ROC found itself in trying to govern a war-torn and weak country, internationally it enjoyed widespread support from the Allied powers, especially the United States. From the US perspective the ROC was the obvious choice to back in East Asia because it opposed both Japan, an Axis power, and the Communist Party. Even though the ROC was a brutal authoritarian dictatorship, the Allies still vastly preferred it to a communist administration, even though the United States allied with the Soviet Union during World War II. The ROC itself eventually worked with the CCP to fight against the Japanese Army, but the KMT and the CCP returned to civil war once World War II ended.

Ironically, in the 1930s and early 1940s the CCP, including Mao Zedong himself, signaled strong sympathy for an independent Taiwan. In a famous 1936 interview with Edgar Snow, Mao said, "If the Koreans wish to break away from the chains of Japanese imperialism, we will extend them our enthusiastic help in their struggle for independence. The same thing applies for Taiwan."[31] Multiple reports and writings by the CCP at the time directly stated or inferred strong support for an independent Taiwan vis-à-vis resistance to Japanese imperialism.[32] As Yuan Hsiao and Lawrence L. Sullivan note, however, this support for independence could have simply been limited to Japanese opposition and the CCP still likely saw Taiwan as part of the CCP's intended territory. But these comments by Mao at least acknowledge that the CCP's opposition to an independent Taiwan was neither an inevitable outcome nor a predetermined one by CCP ideology. At one point the CCP may have seen Taiwan as politically or culturally separate but still deeply connected to China. Dogmatic opposition to Taiwanese independence in any way, shape, or form, however, became ingrained in CCP ideology after China's decision to contest its borders and sovereignty following the end of the Chinese civil war.

By the early 1940s the ROC had been internally ravaged by the ongoing civil war, but it maintained its standing internationally and continued to receive strong support and even resources from the United States. Meanwhile, Taiwan was under Japanese rule and largely left out of China's ongoing wars, save for the battalions of Taiwanese serving under the Japanese Imperial Army.[33] The last time Taiwan was part of China was the eight years it was a province under the Qing dynasty. Until 1945 it was never governed by a modern Chinese state.

Creating a Contested Taiwan

Understanding Taiwan's contemporary contestation requires understanding the effect of two connected processes: how Taiwan was handled by the international community following Japan's surrender and how the KMT treated Taiwan after its arrival. The beginning of what would ultimately change Taiwan's path started with the Cairo Conference in 1943. This conference, between the UK prime minister Winston Churchill, US president Franklin Roosevelt, and Generalissimo Chiang set the stage for how the Allied powers planned to push back against Japanese aggression and outlined what exactly would happen to the countries Japan had colonized and occupied after it was defeated. At the end of the conference a communiqué was released that stated explicitly:

> Japan shall be stripped of all the islands in the Pacific which she has seized or occupied since the beginning of the first World War in 1914, and that all the territories Japan has stolen from the Chinese, such as Manchuria, Formosa [Taiwan], and the Pescadores, shall be restored to the Republic of China. Japan will also be expelled from all other territories which she has taken by violence and greed. The aforesaid three great powers, mindful of the

> enslavement of the people of Korea, are determined that in due course Korea shall become free and independent.[34]

Despite not having any legal binding, the communiqué set the stage for how Taiwan would be dealt with at the end of the war. Even though Taiwan was not originally belonging to the Republic of China, it would "be returned," along with Manchuria and the Pescadores (modern-day Penghu). Korea, however, like most other former colonized countries, would be granted independence. When Japan surrendered in 1945 it forfeited Taiwan along with all other colonized parts of East Asia in accordance with the parameters of the surrender agreement. The Potsdam Declaration, which outlined Japan's expected actions, even evoked the Cairo Declaration when denoting Japan's newly reduced sovereignty in East Asia. Subsequently, in line with the Cairo Declaration, the transfer of power over Taiwan went from Japan to the ROC once Japan fully surrendered.

Cairo Declaration Complications

The Cairo Declaration, unbeknownst to those who celebrated its release in 1942, later became a contentious document that further created contested conditions for Taiwan. Without jumping too far ahead of the story, in 1951 Japan signed the Treaty of Peace with Japan (informally known as the San Francisco peace treaty), a formal peace agreement and further renouncement of its imperial practices, which declared:

> (a) Japan, recognizing the independence of Korea, renounces all right, title and claim to Korea, including the islands of Quelpart, Port Hamilton and Dagelet.
> (b) Japan renounces all right, title and claim to Formosa and the Pescadores.[35]

Unlike Korea, Taiwan (formerly Formosa) was not declared independent or part of the ROC. This occurred because in 1951 there were two competing governments that laid claim to Taiwan: the PRC government, which had recently won the Chinese civil war, and the ROC government, which had fled to and was the acting government on Taiwan. What made the global dynamic particularly awkward was that the US representatives wanted ROC representatives to be present at the signing of the treaty, but the British wanted PRC representatives present.

Some see the San Francisco peace treaty as a document that supersedes the Cairo Declaration and thus does not legitimize the ROC's claims over Taiwan.[36] Others disagree and say that the Cairo Declaration is the last legitimate document confirming the ROC's claims to Taiwan.[37] The PRC at the time argued that the Cairo Declaration was the sole document that justified Chinese claims over Taiwan, and that Taiwan thus belonged to the People's Republic of China, not to the Republic of China.[38] For decades leaders all over the world debated whether or not the Cairo Declaration was sufficient proof that the ROC held authority over Taiwan. Many in the UK pushed back, not because they were in favor of Taiwanese independence but because they did not recognize Chiang's KMT as the new legitimate governing body of China, of which Taiwan was considered a part. For the UK, the status of Taiwan was still undetermined and not recognized as under the formal authority of the ROC or the PRC.[39]

Since the ROC had no representatives present at the signing of the San Francisco peace treaty, the party eventually signed its own peace agreement with Japan a year later, in 1952. That treaty states:

> For the purposes of the present Treaty, nationals of the Republic of China shall be deemed to include all the inhabitants and former inhabitants of Taiwan (Formosa) and Penghu (the Pescadores) and their descendants who are of the Chinese nationality in accordance with the laws and regulations which have been or may hereafter be enforced by the Republic of China in Taiwan (Formosa) and Penghu (the Pescadores); and juridical persons of the Republic of China shall be deemed to include all those registered under the laws and regulations which have been or may hereafter be enforced by the Republic of China in Taiwan (Formosa) and Penghu (the Pescadores).[40]

This treaty's wording effectively transferred citizenship of those living under Japanese rule to the ROC and is seen by some to legitimize the ROC's claims to Taiwan or, at the very least, affirms that the PRC's claims over Taiwan are less legitimate. Ultimately a treaty between just the ROC and Japan was not influential in the foreign policy of the United States, Great Britain, or the United Nations. For the ROC, though, the treaty was an important supplement to the San Francisco peace treaty, especially since the ROC was extremely concerned over the question of which countries would back which China. Meanwhile, the PRC continued to argue that the Cairo Declaration justified its own claims over Taiwan.

The ROC's membership in the United Nations, with a seat on the Security Council, made the challenge even more troublesome. Though the world, through the UN, recognized the ROC, Taiwan's status continued to be in question in the minds of all of the international community after World War II. The Soviet Union protested at the UN over the lack of recognition for the PRC over the ROC, in part contributing to the outbreak of the Korean War. As a member of the Allied Forces, the ROC was granted UN membership upon its founding but calls for switching recognition to the PRC as the formal representative of China grew as time went on. Eventually, as the PRC grew in strength and influence and the ROC's hopes of returning to China looked more and more like a pipe dream, the world began to discuss the need for a formal switch from recognizing the ROC to recognizing the PRC.

Ultimately, the Cairo Declaration and the San Francisco peace treaty created deep contention and threw the question of Taiwan's status into the international spotlight. For some, the two treaty documents are proof that the question of Taiwan is unanswered and that there is no historical precedent for either the ROC or the PRC to claim Taiwan. For others they are proof of the ROC's jurisdiction. Still others see them as contemporary justification for the PRC's claims. Eventually, the US and the UK agreed that the United Nations should ultimately decide the status of Taiwan and whether jurisdiction should be given to the ROC or the PRC. Ultimately the question of Taiwan's position was left unresolved. Despite the fact that most other former colonial countries (such as Korea) had the international system's support for their formal independence, Taiwan was instead thrown into an international gray zone.

The purpose of recalling the role these two documents played in creating the international conditions for Taiwan's contested status is not to argue whose interpretation of which treaty is correct. It is beyond the scope of this project to even offer an inference over the international legality of the two documents or the claims made by different states that invoke them. Even if a consensus among nations were found and justification were made, one of the major parties would be unsatisfied, be it the PRC, the ROC, or any other major player invested in Taiwan's status. Simply stated, like international recognition, the legal distinction of who *technically* has the legal claim over Taiwan does not resolve the underlying tension of contestation. Whether or not the PRC's claims are legal or the ROC's right to Taiwan is factually reflected in the signed documents or an international ruling, or a legal justification is made, the two parties will continue to lay claim to Taiwan.

It is important to underscore that at no point in these international debates did any Taiwanese representative have a voice or say in the fate of their home. Only the foreign KMT government and Chiang's regime advocated for Taiwan's autonomy away from the PRC, but not on behalf of the Taiwanese people. Instead, it was aimed at continuing the legacy of the ROC. The status under which Taiwan was placed was entirely concocted by outside forces. Even in 1942, when the Cairo Declaration was written, the ROC was not yet in control of Taiwan. Taiwanese people have never had agency over the international question of their country's contested status, even when the ROC was backed by the United States.

It is this question of Taiwan's agency and its unresolved status that must be addressed. While Taiwan's contested status can be seen through the lens of international relations and foreign policy, the international stage is only half the puzzle for contested states. To fully understand how Taiwan became contested, we must look at the domestic conditions as well. While the debates of great powers helped make Taiwan contested in the international dimension, the power dynamic between the contesting state and the contested people defines the domestic dimension. How did questions of identity and territorial integrity become the defining political question within Taiwan?

Taiwan in 1945

To understand the development of Taiwanese identity in relation to Chinese identity, we must briefly rewind back to the time before the KMT lost the civil war. In 1945, upon learning of Japan's surrender, many in Taiwan were optimistic about the idea of KMT governance.[41] Under Japanese occupation even the most privileged were second-class citizens. A prevailing perception among Taiwanese elites was that under ROC rule they would have more say over Taiwanese politics at best, and, at the very least, living conditions would improve for everyone. Especially for those Taiwanese who were hopeful about embracing a Chinese identity, the idea of KMT rule seemed palatable.

From the KMT's perspective, the return of Taiwan was a geopolitical victory. But the Chinese Nationalist Party underappreciated the distinct fifty-year gap that Taiwan had experienced away from Chinese rule. Taiwan had spent the previous five decades becoming a version of Japanese citizens, not Chinese citizens. They did not experience the Xinhai Revolution nor either war that the rest of China endured. Instead, Taiwanese civil society was rooted in its Japanese colonial experience. To the dismay of its leaders, which had spent the better part of two decades fighting the Japanese Imperial Army, the KMT arrived in Taiwan to find not long-lost Chinese brethren who shared a common language, political views, and sense of contemporary cultural identity, but a version of the enemy with which they had long been in conflict. Taiwanese did not speak standard Chinese. Instead, they either spoke Taiwanese Hokkien, Hakka, various Indigenous languages, or Japanese. Even though the Taiwanese were never fully accepted as Japanese, the KMT immediately felt deeply suspicious that the people would ever be considered fully Chinese.[42]

The KMT thus had two main goals in Taiwan: de-Japanization and Sinicization.[43] Once in power, the KMT immediately established a system of domination over the Taiwanese people, who the KMT saw as "enslaved" by their Japanese upbringing. Japanese as a language was banned. Standard Chinese was made mandatory, and all aspects of China and Chineseness became the focus of education. The person made governor of Taiwan by the KMT, Chen Yi, was almost immediately disliked by local Taiwanese. His government was seen as corrupt, incompetent, and ineffective, but also deeply discriminatory against Taiwanese people.

From a Taiwanese perspective, this was not the colonial reversal moment they had hoped for. Historian James Lin describes this moment as Taiwan's "missing decolonialization."[44] The recolonization of Taiwan, conducted by a different foreign power that set up systems of discrimination and oppression against the local population, seemed just like the previous Japanese regime.

The KMT, which held a deep distrust and dislike of anyone who was overtly Japanese, especially disliked the Taiwanese elites, who had essentially spent the previous fifty years assimilating in order to maintain their status under Japanese colonial rule. Under KMT rule, these Taiwanese elites were rendered both illiterate (because they could not speak standard Chinese) and powerless, and thus they were seen as potential enemies to the KMT.

Taiwanese perceptions of the KMT worsened following one of the most important political events in contemporary Taiwanese history: the 288 Incident in 1947.[45] The event that catalyzed the 228 Incident was seemingly minor: a woman who was illegally selling cigarettes next to a government building in Taipei was arrested by two police officers for the act. A mob of protesters stepped in to defend the woman and a bystander was shot by one of the policemen. A riot ensued, and the story of the event spread throughout the island, despite the propaganda department's best efforts. Over the next week numerous antigovernment protests broke out in response to the event.

The anti-KMT protests grew to such a degree that the government all but lost authority over the island. Even after two years of living under this new discriminatory government, the Taiwanese were able to subdue the KMT's forces, which only had minimal troops stationed on the island. The majority were still in China fighting the civil war against the CCP; Taiwan was hardly a priority for them at that point. For a moment the Taiwanese people felt like they might finally be able to have a say in the future of their country. Taiwanese elites even established the "Taiwanese Resolution Committee" to negotiate with the KMT to gain more autonomy and better treatment for Taiwanese people. Once word of the chaotic protests and subsequent loss of authority that had ensued on Taiwan reached China, however, the army sent mass reinforcements to the island. No negotiations with local Taiwanese ever occurred.[46]

Instead, in March of 1947 the army began to swarm cities in Taiwan. Random killings and violence ensued all around the island. Any elite who had tried to form any sort of political resistance to the KMT was immediately targeted. The exact number of Taiwanese who died is unknown, but an estimated twenty to thirty thousand Taiwanese died during the crackdown. After the KMT regained control of Taiwan, the subjugation of Taiwanese people continued.[47]

In 1949 the KMT lost the civil war in China to Mao and his Communist Party. In the year leading up to the final defeat of the KMT, its allies began fleeing en masse to Taiwan. In late 1949 Chiang Kai-shek himself fled to Taiwan, fully surrendering China to Mao and the newly established PRC. Despite the KMT's evacuation to Taiwan, the party's leaders maintained that it was the true governing body of China and would one day retake it for themselves. Until such a time, the KMT and the ROC would both exist in Taiwan.

Life for Taiwanese people under the KMT after 1949 did not improve. Instead, martial law was enacted and maintained for nearly forty years, one of the longest-running periods of martial law in modern global history. Taiwanese people were denied basic freedoms, including freedom of speech, assembly, and travel. The KMT, which had just finished fighting the Japanese and were defeated by the Communist Party, was highly suspicious of seemingly everyone. For the Taiwanese, the KMT and those who fled with it still saw the remnants of their Japanese cultural attachments as a "remaining poison" within those who had "lost their Chineseness." But even Chinese citizens who fled with the KMT were closely monitored out of fear that potential communist sympathizers and spies were among them. While most former colonies in the world were given the opportunity for decolonization and eventual independence, Taiwan was instead recolonized by Chiang Kai-shek, who created an authoritarian, paranoid police state. The KMT did create local elections for low-level positions that held very limited political power.[48] Such small liberalizations gave Taiwan the image of a "free China," despite the strong authoritarian system that remained in place for decades. This era is referred to by many as the "White Terror" because of the intensely unfree and unfair society that the KMT created.

One of the most important social constructions brought on by the KMT's control of Taiwan was the creation of two new identity groups within Taiwan: the *benshengren* and the *waishengren*. The *waishengren*, literally translated as "people outside the province," comprises the Han who came with the KMT to Taiwan after 1949. The *benshengren*, or "people from the province," comprises the Han who were already living in Taiwan before the KMT's arrival. Indigenous Taiwanese were largely left out of this distinction.

The dynamics between these two groups were deeply complex. The *waishengren* were perceived by those already in Taiwan to be the privileged class, while the *benshengren* were seen by the *waishengren* with deep skepticism as former Japanese subjects and culturally different and even inferior. At first the *waishengren* were exclusively granted positions of power and the *benshengren* were often discriminated against for their clear cultural difference. While the *waishengren* certainly enjoyed privileges unavailable to the *benshengren*, most *waishengren* themselves were not elites. The average *waishengren*, essentially a refugee living in a foreign home—having just fled the end of the civil war—were continually surveilled by the KMT government, which was weary of communist infiltrators.[49] Meanwhile, the *benshengren* were forced to once again accept a second-class position in society as the ROC exodus arrived in Taiwan. Both the *waishengren* and the *benshengren* suffered different kinds of structural inequalities under the KMT's authoritarian government, but their identities became salient as a way to distinguish different parts of civil society from each other. As time went on, some *benshengren* went on to join the KMT. The KMT's reconstruction of Taiwanese civil society and the reeducation of Taiwanese, through the imposition of the Chinese language and a China-centric education, ultimately instilled a new Chinese identity and association with the ROC within Taiwan. Even though some Taiwanese before the KMT authoritarian era may have identified with China or even with the ROC, it became a state requirement for citizens to do so, regardless of whether you were *benshengren* or *waishengren*.

Despite the KMT's efforts to instill a fully Chinese identity on Taiwanese people through education and language policies, many *benshengren* resisted.[50] As time went on, civil society began to grow, a strong middle class formed, and people of all backgrounds began to participate in social and political life. This growth in part contributed to the conditions for Taiwan's eventual democratization, but importantly it also began to instill a sense of identity among those who lived in Taiwan. In the 1970s, organized resistance against the KMT began to form. A group called the *tangwai* began to advocate for a different political future for Taiwan that pushed against the KMT's authoritarian rule. The full story of the *tangwai* and their role in today's contemporary politics is discussed in a later chapter, but it is important to emphasize here that a key part of *tangwai* politics is political freedom for Taiwanese people living on Taiwan. For some this has taken the form of advocating for Taiwanese independence; for others it is about self-determination, meaning Taiwanese having a say in what their future ought to be, often framing Taiwan as the "free China."[51] This continuation of the Taiwanese identity, which first sprouted during the Japanese colonial era, is a growing iteration of "Taiwan for the Taiwanese." Who and what the Taiwanese were defined as is not necessarily clear, since the *tangwai* are made up of multiple factions. But the *tangwai*'s main division in identity formed around support for or against the KMT.

Debates by Taiwanese intellectuals and the literati in the 1970s and 1980s were centered around what it means to have a Taiwanese or Chinese "consciousness," what types of connections people in Taiwan have (or do not have) with China, and how this ought to affect the sociopolitical goals of the *tangwai*.[52] At the time, some Taiwanese saw Chinese people as a "ruling and oppressing people" while they themselves were a "ruled and oppressed people." Others sought to advocate for a Taiwanese identity that balanced both a local Taiwanese consciousness and a Chinese national identity. Others advocated for a Taiwanese identity sans any Chinese consciousness. Although specific interpretations of Taiwanese consciousness varied, most fundamentally agreed that Taiwan had evolved separately from China due to different historical, social, and political paths over the previous century, and that this ought to be reflected in local identity.

Unrecognition of the ROC

Concurrent with the questions of Taiwanese identity at home, the KMT was dealing with an existential challenge internationally. The rise of the PRC had caused most of the world to eye rapprochement with Mao. Beginning in the 1970s, US president Richard Nixon visited China and began official talks to open the possibility of establishing formal diplomatic relations between the United States and China.[53] One of the PRC's key demands for establishing formal relations was that the United States had to pull its recognition of the ROC as the legitimate and authoritative governing body of China. This was not a demand made only to the United States. Every country that wanted to establish formal ties with China had to first end formal ties with the ROC.

For the PRC to consider joining the United Nations, which was something most major powers also wanted, the UN had to switch recognition from the ROC to the PRC.

The reason the PRC made such strong demands over rescinding recognition of the ROC was because the ROC claimed Taiwan as part of its territory. Even though the PRC was barely more than twenty years old, it still baked into its state-building project and identity the idea that Taiwan was an inseparable part of its territory. At early points in Mao's rule he did propose dropping Taiwan as an issue or, as noted earlier, recognizing its independence efforts in opposition to Imperial Japan. But once the KMT fled to Taiwan, Mao made it a point to include Taiwan into the growing mythos of the PRC's new nationalism. From the PRC's perspective, the civil war would not be truly concluded until the KMT was fully defeated and Taiwan was governed by the PRC. Even though the Chinese civil war had ended and the KMT had fled to Taiwan, the PRC still made multiple militaristic attempts to take Taiwan and its surrounding islands, climaxing twice, in the First and Second Taiwan Strait Crises. Despite their unsuccessful attempts, Mao spent the next twenty-plus years rhetorically making Taiwan part of the PRC's identity. Though in reality it was not part of the PRC, it was something the PRC needed for the state to be fully realized. This language of "national rejuvenation" and the need for Taiwan to be part of the PRC for the "rejuvenation process" to be complete is something still heard today.

The PRC justified its claims over Taiwan in two ways. The first claim was a kind of cultural essentialism, which stated that Taiwan had always been part of China and that the PRC, as the legitimate and authoritative ruler of China, had rightful jurisdiction over Taiwan. The second claim arose out of the Cairo Declaration. The PRC argued that the document, which states that Taiwan was to be returned to China, makes the PRC the legitimate ruler. From the PRC's perspective, if the world switched recognition from the ROC to the PRC, then it would not matter whether the Cairo Declaration technically says the "Republic of China" because that would mean it no longer is recognized as *China*.

China's claims over Taiwan put the United States and much of the world in an awkward position, because the United States had no desire to break off ties completely with the ROC. The ROC had become increasingly important to the global economy, plus it was a critical geostrategic ally of the United States. Most important, and for the same reasons, the United States did not want the PRC to take Taiwan or for Chiang Kai-shek to attack the PRC. From the PRC's perspective, any relationship that the United States had with the ROC was viewed as a slight against the PRC.

The first step in the transition was how to respond to the PRC's claims over Taiwan. The solution by the United States was to *acknowledge* the PRC's claims without *recognizing* or *challenging* the PRC's claims.[54] In the first of three communiqués released by the PRC and the United States, this approach was formally taken by the United States.[55] Meanwhile, the PRC declared that there was only one China—the one led by the PRC—and that Taiwan was part of that China. This is where today's One China Policy by the United States and One China Principle by the PRC originated. Not until the second communiqué in 1979 was the deal finally sealed, and globally the world ceased to recognize the ROC as a state and instead recognized the PRC as the official China. From that point on, Taiwan was unrecognized.[56]

Democratization in Taiwan

Despite losing its international status, life continued in Taiwan. Identity was not the only thing rapidly changing in Taiwan in the 1970s. Taiwan was modernizing, economically, culturally, and politically. The conditions for democratization were slowly becoming apparent, despite the PRC's continued authoritarian path occurring just across the Taiwan Strait. There was no singular variable or factor that led to democratization. Although many claim that it was singularly the KMT's reform or singularly grassroots activism that led to democracy in Taiwan, the reality is that a myriad of critical variables coincided to create the necessary conditions for regime change. For example, decades of land reform, a growing middle class, and limited but meaningful electoral experiences during martial law all played a key role in creating Taiwan's democratization.[57] Of course, reformists within the KMT, who perceived democratization to be the path that would allow them to maintain power over Taiwan, did as well.[58] Finally, a strong and robust grassroots pro-democracy movement by the *tangwai* played a pivotal role in promoting democracy within Taiwan's civil society.[59] In the late 1980s martial law was officially lifted. In 1996 Taiwan held its first free and fair presidential election.

The Wild Lily Movement

Social protest was one of the key means by which Taiwanese civil society participated in the democratization process. Although we typically think of the *tangwai*'s role in democratization, other meaningful separate mass movements also mobilized during Taiwan's democratic transition. For scholars of Taiwanese social protest, one of the biggest protodemocracy social movements outside of the *tangwai* movement was the Wild Lily Movement. This protest in the 1990s was the first major clash between Taiwan's president, Lee Teng-hui, and social movement activists, which would go on to define Lee's sympathetic attitude toward pro-Taiwan activists. The Wild Lily Movement was one of the biggest moments for student activists and also for the DPP, whose members participated fully but separately from the student activists.[60] The protests started when student activists were unhappy with the direction Lee was taking Taiwan's democratic reforms. Even though Lee was known for his reformist attitudes within the KMT, activists believed he was not reformist enough. Thousands of students eventually mobilized in protest, with four key demands:

1. Dissolve the National Assembly.
2. Abolish the "Temporary Previsions Effective During the Period of National Mobilization for Suppression of the Communist Rebellion" (law establishing marshal law).
3. Hold a national conference to discuss constitutional change.
4. Set a timetable for political and economic reforms.[61]

The movement grew, even leading a few participants to engage in a hunger strike; eventually Lee agreed to meet with the protesters. Although he acknowledged their movement, dedication, and patriotism to Taiwan, Lee did not actually make any meaningful concessions or policy changes because of the protests.[62] Lee's acknowledgment of the protesters' efforts and his desire to demonstrate that he shared their values was enough to demobilize the Wild Lily Movement. Even though it is celebrated as a key moment during democratization, the political impact of the Wild Lily Movement was limited. It is another example of a mass movement mobilizing in Taiwan out of which no new political parties formed despite the movement's strongly stated separate identity from the DPP. The protest, however, still left a critical imprint on social activism in Taiwan, because it was one of the first major movements that later Sunflower Movement protestors participated in, including Fan Yun, the eventual founder of the Social Democratic Party.

Taiwan, a Contested State

Two conflicting stories about Taiwan have played out over the same time: one between the PRC and the ROC, and one between the KMT, the Taiwanese people, and the various forces that colonized Taiwan. This combination of international fighting over where Taiwan exists territorially and the domestic unrest over who the Taiwanese are makes Taiwan a contested state.

What makes the recognition aspect of Taiwan's contested status unique is that it came out of the global community's unanimous decision to *un*-recognize the status of the ROC. Unlike most contested states, which want to gain recognition they never had in the first place, the ROC had recognition but lost it. In other words, it was the international community that collectively decided to demarcate Taiwan as an unrecognized state. What the ROC does have in common with other contested states, however, is a background of war that ultimately led to its unrecognized status. Because of the civil war between the PRC and the ROC, Taiwan as the ROC is unable to be included in the international order. But the issue of recognition is only one of the key variables that makes Taiwan contested. The second is its contested identity.

What makes Taiwanese contested identity different from other contested states is the existence of many "contesting parties" to the case of Taiwan. It is not simply Taiwanese identity versus Chinese identity. It is Taiwanese identity versus a Republic of China Chinese identity versus a People's Republic of China Chinese identity. The initial resistance to Chinese identity came as a form of resistance to the KMT and the ROC's understanding of Taiwanese identity.

As a result of centuries of combined international and domestic layers of contestation, today it is possible to see Taiwanese identity as unique, from both ROC Chinese and PRC Chinese identities. The ROC Chinese experience was painted from the memory of Chinese fleeing the mainland with the KMT and becoming part of the privileged class on the island of Taiwan. By contrast, the Taiwanese experience was colored by Japanese colonialism, the 228 Incident and the White Terror, and a continued feeling as an oppressed, unequal group. The PRC Chinese experience, as well as its political and cultural life, is largely defined by the experiences of the PRC since 1949. PRC Chinese identity is shaped by Communist Party rule and defined by the ways in which Mao and subsequent party leaders intertwined party principles with Marxist-Leninist ideals. By contrast, Taiwanese identity is defined by democracy, meaning living in a system with not just free and fair elections but one founded on a memory of the struggle and transition away from authoritarianism and toward democracy.

What this means for Taiwan as a contested state is that there are thick, complex layers to each contested question. First, where is Taiwan? Is it geographically part of China, as defined by the ROC's territorial claims, or by the PRC's territorial claims, which are not the same? Does Taiwan geographically consist of the main island and surrounding smaller islands, that is, no direct connection to continental China? Some in Taiwan contest Taiwan geography by insisting that only *some* of the surrounding islands are part of Taiwan. Second, what does it mean to be Taiwanese? Can those who identify with the ROC be included in the Taiwanese ethnic umbrella? Can one be both Chinese and Taiwanese? According to those seeking independence for Taiwan, the answer is yes. What about Indigenous and non-Han Taiwanese? What role do minorities have in creating a Taiwanese identity that fits the larger state-building project? What exactly *is* Taiwan's state-building project? Is it a mission to create a state that will one day unify with the PRC, or is it a mission to create a separate Republic of China? Should the ROC become fully independent or maintain its contested status, or should Taiwan abolish the ROC and create a new Republic of Taiwan?[63]

No consensus on these questions exists in Taiwan. Rather, they are the defining political questions that penetrate every aspect of Taiwan's socioeconomic and political life. Since Taiwan's democratization, these questions of identity and territory have manifested as electoral political actions and social unrest. Unlike other states that are not contested and that define their political spectrum over issues such as taxes or wealth redistribution, Taiwan's political spectrum is conceptualized by where a given political actor falls along Taiwan's contested issues.[64] Some extreme positions on this spectrum, however, are increasingly rejected by civil society. For example, support for immediate unification with the PRC has become so low that 98 percent of Taiwanese opt for anything but unification with the PRC. Identities have also changed over time. Once democratization occurred and Taiwanese were safe and free to publicly identify as Taiwanese, the number of people who identify as Chinese began to decline. Today the majority of people see themselves as Taiwanese, not Chinese, with the remainder identifying as both Taiwanese *and* Chinese. The smallest demographic group is those who identify as Chinese only. The vast majority of Taiwanese support the political status quo, not formal independence and especially not unification with the PRC.[65] While the status quo, however defined, helps keep the peace in the Taiwan Strait, it ultimately cannot provide a meaningful answer for Taiwan's larger questions of who and where. So long as Taiwan remains contested within the status quo, its politics will continue to be defined by questions of identity and territory.

THREE

Mobilizing without the Missiles

In 2012 Ma Ying-jeou successfully won reelection to parliament, securing the KMT's majority in the Legislative Yuan and triumphing over the DPP once again. Ever since former president Chen Shui-bian's corruption scandal, green-leaning politics had failed to successfully mobilize and win back control of parliament or the presidency. The DPP was in disarray. For pro-independence activists, the idea that the formal political arena could lead to meaningful change became increasingly bleak. As one founding member of the NPP put it, "Leading up to the Sunflower Movement, activists saw politics as extremely rotten, so if you were to suggest you wanted to enter politics you'd be laughed at. It would be to get your hands dirty. We had never really wanted to enter formal politics."[1]

Something changed in 2013 with the introduction of the Cross-Strait Service Trade Agreement bill. Fear was in the air in a way activists had not felt before. In an interview this same founder of the NPP was able to put his finger on this fear: "It was not that the CSSTA made us aware of the fear of China. Before the Sunflower Movement, Ma had already brought so much of China—people, money, investment—and we were already afraid. But when the CSSTA bill passed, we were afraid it would break Taiwan."

Fear of the CSSTA's passage weighed heavily on the minds of those seeking to protect Taiwan's sovereignty. "It was a bad time for activists . . . the KMT was still seen as the dominant party, and the DPP was seen as incapable. We were honestly scared. If we lost the 2016 election, we believed there would be no 2020 election. The KMT would sell us out to China by then."[2]

Despite their years of hesitancy to enter formal politics because of their disillusionment with the DPP and their frustration with the KMT's dominance, a sense of dread and desperation for change began to emerge among activists. "If we did not protect the presidency or the Legislative Yuan, by 2020 every pro-democracy movement or organization in Taiwan would be overrun by the KMT and the CCP. This threat was felt by some of us, and we decided we needed to do something."[3] That "something" was eventually the formation of movement parties, despite past reluctance to entertain the idea of formal political engagement.

The fear of China and the threats felt coming from the PRC struck me as unexpected. Typically when we theorize about China threatening Taiwan, we think first of traditional security issues, such as threats of war or military intimidation. But the kind of fears that activists were talking about were not related to the military. Instead, activists described two feelings of dire threat. The first was a general fear over the KMT "selling" or "giving" Taiwan to China. The second was even more abstract. It was not simply fear of the KMT giving Taiwan to China, but anxiety about what China would do to Taiwan, its democracy, and the lifestyle that Taiwanese people had become accustomed to, including the right of Taiwan and Taiwanese people to continue to exist as Taiwan and Taiwanese people.

Military threats are neither new nor uncommon for Taiwan. Since 2020 thousands of People's Liberation Army fighter jets have flown into Taiwan's air defense identification zone (ADIZ). But threats from China like these long predate the modern age. Once the KMT arrived in Taiwan in the 1940s, the concept of "threats from the PRC" have been baked into Taiwanese identity.

Although Chinese military threats have increased in both quality and quantity over the years, few in Taiwan ever pay them particular mind. In the hundreds of hours of interviews conducted for this book, no subject ever expressed a need or desire to mobilize or take any sort of political action based on China's military threats. But the CSSTA, a trade bill, was felt by many activists to be the most existential threat to Taiwan they had ever faced.

Threats are a critical part of the puzzle surrounding contested states and movement party formation. Why do some threats mobilize activists while others do not? Why did the CSSTA inspire activists to enter formal politics while decades of military threats from China had led to no political action? Why did a trade bill spark such a massive watershed moment while thousands of military actions largely have gone unnoticed?

Threats and Contested States

In a contested state, the fundamental idea of "threat" is perceived differently than in a non-contested state because threats made by the contesting state are an everyday ordeal. Threats made by the contesting state are frequent, varied, and clearly intentioned. They are a regular feature of everyday life in places like Taiwan. The PRC, for example, makes regular announcements of its intention to "unify" Taiwan through both military and nonmilitary means. When threats become a daily occurrence, the very psychological approach and reaction of citizens who endure them changes. Were the PRC to openly threaten the United States with military action, it would be reasonable to expect Americans to respond hysterically. But in Taiwan, where China regularly makes military threats, citizens rarely even have a response.

There are three kinds of threat that contested states face: rhetorical threats, military threats, and threats through domestic co-optation. Military and rhetorical threats do not influence Taiwanese civil society in ways that they would in non-contested states, but domestic co-optation does have a mobilization effect that increases the likelihood of movement party formation.

Conceptualizing Contested Threats

Social scientist Charles Tilly defines "threat" as "the probability that existing benefits will be taken away or new harms inflicted if the challenging groups fail to act."[4] When talking specifically about threat to a contested state by a contesting state, however, more conceptual specification is necessary. Threats are one of the most normalized interactions between contesting and contested states. The normalization of threatening behavior by the contesting state toward the contested state is what also makes sets of threats qualitatively different from non-contesting states. Were any non-contested state to be regularly threatened with the same frequency and magnitude as contested states, an international incident would likely ensue. But because contested states exist in a marginalized position, such threats either go unnoticed by or are acceptable enough to the international order that they do not warrant intervention. Said differently, in today's international order it is normal and acceptable for a contesting state to threaten a contested state, while using the same type of threat toward a non-contested state would be interpreted as a clear act of aggression, if not war. For a contested state, these daily threats are barely noticed. Although the governments of contested states certainly pay

FIGURE 2. A Typology of Contesting State Threat

TYPE OF THREAT	DEFINITION	EXAMPLES	EFFECT ON CIVIL SOCIETY
Domestic co-optation	Infiltration of contesting state into democratic institutions	2008 KMT-ARATS meeting 2012 Want Want's media 2014 KMT-sponsored CSSTA	High
Military	Signal of intent to punish or invade	1996 Third Taiwan Strait Crisis 2004 Routine invasion drills 2019 PLA missile test and air force drill	Intermediate
Rhetorical	Verbal threats of punishment or invasion	1984 Deng Xiaoping public address 1999 Jiang Zemin public address 2019 Xi Jinping public address	Low

attention and react accordingly to all types of threats, understanding why only some threats are felt at the grassroots level is important, especially when the consequences of threats can lead to sweeping changes in a contested state's political institutions.

Chinese threats, in particular, have been fundamental to Taiwan's political development, even before democratization. The KMT's constant anxiety about the PRC waging war against Taiwan, along with an irrational fear of communist infiltrators or turncoats within Taiwanese society, were both justifications for the authoritarian regime's harsh repression.[5] Today, China has continued to use its position as a contesting state to influence, construct, and disrupt political and social life in Taiwan. The daily threats that Taiwan faces are by no means unique to Taiwan. Scholars of Eastern European democratization have long accounted for how fears of Sovietization or Russification have affected democratization, consolidation, and other domestic political features of countries in Eastern Europe.[6] The nature of threats by the contesting state in Eastern Europe has also changed over time. Beyond affecting institutional development within fledgling Eastern European democracies, the post-Soviet era has in part been defined by threat from Russia. For example, several Baltic states in the early 1990s defined their foreign policy and military strategies based on perceived threat from Russia.[7] Although Russia's mere existence instilled a constant fear, its effect on domestic politics varied. Erik Noreen and Roxanna Sjöstedt argue that political elites have sometimes used Russian threats to their advantage, but have downplayed Russia's threat at other times, depending on their own political goals.[8] Russian threats have particularly defined modern Ukrainian politics.

Not All Threats Are Created Equal

Different types of threat from the PRC affect Taiwan differently. The first type, rhetorical threat, has been a constant throughout Taiwan's post-1949 history. From Mao to Xi Jinping, the so-called Taiwan question has been a pillar of the CCP's ethnonationalism and is a central talking point for party leaders. These include formal writings in party documents, op-eds written in party-controlled newspapers, speeches made by party leaders, and expressions in other media and venues. The intended audience of rhetorical threats toward Taiwan, however, is not always the Taiwanese people. Instead, they are often geared toward Chinese citizens. As William Callahan contends, the CCP produces a kind of nationalism for its citizens to consume that is meant to reinforce PRC identity and party legitimacy.[9] Rhetorical threats are meant for Chinese citizens, rather than Taiwanese citizens, because the party has created a mythos of "retaking" Taiwan to which the party must continually pay lip service.[10] Since the founding of the PRC in 1949, it has loudly, openly, and consistently threatened Taiwan through this kind of rhetorical intimidation. Yet every time such a statement is made in PRC newspapers, party documents, or by party leaders in speeches, Taiwanese society shows little reaction. People in Taiwan rarely even notice these threats, let alone react with any kind of collective action. One can reasonably conjecture that rhetorical threats have a minimal effect on Taiwanese civil society.

Military threats, unlike rhetorical threats, show a higher-level commitment to the threat being made by the PRC. Military threats often come in the form of missile testing off Taiwan's shores, troop and force drills meant to simulate an invasion, or People's Liberation Army jets or ships circling and entering Taiwan's ADIZ. Some argue that China's military threats are similar to its rhetorical threats in that they are geared toward China's domestic audience more than toward Taiwan's domestic audience. Edward Friedman argues that "China's missile exercises against Taiwan were served to the Chinese people as a television spectacular."[11] Susan Shirk agrees: "[The PRC] had made Taiwan a litmus test of the nationalist legitimacy of the communist regime . . . taking action to reunify with Taiwan plays a special role in maintaining the legitimacy of the party."[12]

Others agree that the intended audience is indeed Taiwan's citizens. Bruce Jacobs argues that the Third Taiwan Strait Crisis was geared specifically toward deterring Taiwanese voters from electing the DPP's candidate.[13] Some suggest that military threats are a kind of cognitive warfare aimed at Taiwanese voters to make them feel more helpless or have less faith in their government's ability to defend their country.[14] Ja Ian Chong, David Huang, and Wen-Chin Wu have shown that the PRC's threats toward Taiwan do lead to Taiwanese citizens taking a colder view of the PRC.[15] The specific threat of war appears to push Taiwanese voters to support certain policies or political parties during election season. For example, some public opinion polls show that support for independence would likely increase if there was no threat of war.[16] Although a hypothetical question, it demonstrates the effect that looming military threats have on voting behavior. We should subsequently expect military threats to have some effect on civil society overall, but the kind of effect may vary.

A domestic co-optation threat in Taiwan occurs when internal democratic institutions are coercively used by the PRC or pro-China forces to either weaken their democratic integrity or create channels for the PRC to exert influence on Taiwan's domestic politics. This kind of threat is different from rhetorical and military threats because it is an indirect challenge to Taiwan's status. Rhetorical and military threats can be easily identified, while domestic co-optation is often more subtle and thus more difficult to detect. This kind of threat occurs when pro-China forces purposefully co-opt parts of Taiwan's democratic system or civil society organizations to undermine or weaken Taiwan's democracy, with the purpose of making the PRC's goal of unification easier. Unlike military or rhetorical threats, a domestic co-optation threat solicits a qualitatively different kind of response from civil society and is more likely to lead to protest or backlash from Taiwan's citizens.

Social movement theory can help explain why domestic co-optation threat mobilizes while rhetorical and military threats do not. When democratic institutions within Taiwan are coerced into pushing a pro-PRC agenda, threat is felt for two reasons. First, domestic co-optation may affect the daily lives of Taiwanese citizens in ways that rhetorical and military threats do not. When institutions like the press are co-opted by pro-PRC organizations, it has the potential to directly threaten fundamental aspects of Taiwan's democracy, like freedom of speech or freedom of the press. Or, say, if a trade bill designed to take control of large swaths of Taiwan's economy passes, it has the potential to alter or destabilize parts of people's everyday lives. This kind of disruption to everyday life is known as "quotidian disruption." The "breakdown most likely to be associated with movement emergence is that which penetrates and disrupts, or threatens to disrupt, taken for granted everyday routines and expectancies."[17] When pro-China forces threaten to alter democratic institutions that are taken for granted within Taiwanese society, and when these changes have the potential to alter the daily lives of Taiwanese citizens, we can expect an actual response from civil society.

Second, a domestic co-optation threat creates the political context for mobilization that other types of threat do not.[18] When the CCP uses rhetorical or military threats, there are no institutional channels for civil society to challenge the threats or express their grievances in response. However, when domestic institutions such as political parties or other organizations that advocate on behalf of the CCP threaten Taiwan's democracy from within, an opening is created for opposition parties and social movements to mobilize directly against the co-opted institutions. In other words, social movement organizations cannot affect the CCP directly, but they can affect the institutions advocating on behalf of the CCP. When domestic co-optation threat is felt, citizens have agency to respond to the threat.

Quotidian disruption theory posits that the sheer repetition and normalization of military and rhetorical threats causes no disruption to Taiwan's daily existence and thus would have a minimal effect on mobilization. Instead, they become a normal, everyday part of life. Domestic co-optation, however, is not an abstract idea among Taiwanese citizens. Unlike a rhetorical or military threat that is made far away from daily life, domestic co-optation directly affects everyday domestic politics. Military and rhetorical threats, meanwhile, leave citizens at the mercy of government-to-government interactions. No amount of mobilization in Taiwan will deter military or rhetorical threats. Only when the threat from China is felt through a domestic institution and has the potential to affect everyday life in Taiwan are citizens likely to mobilize.

Third, Taiwanese civil society organizations, including social movements and lobbying groups, have limited to no control or sway over Communist Party rhetoric such as, for example, a decision to conduct military exercises. Instances of rhetorical and military threats never actually lead to any sort of domestic backlash. Although Taiwanese politicians often release official responses to rhetorical and military threats from the PRC, nothing changes domestically. Despite years of weapons tests, invasion drills, and air space incursions, none of these threats have ever materialized into an actual attack or invasion. Although these threats are often seen as credible, the regularity and lack of actual follow-through has led to Taiwanese society remaining unaffected when they occur. This habitual threat pattern by the PRC is exacerbated by the inability of Taiwanese voters to influence their occurrence. Put simply, Taiwanese do not feel rhetorical or military threats because they are often abstract and far away.

A comparative historical analysis of two critical junctures in Taiwan history, defined by climaxes of varying kinds of threat, show that military and rhetorical threats have a null effect on social movement mobilization while domestic co-optation threat can and does solicit social movement mobilization. Two case studies follow, with data drawn from interviews of activists, organizers, and politicians and several primary and secondary sources, including newspaper articles from the past five decades, personal writings from state elites, and other contemporary studies of Taiwanese history.

Case 1: The Third Taiwan Strait Crisis

Taiwan's first direct presidential election nearly brought catastrophe to the country. China's near-decision to bomb Taiwan into literal nonexistence did not simply happen by chance circumstance. Democratization set the stage, the rise of pro-independence opposition parties wrote the script, and KMT president Lee Teng-hui played the lead role. Despite the fact that the crisis led to an international incident that redefined cross-strait relations, the event nevertheless had no major mobilizing effect on civil society. Rather than cause mass panic or major domestic instability, it simply became a topic of discussion during the 1996 election.

Democratization Continues

After decades of contention, Taiwan began to democratize in the late 1980s. Regime change from the KMT's authoritarian martial law system to a multiparty democracy brought three critical changes to Taiwan with regard to the Chinese threat. First, Taiwan's political identity became radically different from China's. Although the KMT and the CCP had been mortal enemies for decades, the governments were alike in their authoritarian nature and the limits they imposed on an individual citizen's ability to participate in politics. By changing the political regime, Taiwanese citizens became institutionally different from Chinese citizens. Taiwanese citizens could now access formal politics through multiple forms of political participation that Chinese citizens did not have access to. Most important, by democratizing, Taiwan complicated the prospects of unification under either the PRC or the ROC. The CCP were forced into coercing the KMT into unification, but also coercing Taiwanese citizens, who now had agency in the country's future.

Second, democratization cemented a Taiwanese consciousness within civil society. Although Taiwanese identity did not emerge during democratization, only following democratization did that the identity became

FIGURE 3. Effect of Military Threat on Civil Society

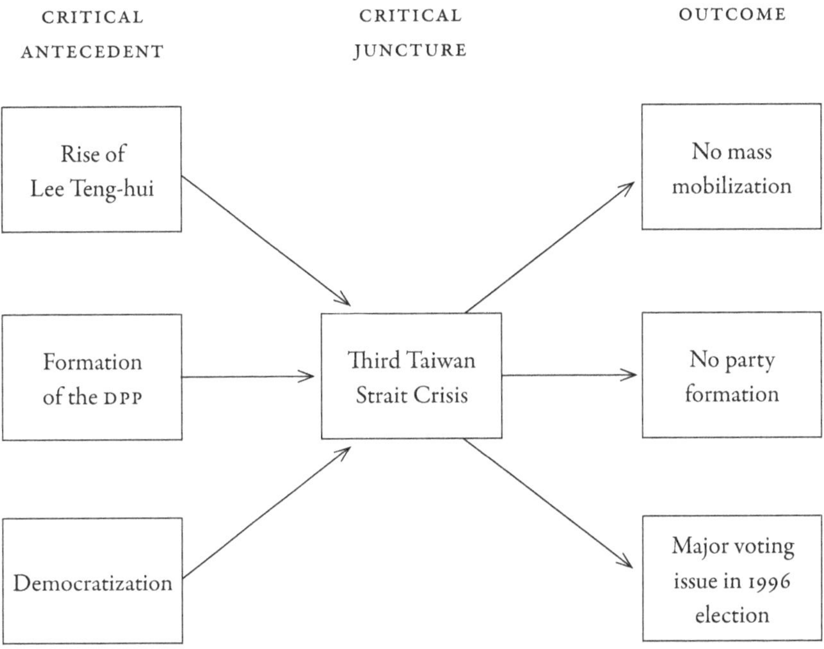

legitimate in the eyes of the ROC government, which now had to accept those who identified as Taiwanese (not Chinese) as legitimate players in Taiwanese politics. Those who advocated for a Taiwanese consciousness went from being illegal enemies of the state to those who defined Taiwan's fundamental political spectrum during elections. The rise of Taiwanese identity matters when discussing the threat from China because identity itself came to define the primary political cleavage within Taiwan.[19] Democratization cemented the political spectrum with advocacy for a Taiwanese state at one end and unification with China (under either the ROC or the PRC) at the other. Although the KMT and the CCP maintained a cold, mutually antagonistic relationship throughout democratization, the formation of the Taiwanese-versus-Chinese identity litmus test eventually sowed the seeds of KMT-CCP rapprochement.

Formation of the DPP

Democratization would not have been nearly as anxiety-inducing for the CCP (or, to a large degree, the KMT) had there not been such a strong, fully functional opposition party already formed by the time it took effect. The formation of the DPP began with the *tangwai* movement toward the end of the KMT martial law era. The rise of the opposition party took decades of activism, through both formal and informal channels. Despite years of factional disagreements over using formal and informal political channels, the movement was able to cooperate and come to each other's aid as needed. For example, it was the moderate faction of lawyers who defended the radical faction of activists in court following the 1979 Kaohsiung Incident (a KMT crackdown over a *tangwai* protests).[20] In 1986 in Taipei, during a meeting over how to combat the KMT in the upcoming local elections, the *tangwai* movement officially declared itself the Democratic Progressive Party, despite the party's illegal status under martial law.

When it entered the formal political arena, the DPP was not necessarily viewed as a political threat by the KMT. Ironically, the party enjoyed more public support before democratization than immediately after. In early democratic elections for local office, the issues of national identity and relations with China mattered, but they were not the only issues, nor were they yet the dominant issues. Dafydd Fell's analysis of Taiwan's early electoral rhetoric and campaign politics demonstrates how social welfare and corruption were two of the most critical issues during the first election.[21] Part of the DPP's early success was not necessarily a result of pro-independence or pro-Taiwan identity rhetoric but rather resulted from focusing on KMT corruption and making it a campaign issue. As the presidential election approached, the party shifted its focus to pro-independence politics, which ended up hurting its domestic support. As former DPP leader Huang Hsin-chieh commented on the DPP's pro-independence platform, with the luxury of hindsight, "The people were not ready for us."[22]

Rise of Lee Teng-hui

The election of Lee Teng-hui was the match that lit the fire set by democratization and the DPP. Lee angered China, not because he was a pro-independence green politician but because he was a reformist KMT politician with a strong Taiwanese consciousness. His run for the presidency in 1996, Taiwan's first directly held election, led to the missile crisis and forever changed the nature of the military threat from China.

Before the election, Lee was already serving as Taiwan's unelected president, in addition to his role as KMT chairman. Lee was a longtime KMT politician and, among the party's elites, was responsible for much of the ROC's liberalization, which contributed in part to Taiwan's democratization. Lee pushed for popular elections, he freed former marshal law–era political prisoners, and he appointed Taiwan-born officials instead of appointing only officials with mainlander backgrounds. His liberal nature and push for reducing the KMT's centralized power made him extremely unpopular within some KMT circles but extremely popular within some "deep green" DPP circles. Although Lee was a lifelong KMT politician, many saw his pro-reform stances as almost treasonous to the ROC.

The CCP viewed Lee as a threat to unification. The PRC saw Lee's actions as contrary to the PRC's One China Principle at best and sympathetic toward Taiwanese independence at worst. One editorial in the *People's Daily*, the PRC's state-run newspaper, attacked Lee, saying: "The real danger is allowing Lee's attempts to continue with the 'Taiwan independence' stances unchecked, thus jeopardizing the efforts to reunify the motherland."[23] Although the DPP's Peng Ming-min and a few former KMT officials also ran as candidates in the 1996 presidential election, none were as controversial as Lee. Some factions within the KMT were outraged at their party's candidate, leading to an exodus of KMT officials from the party, including some who were forcibly removed.

The spark that truly lit the flame of the crisis, however, was Lee's visit to the United States. The understanding between China, Taiwan, and the US was that no standing Taiwanese leaders would visit the United States under the guise of a formal visit. Lee, who earned a PhD from Cornell University, was invited to his alma mater to give a speech. Lee accepted the invitation and flew to New York, which China saw as a direct provocation. Subsequently, a week before Lee's presidential campaign officially began, China began a series of missile tests in the Taiwan Strait, causing a global panic that war was imminent between Taiwan and China. Known as the Third Taiwan Strait Crisis, this was the first time the CCP launched projectiles near the island.[24] Although the tests were meant to intimidate rather than damage Taiwan, the shells landed dangerously close to the major ports of Keelung and Kaohsiung. Over the course of a year, three sets of PRC missile tests were launched to intimidate and signal threat to Taiwan. Between 1995 and 1996, China conducted three sets of missile tests, ran an invasion simulation off the coast of China, and moved hundreds of thousands of troops to a location off the coast of Fujian, roughly 180 kilometers from Taiwan. For almost a year Taiwan seemed like it could be on the brink of war.

The first set of missiles were launched near the beginning of the presidential campaign, changing the tone of the election. The Chinese threat became a central theme of the debates and campaign speeches. Two candidates, both former KMT members, hammered Lee over how he had angered China during his US visit. During one major debate held close to election day, one candidate accused Lee of refusing to identify as Chinese at the expense of antagonizing China and also argued that China left Taiwan alone because Taiwan's ROC government had identified as Chinese while Lee's actions were endangering them all.[25] Following the debate, campaign rhetoric was heavily focused on the Chinese threat. A number of campaign ads from Lee's competitors echoed similar sentiments, with such phrases as "Choosing Lee is choosing war" and "War is not child's play, if we elect the wrong president, war games could become real. . . . Our vote decides whether we live or die."[26] Meanwhile, Lee responded to his former KMT competitors by saying, "Is the new leadership Jiang Zemin? Is the new order the People's Liberation Army?"[27] and "Please vote for Lee who will not bow down to Chinese Communist attacks and threats, who dares to say we want a dignified existence and have the ability to plan a complete relationship between the two sides of the Taiwan Strait."[28] Even the DPP attacked Lee: "Lee Teng-hui says he is a Taiwanese as well as Chinese. We do not know if he identifies with Taiwan or China. Does he want independence or unification?"[29]

Electoral Effects of the Crisis

Surprisingly, as Chinese missile threats became real and attacks from the KMT, the CCP, and the DPP against Lee increased, his popularity also increased.[30] In the end, Lee won with over 56 percent of the vote. The next-largest vote share went to the DPP candidate, Peng Ming-min, who took 22 percent. The two former KMT candidates together did not receive 15 percent of the vote. China's military exercise, threats of invasion, and rhetorical condemnation of Lee and the DPP did not stop the public from supporting Lee on election day.

Most critical, however, was the overwhelmingly quiet response from civil society organizations. There was no mobilization by social movement organizations or political parties against the PRC's military or rhetorical threats. There was no mass protest against China's direct threat of war, regardless of how serious or credible they seemed. Although the Chinese threat was certainly the most salient point of discussion during the presidential election, it did not cause any meaningful change in daily life within Taiwan. The only changes that occurred were some fluctuations in Taiwan's stock market and mass purchase of plane tickets by some wealthy Taiwanese to leave the island in the event that war did occur.[31]

Case 2: The Sunflower Movement

After nearly two decades of military and rhetorical threats, none of which had any major mobilizing effect on domestic politics, a new form of threat emerged within Taiwan: domestic co-optation. The rise of the domestic co-optation threat began when two mortal enemies, the CCP and the KMT, stopped seeing each other as bitter rivals and instead reframed their relationship as a lucrative partnership. Once pro-independence activists in Taiwan recognized this threat, mobilization against the CCP's presence in domestic politics began to increase in ways that military and rhetorical threats had never caused. While pro-China forces have always existed in Taiwan, the PRC's access to them was fairly limited until 2005. But the PRC was able to access domestic politics in an accelerated way after the KMT and the CCP normalized their relations. Each time a major form of the domestic co-optation threat spiked, whether through trade bills or pro-China organization buyouts, social movement mobilization occurred in response. The Sunflower Movement was the climactic result of six years of protest against Ma Ying-jeou's government, which was responsible for formalizing pathways for the domestic co-optation threat to grow within Taiwan's democratic institutions.

Normalization of KMT-CCP Relations

Even though the KMT lost control of the executive branch to the DPP in the 2000 and 2004 elections—resulting in the first peaceful political transition since Taiwan's democratization—the former authoritarian party continued its plans for increased cross-strait relations. In 2005 Lien Chan and James Soong, the failed KMT president and vice president hopefuls, respectively, who twice lost to the DPP's Chen Shui-bian and his vice president, Annette Lu, traveled to China to meet with CCP leaders, including then-president of China Hu Jintao. This was the first time since 1945, when Chiang Kai-shek and Mao Zedong met in Chongqing, that such high-level officials from the KMT and the CCP had met.

Lien Chan, a lifelong KMT politician and the party's chairman at the time, was Lee Teng-hui's vice president. James Soong had a more complicated relationship with the KMT. A former high-ranking KMT member, Soong had been kicked out of the party after unsuccessfully challenging Lien for the presidential nomination in 2000. In response, Soong and his followers formed their own new political party, the People First Party (PFP), which adopted a platform nearly identical to the KMT's. In 2000 Soong ran as a third party-candidate for president against Lien. Having two popular pro-China candidates running against each other led to a split within the KMT vote, resulting in the DPP's first presidential victory.[32] Having learned from their mistake, in 2004 the KMT ran Lien and Soong together with the hope of reuniting the pan-blue vote. In an extremely contentious race, the DPP won by only twenty thousand votes.

Despite losing the presidency a second time, the KMT was not deterred from continuing to promote its vision of strengthening cross-strait relations. Although the KMT and the CCP had historically been mortal enemies, Taiwan's democratization had given them a new shared enemy: the DPP. To both the KMT and the CCP, the DPP, and especially Chen Shui-bian, represented the de-Sinicization of Taiwan and threatened their goals for Taiwan's future. Although the two parties disagreed about whether the PRC or the ROC ought to rule Taiwan's future, they agreed that Taiwan and its people were part of China. In addition, and beyond their political incentives, the KMT and the CCP saw the potential for creating a robust economic relationship

FIGURE 4. Effect of Domestic Co-optation Threat on Taiwan

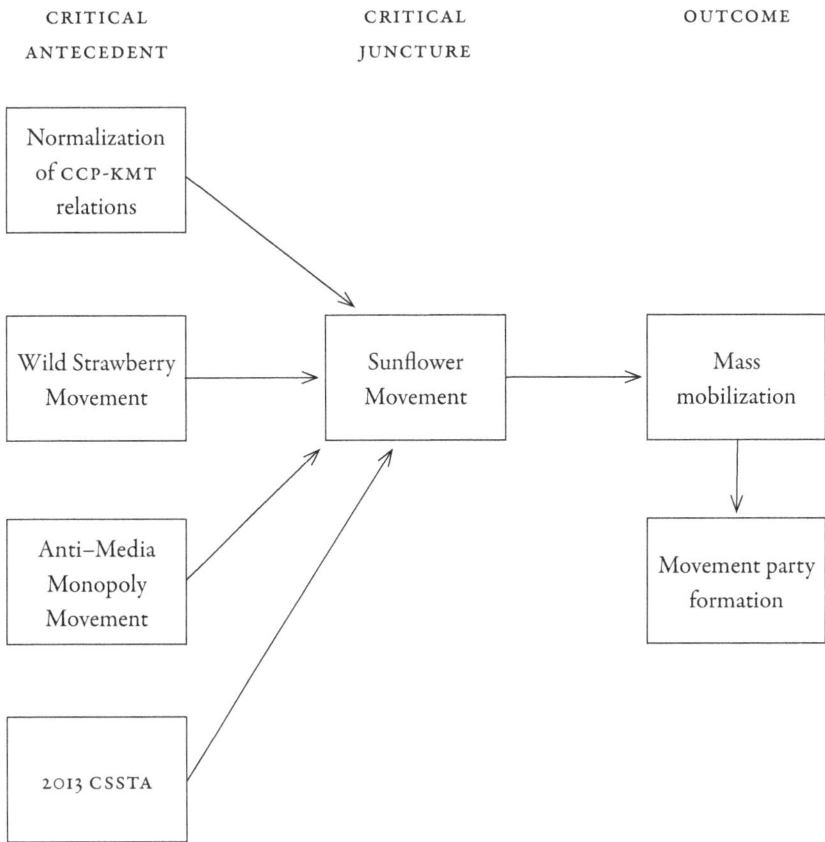

between Taiwan and China, which in no small way would help them achieve their political goals.

A year after their second defeat, Lien and Soong took turns visiting China. Both met with Hu Jintao and other high-ranking CCP officials, and each returned with a new set of accords. Lien and Hu first created a five-point "Vision for Cross-Strait Peace" that included:

1. Recognition of the 1992 Consensus.
2. The need for formal peace agreements.

3. Cross-strait interaction, such as direct flights and increases in trade.
4. A push for Taiwan's participation in international organizations.
5. Establishing a system for party-to-party talks [KMT-CCP not DPP-CCP].[33]

Meanwhile, Soong's visit resulted in a six-point communiqué that was not considerably different:

1. Recognition of the 1992 Consensus.
2. Opposition to Taiwanese independence.
3. Ending the military standoff between the two sides, facilitating a peace agreement, and establishing a means for addressing military affairs between the two sides.
4. Strengthening economic and business ties, including establishing a free-trade area between China and Taiwan.
5. Pushing for Taiwan's participation in international organizations.
6. Establishing a forum for experts from both sides of the Taiwan Strait.

The domestic political responses to Lien and Hu's and Soong's visits were harsh. Former president Chen Shui-bian condemned the trips, while other DPP politicians tried to downplay their importance. One DPP politician characterized the trips as the KMT effectively "paying tribute to the Chinese government." Former president Lee Teng-hui also criticized the trip, saying that the KMT envoys were in "collusion with the Chinese Communist Party and sell-outs of Taiwan."[34] The Taiwan Solidarity Union, a pro-independence party, even unsuccessfully attempted to sue Lien and Soong.

Ultimately the accords reached by Lien and Soong were not legally binding and led to no immediate or formal changes to Taiwan's domestic policy. So long as the DPP was in power, the agendas laid out by the KMT were simply unrealized ideas. But once the KMT returned to power in 2008 through the election of former president Ma Ying-jeou, the KMT was able to quickly and aggressively pursue the Lien and Soong agendas.

The KMT and the CCP had been mortal enemies since 1927. The KMT's legitimacy throughout Taiwan's martial law era was largely justified as a mechanism for protecting Taiwan from the CCP. Through Lien and Soong's two trips, however, the KMT opened channels to reconnect the two political parties. These two organizations had reawakened a long-lost friendship—a friendship that terrified pro-independence forces within Taiwan. This rapprochement of relations between the KMT and the CCP set the groundwork that has redefined cross-strait relations to this day.

Domestic Co-optation Threat

When the CCP and the KMT normalized relations, the tone for what unification with China could look like changed. Instead of seeing unification as something done forcefully and at the point of a gun, it was soon seen as potentially a soft takeover through economic and political coercion. The CCP no longer had to use military force to unify Taiwan. Instead, it could utilize its business and political channels within Taiwan, established through its renewed alliance with the KMT, to influence domestic politics. Before Ma Ying-jeou's rise, unification was mostly an abstract goal; policies that pushed Taiwan toward China were minimal. Under Ma, economic and political policies that tied Taiwan and China closer together had the potential to create real implications for Taiwan's autonomy and sovereignty. For pro-China policies to pass and be successful, however, local institutions within Taiwan had to advocate for them. Institutions that became coercive tools for a pro-China policy created a new kind of threat: domestic co-optation.

Even before Ma was inaugurated, KMT-CCP meetings continued to take place, with the new KMT party chairman, Wu Po-hsiung, meeting Hu Jintao several times. Once Ma entered office, the first major change was the chartering of direct flights between Taiwan and China, which welcomed a new era of Chinese tourism to Taiwan.[35] The second, which began in June 2010, was passage of the Cross-Strait Economic Cooperation Framework Agreement (ECFA), which was signed by unofficial organs representing the ROC and the PRC in Chongqing, China. This trade bill was not unanimously welcomed domestically. Government officials did not know whether the agreement was technically a free trade agreement, and perceptions on the Chinese side seemed to indicate that it was a step toward unification rather than a shared way to grow economic interactions. For some Taiwanese, fears of Ma ceding Taiwanese sovereignty for economic gain began to rise. Somewhere between thirty and one hundred thousand people protested outside the Legislative

Yuan, and some DPP and KMT legislators broke out into a brawl after the ECFA passed.[36] Although no long-lasting political movement formed out of these protests, such pro-China economic trade bills came back to haunt Ma in 2014.

Wild Strawberry Movement

Months after entering office, Ma invited Chen Yunlin, the head of the Association for Relations Across the Taiwan Strait (ARATS), the unofficial organ through which the PRC interacts with Taiwan, to visit Taiwan in person. Chen became the highest-ranking official from the PRC to ever be welcomed to Taiwan by the ROC government. When Chen arrived, hundreds of protesters demonstrated against his appearance. To the surprise of the Taiwanese public, the police cracked down and forcibly removed the protesters, citing the lack of a formal permit. The venue where Chen Yunlin spoke did not contain any Taiwanese, that is, ROC flags and the ROC anthem was not played. Anyone who did have an ROC flag was removed from the event. In the following days, protests erupted all around the island, with citizens angry at the Ma government for repressing dissenting voices and for moving relations closer to Beijing. The Wild Strawberry Movement was born.[37]

The Wild Strawberry Movement aimed to address two key grievances: the CCP's encroaching relationship with the KMT and the swift reaction by the police. The movement's protestors mobilized over not just the presence of the CCP, but also the way the KMT rolled out the red carpet for Chen Yunlin at the expense of allowing any symbolic pride for Taiwan or the ROC. This was compounded by the police's swift removal of protesters from a CCP-related event specifically. Many saw the police crackdown as violating Taiwan's freedom of speech and freedom of assembly, which especially enraged activists, who considered it an abuse of power and an attempt to silence dissent. Protesters' demands focused on forcing Ma to apologize for the police's behavior, obtaining the resignation of the directors-general of the National Police Agency and the National Security Bureau, and reformation of the public assembly law.[38]

Despite the timing and theme of the Wild Strawberry Movement, it did not lead to any major political changes within Taiwan or the formation of any new political parties in Taiwan. Although the Wild Strawberry Movement was not long-lasting, it was a foundational social protest for the Sunflower Movement's leaders. Activists who eventually went on to lead the Anti–Media Monopoly and Sunflower Movements first experienced social protests during the Wild Strawberry Movement. Wild Strawberry was also the first major social movement that directly protested the PRC's growing influence in Taiwanese civil society.

Anti–Media Monopoly Movement

Political parties like the KMT were not the only institutions pushing for closer relations with the PRC and which ultimately mobilized civil society. Taiwan's media industry, especially the businesses that profited from Ma's economic deals with China, also became the target of mass mobilization for their increasingly pro-China leanings. Despite democratization, many of Taiwan's media conglomerates were explicitly pro-China and advocated for unification with China. Many of these conglomerates, such as Want Want Group, were becoming juggernauts of the media industry and their unabashedly pro-China leanings were not subtle. For example, in one interview, Want Want chairman Tsai Eng Meng said, "Whether you like it or not, unification is going to happen sooner or later," and he later further commented that the Tiananmen Square Massacre never happened.[39] When Tsai began to make aggressive moves to buy out other media organizations and conglomerates, activists began to worry.

Want Want began purchasing independent media companies in 2008, with no government opposition or legal barriers in place to challenge its disproportionately large media market share. Want Want acquired the next-largest media company in Taiwan, the China Times Group, and its attempt to bid on the second-largest cable television provider, the China Network System, ignited protests. In a complex move, Want Want also attempted to become a key shareholder of Next Media, which owned Apple Daily, a news outlet formerly run by Hong Konger Jimmy Lai, whose often green-leaning media content in Taiwan was one of the major outlets critical of both the DPP and the KMT.[40] With no laws or policies to address the structure or actions of the monopoly, activists saw Want Want's actions as extending Chinese influence in Taiwan and thus a threat to Taiwan's democratic institutions, especially freedom of speech and freedom of the press.[41]

From 2012 to 2014 the Anti–Media Monopoly Movement protested Want Want's intentions to control a disproportionately large amount of Taiwan's media industry. It was rooted in "the convergence of debates over freedom of the press, Cross-Strait relations, and distrust of Taiwan's political institutions."[42] Although the movement itself was focused on blocking Want Want's purchases, the broader focal points of the movement were freedom of the press, anti-trust laws, and Chinese interference. The protest was also the first major social movement in which activists like Lin Fei-fan, Chen Wei-ting, and Huang Kuo-chang became known as major figures. Despite Want Want's best efforts to stop the protests, including suing the movement's leaders, the buyout was eventually blocked. Notwithstanding the fear of dire consequences over Chinese influence in Taiwan's media industry, no major organization or political party formed out of the movement.

A New Sunflower Blooms

The same year that Want Want's buyout was blocked, the KMT convened with the CCP in Shanghai to write a new trade bill, the Cross-Strait Service Trade Agreement. The bill itself was a follow-up to the ECFA bill that was passed at the beginning of Ma's presidency. Just as the ECFA sparked protest, so did murmurs of CSSTA's passage and what it might do in Taiwan. Just as the Wild Strawberry Movement and the Anti–Media Monopoly Movement both sparked fear of how Chinese influence could co-opt Taiwan's democratic institutions, activists feared the implications of the CSSTA. Unlike the previous two movements, however, the CSSTA was negotiated in China behind closed doors and the contents of the bill and its implications were a black box to outsiders. Once it was finally introduced, the KMT's rushed and semi-legal passing of the bill during the 30-Second Incident only cemented activists' perceptions that the bill was directly threatening Taiwan's democracy.

The Sunflower Movement was the climax of eight years of domestic co-optation threat felt by activists in Taiwan. Fell describes the movement as "not having come from nowhere . . . rather, it represented the culmination of social tensions that had been building up since the autumn of 2008."[43]

Although all three movements were mobilized by PRC coercion within Taiwan's democratic institutions, the CSSTA and the subsequent Sunflower Movement were the largest and most consequential for Taiwanese politics and arose explicitly in response to fears of domestic co-optation by the PRC. During the Sunflower Movement, rhetorical frames and slogans revolved around anti-KMT and anti-PRC sentiments, highlighting this fear, including "until the KMT falls, Taiwan will never be okay."[44]

Anti-KMT sentiment, however, encased a number of grievances with the party: corruption, historical persecution of those who advocated for Taiwanese independence, and the party's growing friendship with the CCP. Opposition to the KMT was a proxy for opposition to the CCP. Although the CCP was working with the KMT to propose policies such as the CSSTA, it was primarily the KMT that pushed the pro-China policy agendas domestically. For many pro-independence activists in the Sunflower Movement, advocacy for independence had much more to do with opposition to the KMT and its pro-China agenda than it did with a response to the CCP. To them, China and the CCP were together a sort of ambiguous yet overarching institution they opposed. The KMT, by comparison, was the tangible institution actually advocating for a pro-China agenda. Ma and the KMT represented the threat of the PRC in a way that could concretely affect Taiwan and its democracy.

The nature of the domestic co-optation threat that mobilized the Sunflower Movement was different from the Anti–Media Monopoly or the Wild Strawberry Movements. Sunflower faced a critical level of domestic co-optation threat that activists had never felt before. Although these feelings most certainly were the result of compounding threats from the previous two movements, the Sunflower Movement itself was the climactic result of years of fear over a domestic co-optation threat.

Threats and Movement Party Formation

The material and actualized nature of this kind of Chinese threat is why domestic co-optation threat mobilized so heavily during the Ma era, but also why it is necessary to conceptually separate it as its own kind of threat that is different from military and rhetorical threat. Despite the lack of party formation during the Wild Strawberry or Anti–Media Monopoly Movements, the underlying domestic co-optation threat from China was the consistent feature that led to activists mobilizing to protest. Activists connected these movements beyond just their shared cohorts. Participants of all three of these movements recognized the consistent underlying nature of the domestic co-optation threat from the PRC.[45] For Wild Strawberry, it was both the lavish reception given to the CCP officials combined with the police crackdown on civil society's right to protest specifically at a pro-CCP event that led to action. During the Anti–Media Monopoly protests, Want Want showed a clear pro-China agenda and attempt to buy out and silence any voice in the media who held different values. For the Sunflower Movement, it was not just about the KMT pushing for a pro-China agenda, but specifically the way the bill was designed in China, behind closed doors and in coordination with the CCP, and the way it was passed, bypassing Taiwan's democratic norms. As succinctly put by one activist who participated in all three movements, "The three movements together have the same background and were based on the same set of appeals: protesting against China and its attempts to force Taiwan to unify."[46]

Why does a domestic co-optation threat mobilize while military and rhetorical threats do not? The normalization and lack of commitment or follow-through from China had become such a constant for activists that they did not feel a dire sense of threat. In all the conducted interviews for this project almost no one paid lip service to military or rhetorical threats by China. Military threats and rhetorical threats often do not even appear on Taiwanese activists' radar. Only the threat of autocratic takeover and the weakening of Taiwan's democratic norms mobilized activists to protest the threat of PRC unification.

It is worth noting that the meaning and implications of these types of threats have changed over time and may continue to change in the future. Military threat was once the key driving force behind how and why the KMT chose to govern Taiwan and how it conducted its foreign policy. Today, this is no longer true. Domestic co-optation by the PRC within Taiwan was once considered impossible, but today it is seen as a threat against the health of Taiwan's democratic institutions.

Discussing domestic co-optation threat and how it can coerce institutions like media or political parties is conceptually tricky because China is not directly threatening Taiwan. Unlike military or rhetorical threats, where the intention and target are usually obvious, domestic co-optation threat is passive-aggressive and indirect. Rather than threaten Taiwan directly, a domestic co-optation threat targets Taiwanese institutions and pushes them to advocate for policies that bolster China's influence within Taiwan. Although the domestic co-optation threat is conceptually different from traditional understandings of Chinese threat, it has had the largest impact on civil society since the KMT returned to power and normalized relations with China.

Complicating and reconceptualizing our understanding of threat has a number of important implications for how domestic politics functions in contested states. Although these three types of threats are archetypes, and certainly can vary widely, they at least demonstrate variation in types of threats and how civil society responds to them. It would be a vast oversimplification to group "Chinese threats" into a monolithic category. When scholars and analysts ask, "Why do some types of threats have certain effects while others do not?," it is conceptually and empirically necessary to specify what kind of threat under consideration because different types of threats affect contested states differently.

Domestic co-optation threat, however, is not a sufficient condition for movement party formation. Although this kind of threat does have a mobilizing effect on civil society, it is not enough to push activists to form new political parties. We know this because domestic co-optation mobilized into protests as soon as such threats became a reality during the Ma administration, but parties did not form until 2014. For over six years, activists constantly protested domestic co-optation threats without ever forming a new political party. The Sunflower Movement, however, was different. This movement arose out of a critical level of domestic threat the likes of which activists had never felt before. Sunflower activists saw the CSSTA as potentially ending Taiwan's democracy. This kind of critical level of domestic co-optation threat is a necessary condition for the type of social movement mobilization that can potentially lead to movement party formation. Together, this critical level of domestic co-optation threat, combined with how activists perceived the DPP as too moderate, created the conditions conducive for movement party formation.

FOUR

Corruption in Contested States

It is perplexing why so many Sunflower Movement activists did not express strong support for the Democratic Progressive Party in 2015. Why would activists of a pro-independence movement not support Taiwan's supposedly pro-independence party? Because for many Sunflower Movement activists, the DPP was not the pro-independence party that people assumed it was. A common phrase heard in the lead-up to the 2016 election was, "I oppose the KMT, but I do not support the DPP."[1] Skepticism and criticism from Sunflower activists toward the DPP were also rooted in the DPP's platform on the CSSTA. Contrary to expectations, initially the DPP was in favor of the CSSTA, with some DPP leaders enthusiastically wanting to negotiate with the KMT about the bill's specifics.[2] Even after the 30-Second Incident, the DPP's only opposition at the time was to symbolically walk out of the Legislative Yuan. Not until after the Sunflower Movement began did the DPP change its stance on the CSSTA, from quiet enthusiasm to loud opposition. Sunflower activists were keenly aware of the DPP's shift in stance and tone on the CSSTA after the protests began, adding to their skepticism of the party and its motives. Conversations often revolved around discussing why exactly activist felt such melancholy toward the organization that was once the pride and joy of pro-independence politics in Taiwan. It became clear that there were two critical variables to understanding why activists were unhappy with the DPP: its platform on independence and corruption within the party.

Activists were, surprisingly, not shy or subtle about critiquing the DPP. "When was the last time the DPP acted like it was a pro-independence party?" J, an activist who formed one of the movement parties that came out of the Sunflower Movement, asked rhetorically. Another activist echoed a similar, extremely common sentiment among the activists: "They [the DPP] have not fought for Taiwanese independence since . . . it has been so long I do not remember!"[3] Another commonly held sentiment was how the DPP was not pro-independence, but actually pro–status quo: "The DPP is all about maintaining the status quo," said E, an activist who was among those who occupied the Legislative Yuan during the Sunflower Movement. He continued, "They won't dare do anything to actually advance Taiwan's status."[4]

Beyond complaints about the DPP's lack of advocacy for pro-independence politics, activists also felt a sense of betrayal over the corruption scandals that had plagued the DPP since the Chen Shui-bian administration. Regardless of whether they believed the Chen corruption scandals or any of the other handful of DPP corruption scandal stories that had broken headlines over the years, DPP corruption had clearly had a negative effect on how Sunflower activists perceived the DPP. "The KMT's values have influenced the DPP," said L, another occupier of the legislature during the Sunflower Movement.[5] He continued: "Now all Taiwanese politicians are used to twisted values, especially DPP politicians." I, another organizer of the Sunflower Movement, expressed disappointment in how the DPP had changed over its life cycle: "The DPP today is not the same that it used to be. They have been playing in the political arena with the KMT for so long that the DPP has learned many of the KMT's dirty tactics . . . The KMT are not the only ones with politicians who practice nepotism and use bribes for favors. The DPP is just as guilty."[6]

Corrupt—a label one does not expect activists to use to describe the DPP—was a commonly held sentiment among many Sunflower Movement participants. Most activists, however, clearly differentiated the KMT as far worse and infinitely more problematic than the DPP. In no way was the DPP seen as being as corrupt as the KMT, and no Sunflower activists ever made such an equivalence. However, the mere presence of any corruption, or a history of problematic scandals within the DPP, has hurt how activists perceive the party. As one activist phrased the problem, "The KMT and DPP are both corrupt. But the KMT set the rules of our government, so the DPP has to act accordingly. Our parents' generation sees the DPP's behavior as acceptable. But that is not good enough for the current generation."[7] Said another activist, "The KMT has second-generation politicians; the DPP also has second-generation politicians. The KMT bribes, the DPP bribes. The KMT engages in dirty politics; so does the DPP. Sure, they have their ideological differences, but the way these parties function? It is the same."[8] At the beginning of the movement the DPP had been in opposition since the Chen era, and its status as an opposition party did not help its image. "The

DPP has stopped pursuing its goals. It has been the opposition party to the KMT for so long, all it knows how to do is oppose the KMT."[9]

Activists felt jaded, hurt, and in a sense betrayed by the DPP. To activists the DPP was not simply another political party that advocated for a policy platform they supported. It was *the* political party that fought against the KMT during martial law, advocated for clean anticorruption politics in the 1990s, and supported Taiwanese independence, or at least once did. It was not simply a matter of whether the DPP was or was not pro-independence or whether it had corruption scandals. For activists, the DPP represented something much more than just a political party. It was the singular political party and vehicle that could solve Taiwan's contested status. When the DPP was no longer viewed as able to address Taiwan's contested status, activists felt the need to forge their own political parties.

Political Parties in Contested States

When a state is contested, political parties hold a qualitatively different meaning than in non-contested states. Parties are no longer simply political vehicles through which citizens can enact policy changes. Instead, they become *the* political vehicle through which citizens can actively change a contested state's status. Political parties in contested states, by virtue of having access to this power and the contested state's constant conversation around its identity and future, carry a particular burden. Such political parties sell to voters not simply a set of values or competing visions of the public good that determine the sorts of policy platforms debated in non-contested states. Rather, they offer an ideology that will *determine* the future of a contested state. For pro-independence voters, established pro-independence parties are *the* political organization on which their hopes of legitimate statehood lie. Without a legitimate pro-independence party, those who seek formal independence are unable to ever meaningfully change the contested state's structural condition.

For decades, Taiwan only had one electable pro-independence party, the DPP. Pro-independence activists and voters saw the DPP as not just another political party, but a shining beacon of hope for those who wanted Taiwan to shed the ROC framework and (or) not unify with the PRC. But over the last three decades of the party's existence, voters within its base of support saw the party shift from pushing for Taiwanese independence to advocacy for the status quo. The importance of this change for pro-independence activists cannot be overstated. By going from pro-independence to supporting the status quo, the party has qualitatively changed both its defining feature and the key reason for many voters to support the party. In tandem with its ideological fluctuations, as the years went by corruption scandals began to plague the DPP's public image. The DPP had originally been seen by its base as the clean, anti-corruption party. What was initially a party formed by pro-democracy, anti-corruption activists became known as a party full of dysfunctional bureaucrats and shady politicians. The DPP had succumbed to "moderation," the process of a political party moving toward the political center while simultaneously becoming more bureaucratized and invested in self-preservation than specific policy outcomes.

For activists, the DPP no longer advocated for Taiwanese independence and was organizationally problematic. The combination of ideological and organizational change created conditions necessary for Sunflower activists to no longer see the DPP as a viable party vehicle. For them, there was no longer a political party that could solve Taiwan's contested status. Activists took matters into their own hands to create new political parties that could be "clean," progressive, and pro-independence.

In a contested state, what exactly does it mean for a party to be moderate? What impact does moderation have on how and why civil society supports a particular party? Tracing how the DPP's formal stance on Taiwanese independence and their public image has changed over time reveals the platform shift that had major consequences for the party because it led to pro-independence advocates feeling isolated from the party. The history of the DPP's corruption scandals hurt its image just as much as, if not more than, changes to its pro-independence platform. The presence of corruption or, at the very least a perception of corruption, is a critical and yet undertheorized variable for why activists might want to start their own party.

What Does It Mean to Be Moderate?

Typically, when political scientists think of a party becoming moderate, they are referring to the left-right political spectrum. A party might begin at the farther ends of the political spectrum and slowly move toward the middle, subsequently softening their political platforms and appealing to a wider cohort of voters. In some instances this move toward the middle is enough to inspire new party formation by disgruntled supporters. For example, in India, the Bhartiya Janta Party (BJP), an exceptionally conservative Hindu nationalist party, formed after the Janata Party became "too secular" in its approach to Hindu nationalism.[10] The BJP formed in the late 1980s as a small conservative challenger to the Janata Party but by 2014 it had grown to become the dominant conservative Hindu nationalist party. What began as a small party outside the mainstream is now a major part of India's political zeitgeist.[11]

Political moderation is not just a matter of moving from one end of the political spectrum to the middle. It is also about changes within a party organization itself: how the party operates and how its growth is seen by its base of support. As social scientist Robert Michels's seminal study of party corruption postulates, "As organizations grow, in particular political parties, they become more moderate, more corrupt, and less democratic over time."[12] Although we typically think of moderation only along the left-right political spectrum, Michels's concept of clean-corrupt party quality ought to be considered in tandem with a shift in platforms. We might consider these two spectrums:

When a party moves toward moderation, civil society does not stay static, especially the party's original base of support. The effect of a party becoming moderate across both axes can lead to a number of responses. For the party, growth and moderation may lead to more electoral successes and organizational expansion. Among the party's original base of support, however, a move toward moderation—from the far end of the political spectrum toward the middle—can be read as a pejorative change and a form of betrayal or abandonment of the party's original goals and ideals. In some cases a moderate party's original base of support may even go so far as to break away from the party and form a new party that is similar to the original party before it became moderate.

The formation of a new party may not necessarily be due to a group's change in ideology, but rather as a movement's desire to return to the party's "original" version. Rather than advocate for a new set of policy platforms, parties that form out of response to moderation are simply offering the

FIGURE 5.
Visualizing Moderation

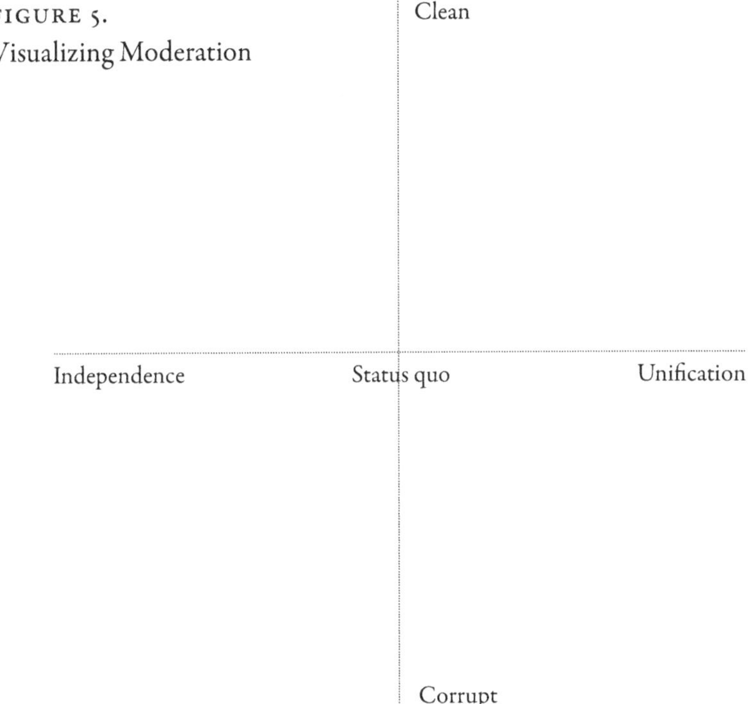

now-moderated party's original platform. Movement parties do not offer a complete change in policy, but rather a return to a "purer" political ideology. For example, the BJP formed not because no Hindu nationalist parties existed, but rather because existing Hindu nationalist parties had become too secular in the eyes of their bases of support. In Taiwan, activists who went on to form new movement parties did not do so because there were no existing pro-independence parties, but rather because existing pro-independence parties had become too moderate and not pro-independence enough.

Corruption

What exactly does "corruption" mean? In a political context, corruption means some sort of moral decay or "perversion of anything from its original state of purity."[13] Formal definitions vary widely and are highly contested, depending on the context. Even in a single country, changes in political systems, party lines, and time can all impact the meaning of corruption. As James C. Scott puts it, "Corruption, we would all agree, involves a deviation from a certain standard of behavior. The first question which arises is, which criteria shall we use to establish those standards?"[14] Actions involving theft, bribery, nepotism, conflict of interest, lying, abuse, error, waste, or involvement with organized crime are all associated with corruption, but not all studies of corruption necessarily involve all these acts.

The other challenge in defining and conceptualizing corruption is the role of public perception and opinion. The citizenry's understanding of corruption may differ from official or legal definitions. The impact of corruption on electoral outcomes is also heavily impacted by public perceptions and tolerance of corruption. Certain types of corruption are sometimes accepted by both political elites and the voting public, at other times by elites only, and at other times unanimously condemned. This white-gray-black corruption spectrum is prevalent across nations, including the United States and Taiwan.[15]

Taiwan itself has a long history of corruption being a voting issue. Although Taiwan's contested status remains the most critical issue during national elections, corruption is the next-most-important issue for many voters.[16] What corruption means in Taiwan has changed throughout years of martial law, democratization, and modern times. Dafydd Fell gives the DPP credit for "taking a latent political issue, corruption, and progressively broadening the scope of what is publicly acknowledged as corruption. Under the [DPP's] relentless anti-corruption attacks, the KMT has been forced to change its positions."[17] Since its formation in 1986, the DPP has utilized corruption as one of its strongest campaign issues. Its emphasis on corruption has changed with each faction's control over the party. Less ideologically strict factions emphasized corruption more, and ideologically strict factions emphasized corruption less.

The DPP's ideological and institutional moderation was a necessary condition for movement party formation following the Sunflower Movement. A comparative sequential method shows the process of how the DPP went from a party that was pro-independence and campaigned on anti-corruption to one that no longer stood for pro-independence while also becoming the focus of major corruption scandals. The comparative sequential method, a type of comparative historical analysis, allows for within-case study of events as they progress over time.[18] By taking seriously not just the change in the political party's platform but also the order of events that led to the change in its platform, it is clear that the qualitative *process* that led to the DPP's ideological and institutional changes, not just the changes themselves, influenced political activists.

The DPP's turbulent changes, going from pro-independence to pro–status quo politics, combined with an increase in corruption scandals over time, led to a major loss of support. This created a perception among activists that the DPP, Taiwan's only major opposition pro-independence party, was too corrupt, too ideologically bland, and too unelectable to be a meaningful party vehicle. Negative perceptions of the DPP, both in terms of political ideology and party quality, were key sources of motivation for movement party activists to consider creating their own political party. Sunflower organizers and eventual party founders all cite their lack of support for the DPP as a fundamental reason behind their eventual founding of and support for post-Sunflower Movement parties. As the DPP became more moderate, the likelihood of activists forming their own parties also increased.

In the 1990s the DPP was seen as a pro-independence, "clean" grassroots-based organization. Over the course of two decades, it moderated into becoming perceived as a pro–status quo and no longer clean bureaucratic organization. This process, however, did not happen immediately, nor in a vacuum. Rather, it was the result of a series of critical antecedents that occurred throughout the DPP's history, which climaxed in movement party activists feeling the need to break away from the DPP and start their own party.

The *Tangwai*: From Outside the Party to Parting the Outside

Although the DPP is only thirty-eight years old, it has gone through radical transformations as a political organization. Its proto-political organization, the *tangwai* movement, had a radically different political ideology compared to the DPP of 2014. *Tangwai* members' political positions, ideals, and goals for Taiwan's future varied widely. Some *tangwai* members advocated for

FIGURE 6.
Activists' Perceptions of the DPP's Moderation

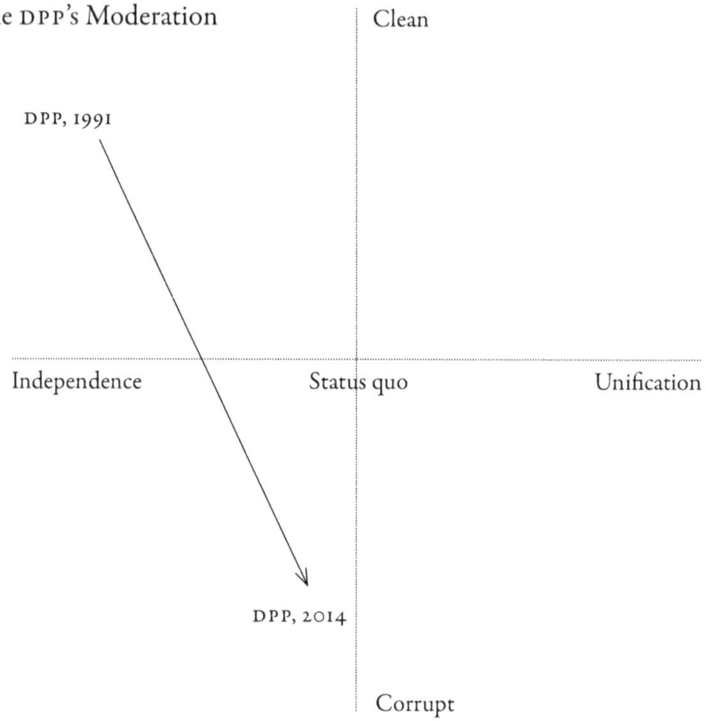

self-determination, arguing that it should be up to Taiwanese people to decide Taiwan's future. Others advocated for specific democratic reforms to the standing ROC framework. Still others advocated for Taiwanese independence.[19]

It is inaccurate to describe the *tangwai* as an exclusively pro-independence movement. There were pro-independence advocates within the movement, but they were never a majority, nor was Taiwanese independence a key *tangwai* platform. *Tangwai* activists had good reason to not openly advocate for independence: under KMT martial law, independence advocacy was illegal and punished extremely. Even mentioning independence could warrant arrest.

The movement is best described as a pro-democracy and anti-authoritarianism movement. *Tangwai*, an expansive umbrella term, permitted members with a wide array of backgrounds to join the cause.[20] First came intellectual groups, including academics, lawyers, and writers, who more normatively advocated for democracy as a political ideal, along with the end of authoritarianism. Second were politicians who had defected from the KMT and were sympathetic to the *tangwai*'s cause or saw the party's declining legitimacy and wanted to capitalize on the *tangwai*'s growing attraction for their own gain. Tactics also varied greatly within these two factions. Some within the intellectual groups advocated for using direct tactics, such as street protests, which occasionally became violent. Others shunned protesting and thought the movement should focus on local elections, that is, where members were able to find small political successes when the KMT permitted them to run.[21]

The ideological stances of the two factions within the *tangwai* may seem similar, but their differences were one of the underlying causes behind the resulting infighting. For example, the goals of self-determination and pro-independence are often portrayed as being comparable or compatible, but they offer two very different approaches to regime change.[22] Self-determination advocates wanted Taiwanese citizens to decide whether and how they wanted to change their political system, regime, name, and so on. To be pro-self-determination was to be willing to accept whatever outcome was decided, so long as it was decided by the will of the people. Pro-independence, however, was explicitly advocating for a specific kind of regime change, where Taiwan would declare itself culturally unique and politically separate from both the ROC and China. Pro-independence advocates did not necessarily accept any other type of regime change or political outcome, even if the majority people were against independence. Despite what were considered by *tangwai* to be drastically different approaches to Taiwan's future, from the KMT's perspective they were the same for all intents and purposes.

Self-determination as a motivating goal was far more popular within the *tangwai* than Taiwanese independence. Of the various competing factions within the *tangwai*, only one, the New Tide faction, was vehemently pro-independence. It is worth emphasizing, however, that *tangwai* preferences for self-determination as opposed to independence are in part the result of decades of structural oppression by the KMT against any sort of independence advocacy. Widespread fear of repercussion from China if Taiwan declared independence had also weakened the appeal of an independence ideology. When the DPP formed in 1986, it knew the barriers to having a pro-independence platform and emphasized during its formative years that it is a pro-self-determination party, *not* a pro-independence party. In 1990 Chen Yung-hsing, a DPP standing committee member, aptly summarized the DPP's formal platform: "The DPP's position on Taiwan's future is the 'people's self-determination,' and it maintains that all inhabitants should jointly determine their common destiny. . . . As Taiwan's largest opposition party, the DPP has the responsibility to reflect the aspirations of the masses of society, to vigorously try to obtain accelerated implementation of constitutional government reform, and to avoid Taiwan's losing its way in the abyss of unification."[23]

When the DPP formed in 1986, it did not write a strongly stated pro-independence stance into its party charter. In fact, the DPP did not have a strong policy platform of any kind. It was loosely formed around two principles: anti-KMT sentiment and advocating for democracy. The party spent its initial five years negotiating exactly how it was going to manifest these two principles. It was only over time that pro-independence clauses were added, between 1986 and 1991.[24] In 1987 the DPP added into its charter the right for Taiwanese citizens to advocate for Taiwanese independence. In 1988, Resolution 417 added that Taiwan's international sovereignty did not belong to the People's Republic of China, which has its capital in Beijing. That same year, the "Four Ifs" clause was added, which stated that if any of the following four situations occurred, the DPP would immediately advocate for independence:

1. If the KMT and CCP held unilateral talks.
2. If the KMT sold out the interests of the Taiwanese people.
3. If the CCP annexed Taiwan.
4. If the KMT does not implement true constitutional democracy.

Although these points are independence-leaning, the Four Ifs clause was not yet an outright declaration of pursuit of independence. Such a pursuit did begin in the early 1990s. In 1990, Resolution 1007 added that Taiwan's actual sovereignty did not extend to China or Mongolia, a stance that directly contradicted the ROC constitution. The biggest change, however, came in 1991, when the DPP amended its party charter to specifically call for a referendum on creating an independent Republic of Taiwan. This was the moment the DPP officially became a pro-independence party.[25] The DPP's pro-independence stance, however, did not last over the following two decades.

How did the DPP go from being a pro-self-determination party to embracing a pro-independence platform? The ideological splits within the party did not subside over time.[26] Since the party's founding in 1986, the divide between independence versus self-determination had only intensified. Factional infighting had dominated both the *tangwai* and the newly formed DPP, with two factions in particular becoming the leading groups: the pro–status quo Formosa faction and the pro-independence New Tide faction.

One key factor that pushed the DPP to embrace a pro-independence platform was the return of pro-independence activists who had been exiled from Taiwan during martial law. When martial law was ended and it was no longer illegal to advocate for independence, hundreds of Taiwanese dissidents who were far more pro-independence than those who still resided in Taiwan were able to return home. Most of these pro-independence returnees joined the New Tide faction and further pushed the DPP to endorse a pro-independence platform.

Factional infighting within the party became fraught, as the pro-independence faction fought factions that were less inclined to embrace a strong pro-independence platform. After a complex internal battle, the New Tide faction was able to briefly establish its dominance, ending with the passage of the 1991 pro-independence referendum amendment. The New Tide faction's push for a referendum on independence was, in actuality, a compromise from its initial desire to seek independence immediately. Despite this compromise, the DPP had officially become a pro-independence party in accordance with its party charter.[27]

Before the DPP established itself as a pro-independence party, its loosely defined pro-democracy and anti-KMT stances had made the party increasingly electorally viable. Once it formally embraced a pro-independence platform, however, the DPP ironically began to struggle to increase its electoral power. Political scientists attribute the DPP's struggle to win elections to two reasons. First, the KMT still maintained a strong structural advantage.[28]

For decades the KMT had built up cross-class and cross-industry networks of support, and the party's history of economic success made them more appealing to many Taiwanese voters.[29] The KMT's dominant role in Taiwan's democratic transition also allowed the party to create the electoral rules that helped safeguard its position in formal politics. The KMT saw itself as still in a position of power when it conceded democracy as a goal and understood that democratic elections would not be the party's downfall.[30]

Second, most Taiwanese did not support Taiwanese independence. This could be related to the aforementioned structural reasons, but Shelley Rigger argues it has to do with a major miscalculation by the DPP's New Tide faction. She describes the New Tide's victory in establishing a pro-independence platform within the DPP as having "won the battle but lost the war."[31] The idea of advocating for a new, independent Taiwanese state was seen by voters as an incredibly risky idea that could potentially harm Taiwan's safety. Despite strong momentum during its founding, the DPP earned only 24 percent of the vote in the 1991 National Assembly elections. In 1996, during the first presidential election, the party improved slightly in the National Assembly elections, earning 30 percent of the votes. However, the DPP presidential candidate, Peng Ming-min, who ran on a hardline Taiwanese independence platform, received only 21 percent of the votes.[32]

From Pro-Independence to Pro–Status Quo

After the 1996 election, the DPP leadership decided its pro-independence stance was not conducive to facilitating electoral success. It began to shift the party's position from pro-independence to pro–status quo via the emergence of more factions within the DPP. Although intuitively more factions may seem like a problem for a political party, the increase of factions within the DPP reduced the New Tide faction's power, resulting in a newfound prioritization of party unity. Infighting among factions gradually decreased during the 1990s.

The most significant change made to the DPP's party platform came in 1999. Called the "Resolution on Taiwan's Future," the DPP made critical changes to its party charter's ideological platform.[33] First, it acknowledged "Republic of China" as Taiwan's official name and government. Rather than seeking formal independence, the party articulated that Taiwan was *already* independent as the Republic of China. If there were to be any major changes to the ROC system, the DPP would support said changes only when accomplished through public referendum. The party itself, if lacking the will of the people, would not pursue formal changes. The resolution also articulated several important pan-green political platforms, including a rejection of "One Country, Two Systems" and the idea of "One China."

This qualitative change—from first rejecting the ROC in favor of a Republic of Taiwan to then accepting the ROC as a means of more moderately advocating for Taiwan's sovereignty without pursuing radical changes—marked the DPP's shift in political stance. This change allowed the DPP to maintain its pro-Taiwan sovereignty leanings while also exonerating the party from needing to pursue formal changes that would alter the cross-strait status quo. It appealed to moderate Taiwanese voters who saw the party's pursuit of independence as too aggressive or too dangerous, while also appealing to voters who wanted to acknowledge Taiwan's de facto independence from China. Whether or not the party did this purely as an electoral strategy or out of genuine concern for the risk that formal independence could bring is debatable, but, regardless of motivation, the change marked a critical shift in the party's development as an opposition party. Since the 1999 resolution, the DPP as a party has not formally pursued independence and has stuck by its status quo stance of acknowledging the ROC's de facto independence without advocating for de jure independence.

The Anti-Corruption Party

Since its formation, the DPP campaigned heavily on a platform of anti-corruption.[34] The DPP was a pro-democracy and anti-KMT party first and foremost, but one of the ways it attracted voters throughout the 1990s was through a focus on anti-corruption campaigns. Regardless of national identity, corruption was largely a valence issue that all Taiwanese and Chinese-identifying citizens could support.[35] The KMT also had no shortage of corruption scandals from either the martial law era or the contemporary period on which to draw, making the party an easy target for the DPP. The DPP, being new, local, and grassroots-led, was seen as a "clean" organization.

Polls from the 1990s confirm that voter preferences for the two parties were in part due to their views on corruption: those who disliked the KMT cited the party's corruption problem, while those who liked the DPP cited it clean image. One survey shows that, as the 1990s progressed, voters saw the KMT as increasingly corrupt and the DPP as less corrupt.[36]

Chen Shui-bian's Presidency

The DPP's pro–status quo stance was further cemented during Chen Shui-bian's first presidential term. Chen, a long-time *tangwai* activist and founding member of the DPP, won the 2000 presidential election and became the first non-KMT president of the ROC. It is important to note that this victory was due to a split of the pro-KMT vote between two candidates. Chen won with 39 percent of the total vote.[37] Regardless, it was a major event in Taiwan's democratic history and an important step toward consolidating Taiwan's political system. The DPP did not win a majority in the Legislative Yuan and would not do so until 2016.

Chen campaigned on a pro–status quo and anti-corruption platform, attempting to downplay the DPP's history of pro-independence advocacy as much as possible. During the campaign he regularly accused his two opponents of coming from a corrupt party that had done little to address corruption. He was able to point to the DPP's performance in the local and national elections during the 1990s, highlighting how he and his party would combat rampant corruption within Taiwanese politics.

Chen's tenure as president heralded an important shift in Taiwanese politics. Despite his pro–status quo stance, he still prioritized a policy of localization (*bentuhua*).[38] Education reform during his presidency incorporated Taiwanese history into school curricula while shifting away from the Chinese-centric history that was favored by the KMT. Taiwan's sovereignty and Taiwanese identity became a focus of his political rhetoric, and he made headlines worldwide for being "provocative" vis-à-vis China. Chen was often portrayed as pro-independence by international media, but his rhetoric during his first term was far milder than portrayed. Notably, Chen said he would be representative of all citizens regardless of their party or personal identity. He also regularly said he would fight for the ROC (not for "Taiwan") to be reincorporated into the international system.[39] To this day media characterizations of Chen and the DPP during his first term still portray both as pro-independence.

Chen further solidified his pro–status quo agenda with his inauguration speech, when he introduced his most important policy: the "Four Noes, One Without" policy. The platform stated that so long as the PRC did not use military force to try to annex Taiwan, Chen and his administration would not:

1. Declare Taiwanese independence;
2. Attempt to change the formal name of the Republic of China;
3. Push for any additions to the constitution that indicated the Republic of China and China are two separate countries; or
4. Push for a public referendum on Taiwanese independence that would alter the status quo.

The one "without" stated:

1. Chen would not abolish the National Unification Council, the official ROC organization charged with promoting unification with China.

This platform defined Chen's first term cross-strait policy.[40] Pro-independence activists were highly critical of his stance, as it was a significant move away from any sort of pro-independence agenda and instead prioritized the relatively peaceful status quo. Internationally, Chen's policy was welcomed by the United States. The American Institute in Taiwan (AIT), the de facto US embassy in Taiwan, even formally stated, "The United States attaches profound importance to these pledges, which are a cornerstone of Cross-Strait peace and stability."[41] Although Chen's domestic policies pushed for a more Taiwan-centric identity, they did not challenge the status quo. Despite the DPP's reputation, Chen had managed to find a way to make a DPP administration palatable to an international audience by spelling out exactly how he would not pursue any sort of independence yet still advocate for Taiwanese sovereignty and identity.

Murmurs of Corruption

Beginning in 2005, the DPP's image began to change. Accusations of corruption began to haunt the party, as rumors of bribery and scandals began to surface.[42] Rumors of the involvement of Kaohsiung DPP politicians Chen Chu and Chen Che-nan in a government bribery scandal came to light, leading Chen Chu to step down as chairwoman of the Council of Labor Affairs.[43] Additional rumors involving insider trading by Chen Shui-bian's family, including his wife and son, began to make headlines. His wife and three other DPP officials were also indicted for forgery and embezzlement.[44] One major study of the involvement of organized crime in Taiwan found that major gangs may have donated to Chen's campaigns.[45] From an administrative perspective, Chen made several political decisions that further hurt his image as a clean politician. Under his administration, premiers were not allowed to pick their own cabinet members though Chen himself selected executives to a number of state-controlled enterprises during his administration. Some DPP politicians saw this as Chen overstepping his boundaries at best and crony capitalism at worst.

One major green political figure in particular, Shih Ming-te, a founding member of the *tangwai* and colloquially known as the "Nelson Mandela of Taiwan," called for Chen to step down. Shih went so far as to form an entire protest movement called the "Million Voices against Corruption, President Chen Must Go," which at its peak mobilized several hundred thousand protesters against Chen.[46] Chen did not step down, but in an attempt to appease the public he ceded some of his presidential power to his premier, Su Tseng-chang, a move that was poorly received by the public.[47] Although pro-China media capitalized on Shih's movement to attack Chen and the DPP themselves, the movement was still a signal that those within the pan-green camp were losing trust in the DPP. The DPP no longer held the same clean image it had in the past.

From Status Quo to Independence

As Chen's second term progressed and corruption scandals focused on the DPP and his family drew more headlines, Chen himself became less and less dedicated to a pro–status quo stance. Textual analysis by Jonathan Sullivan and Will Lowe finds that the number of mentions of Taiwaneseness, sovereignty, and identity increased throughout Chen's presidency, but came at a higher rate during his second term.[48] When running for reelection, Chen did not change his pro–status quo politics, although his comments at a number of DPP rallies and events were seen as leaning more and more toward pro-independence, including the famous 228 Hand-in-Hand rally that was aimed at China.[49]

Chen's major policy changes began in 2006. Even though it was part of his original stated Four Noes, One Without policy, Chen dissolved the National Unification Council then tried to soften the blow by framing the organization as "ceasing to function" rather than declaring its abolition outright. Chen was heavily criticized by the KMT and PRC regardless. Chen argued that the council's dissolution was necessary in light of military threats from the PRC. The PRC responded by claiming Chen's actions would have more dire consequences for Taiwan.[50]

Chen's most drastic step away from pro–status quo politics happened in 2007, one year before the end of his presidency and at the peak of his domestic corruption scandals. He abandoned his Four Noes, One Without policy platform and introduced the "Four Wants, One Without" platform. Contrary to his original status quo–oriented policy, this new platform reflected direct desires for Taiwanese independence:

1. Taiwan *wants* independence.
2. Taiwan *wants* to formally change its name.
3. Taiwan *wants* a new constitution.
4. Taiwan *wants* development.

The one "without" stated:

1. Taiwan is without a political "left" or "right"; it has only "independence" and "unification."

Why did Chen switch from being one of the most vocal pro–status quo politicians in the DPP to embracing an almost antagonistically pro-independence stance? It is possible he was pro-independence all along and only utilized pro–status quo rhetoric and policy as an electoral strategy. He and the DPP could have been trying to put their fingers on the public's pulse to appeal to the largest base possible. It is also possible that Chen was genuinely pro–status quo but wanted to change his image to pro-independence to boost his popularity in the middle of a major corruption crisis. Switching to being pro-independence could have been an attempt to reinvigorate party support. Or, since he was a second term president, perhaps it was because he would no longer be confined by the same pressures to maintain a pro–status quo stance once out of office. Regardless of how Chen truly felt throughout his political career, we know that he was a pro–status quo politician until 2007 and his last year as president marked a clear departure from pro–status quo politics.

Acknowledging Corruption

Chen's lowest moment, however, came immediately after he left office. The day he finished serving as president he was arrested for diverting $30 million of DPP campaign money into a private bank account in the Cayman Islands. Over the next decade Chen, his wife, and those connected to him were the center of Taiwan's most infamous scandal. Chen's corruption charges redefined the DPP. What was supposed to be a clean party born out of movement activism against corruption was now seen as a corrupt, dirty, cartel party that had lost its way. The electoral ramifications of Chen's scandal were also dire. The DPP lost support across the country, and for the next eight years the DPP was badly battered in almost every election.

Chen's corruption scandal was particularly painful for DPP supporters for two reasons. First, the DPP actively campaigned on an anti-corruption platform. Since the DPP's founding, one of the party's strongest, most salient appeals to Taiwanese citizens beyond Taiwanese identity was its anti-corruption position. Anti-corruption was a cornerstone of the DPP's early identity and continued so for many years. Corruption and "black gold" politics were supposed to be something the KMT engaged in and the DPP called out, not the other way around. Second, Chen's scandals came on the heels of his "return" to pro-independence politics. Chen's politics went from being pro–status quo to pro-independence at the same time as his corruption scandals became known. This damaged the pro-independence movement's reputation and left many pro-independence activists feeling more isolated than ever from the DPP. Chen's scandals made the DPP look hypocritical and, because of the sudden timing of Chen's pro-independence advocacy, disingenuous.

Lin Yi-hsiung's Departure from the DPP

Lin Yi-hsiung is considered one of modern Taiwan's most heroic and tragic figures. In 1977 he was one of the first *tangwai* activists to ever win a local election. He was a key member of the movement and remained heavily involved throughout the DPP's party formation in the 1980s. Lin also was a key target of the KMT's attempted repression of the *tangwai*. During the infamous Kaohsiung Incident, a pro-democracy rally that ended in the detention of dozens of pro-democracy activists, Lin himself was arrested and tortured by the police. During his jailing, his mother and six-year-old twin daughters were stabbed to death in his home, despite his house being under twenty-four-hour police surveillance. Police never conducted a full investigation into the murders and the individuals behind the Lin family killings are still unknown today.[51]

During the *tangwai* era Lin was considered neutral when it came to factions. He never formally aligned with any particular group, even when the DPP formed in 1986. Lin did not join the DPP until 1994, despite his constant presence in party affairs. Within the party, his neutral position gave him several advantages.[52] For example, he could navigate between factions and serve as a mediator when conflict arose. Lin was never as outspokenly pro-independence as the New Tide faction, but he also strongly pushed back against the Formosa faction's attempt to tone down the DPP's position. When DPP party chair Hsu Hsin-liang attempted to push the DPP too far away from its pro-Taiwan stance, it was Lin who called for Hsu's impeachment.[53] Lin himself served as the DPP's party chair from 1998 to 2000, and he was partially responsible for Chen's first presidential victory. Despite universal praise for his ability to coordinate between different sides of the party, Lin declined to serve more than one term.

It was a shock when Lin announced his departure from the DPP in 2006. In his official resignation speech he said infighting within the party and increased factionalization had become so intense that hatred within the DPP made "party membership already meaningless."[54] In a rare TV interview around the time of his departure, Lin made note of the DPP's major corruption problems, saying, "Every country has corruption, but that's not the most serious problem, the most important thing is how to face these failures. The current DPP has done nothing but defend itself instead of standing with the public."[55]

Aside from Lin's disapproval of the condition of the DPP, other interparty politics may have also played a role. Lin had attempted to push for a more reformist candidate for party leader who was never given a proper chance by the other factions. Some say he got caught up in an interparty dispute between Su Tseng-chang and Yu Shyi-kun.[56] Regardless of what caused Lin to leave the party, he did so at a time when the public's perception of the DPP was on the decline. The party that Lin had fought to create was no longer one to which he wanted to belong. As one activist and future founder of the NPP put it, "To Lin, the DPP had changed. The people he had known since the *tangwai* movement were not the same people anymore, and the DPP was not the same organization from when it was founded."[57]

After leaving the party, Lin returned to his roots in social activism. He became a leading figure in environmental movements, especially Taiwan's anti-nuclear power movement.[58] He remained on good terms with the DPP and even endorsed some of its candidates during elections. His dissatisfaction with the DPP, however, was well known for years after his departure. Chen's corruption scandals and the DPP's abandonment of its original pro-Taiwan sovereignty goal and subsequent inability to present itself as a functioning opposition party, combined with the KMT's return to power, all pushed Lin toward realizing the need for another kind of opposition party.

Lin was one of the activists who felt a sense of national dread during Ma Ying-jeou's second term. Unsure that the DPP could prevent the KMT from winning another presidential election, Lin decided to act. In 2013 he formed the Taiwan Citizens Union (TCU), the social movement proto-organization that, following the Sunflower Movement, would transform into two political parties: the NPP and the SDP. From a counterfactual perspective, had the

DPP not been plagued by corruption, or had it not seemingly strayed from its original ideals, Lin might not have been so eager to leave the party. Had Taiwan's original opposition party been able to maintain its quality and ideological position from the 1990s, and if Chen's corruption scandals had not ruined the party's image and meaning for him, Lin likely would have remained a member and not founded the TCU.

Why DPP Moderation Mattered

Interviews with activists have made it clear that their perceptions of the DPP were critical in their decision to both start and support new movement parties. The DPP's corruption scandals, its flip-flop position on independence, and Lin Yi-hsiung's departure were all topics frequently mentioned by activists themselves. It is clear that the DPP held a deeply meaningful position among activists, not simply because it was the political party they identified with, but because their faith in the party to advocate for Taiwan's right to exist was dwindling. Furthermore, several activists revealed that disconnection and discontent between social activism and the DPP had been growing for years. As one founding member of the SDP put it:

> For a long time, over last ten-plus years, I have always voted third party instead of the DPP. Usually, I voted Green Party. Sometimes I would vote for the DPP if it came to mayor or other such smaller elections, but third parties have always been my biggest focus, especially given Taiwan's multiparty system. The spirit of small parties is always something I consider worth supporting. Regardless of how well they do as a party, they're a group of volunteers trying to compete against the DPP. Of course, the DPP is just a relatively corrupt version of the KMT. This was certainly a problem. When Lin Yi-hsiung suggested forming a new kind of small party, it was certainly something I was ready to support. From my own research, I've found there to be problems between social movements and the DPP. Of course, all political parties are disconnected from social movements . . . for the sake of competing against the KMT, the DPP became more and more like them. From my position within social movements, competing against the DPP as a more progressive organization was certainly a good cause.[59]

FIGURE 7. Effect of DPP's Moderation on Movement Party Formation

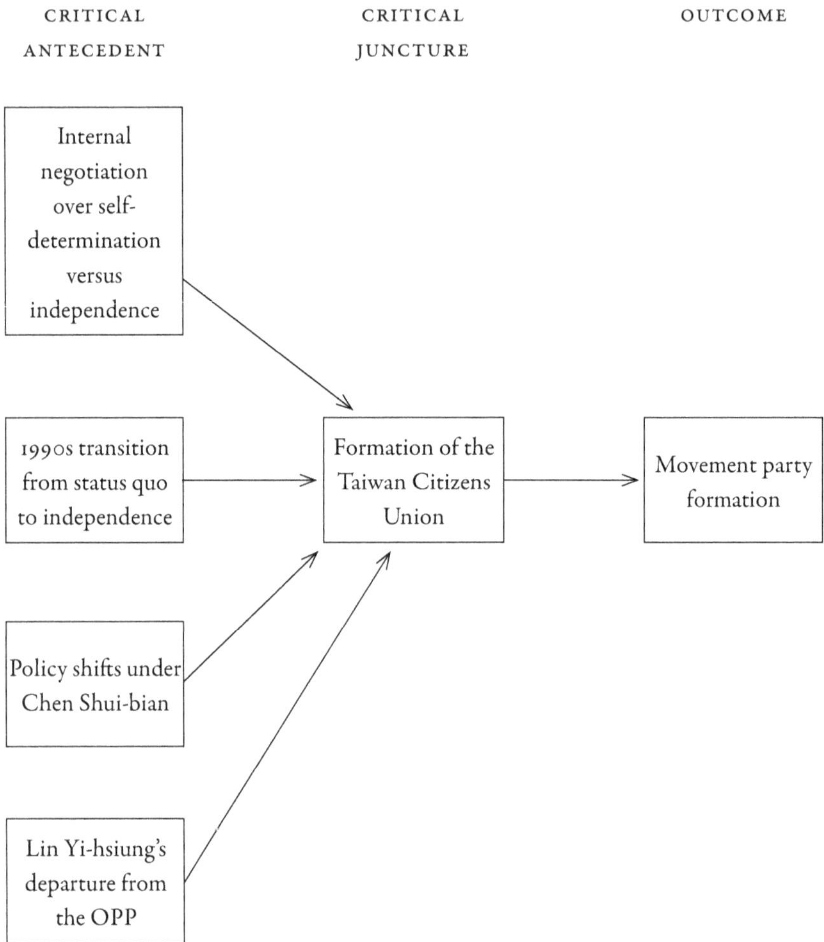

Such feelings of discontent are not limited to just SDP party founders. NPP party founders share an identical sentiment:

> Our desire to start a party began with extreme disappointment in the DPP. I had always kept space between me and the party, but for a long time I would help give suggestions on policy or help with bill writing. But [by the time] the TCU formed, I had lost all hope in the party. Even when discussing our

> disappointment in the DPP, there is an even more important factor: from 2008 to 2013 I realized the DPP's ability to progress with its policy—its agenda-setting ability—was always poor. If you look at different eras in Taiwan's history, it was always social movements who set progressive agendas, it was never the DPP who started them. The DPP would usually support some sort of ambiguous stance until it became needed for them to speak clearly. At the time, we saw two roads that we could walk down. One was to join the DPP and change them from within. The other was to start our own party. From our perspective, there was no way for us to change the DPP. Lin Yi-hsiung himself told us there was no way to change the DPP. Now, of course, I understand why he says this, but in my mind, I still wondered if there was still some way to change the DPP. But by 2014, I realized changing the DPP was impossible.[60]

Whether it was because of party corruption, a lack of representative policy platforms, or other reasons, activists did not see the DPP as a viable party vehicle. The DPP had unintentionally isolated a certain part of its base of support to the point that they were waiting for the moment to fully break away and found their own political parties. Even though this critical sentiment toward the DPP had been brewing for years, it was not until the Sunflower Movement that activists felt the moment was right to be able to meaningfully capture the energy for change.

The DPP's own moderation played an indirect yet critical role in creating the necessary conditions for the formation of new movement parties in 2014. Activists closely followed the DPP's decline, from a clean party to an organization plagued with corruption scandals, especially the party's on-again-off-again advocacy for Taiwanese independence. New party founders were keenly aware of the DPP's problems and were waiting for the right moment to act off their dissatisfaction. The DPP's moderation alone did not lead to the Sunflower Movement or new party formation. The combination of the party's moderation and Lin's subsequent departure from the DPP, however, served as perhaps the most important critical antecedents behind the Sunflower Movement's party formation.

What, then, does the moderation of the DPP tell us about the role that existing political parties play in new party formation? There are two key theoretical takeaways. First, the definition of party moderation should be expanded beyond just a shifting within a state's left-right spectrum. Taiwan's history shows that the quality of a party, specifically whether it is perceived as corrupt or corruption-free, can have just as much of an impact on its reputation as a specific policy platform. Changes on a left-right spectrum still matter, but left-right is not the only spectrum that contributes to a party's move toward moderation. Second, the who, what, when, and how of moderation matters. Although moderation is in part an organizational shift, individual decisions made within a party's structure during the moderation process can have real-world outcomes. Furthermore, once moderation happens, the process is not easily forgotten. The history of a party's shift, both on the left-right spectrum and regarding the clean-corrupt spectrums, leaves lingering memories, especially within a party's base of support.

What can the moderation of the DPP tell us about movement party formation in contested states? Political parties that advocate for the sovereignty of the contested state face the challenge of needing to seem ideologically pure and organizationally clean in order to maintain a strong base of support. When one or both dimensions dwindle, the base of support begins to question the party's commitment or competence. Of course, this may be true for almost all political parties in the world, but what makes political parties in contested states different is that political parties like the DPP are logistically and symbolically much more than a political party. In Taiwan, it is *the* political party that is able to meaningfully advocate for Taiwan's sovereignty within formal politics. Political parties in non-contested states do not have to worry about advocating for their country's independence or legitimacy. Political parties in contested states, however, define themselves based on their advocacy on an independence-unification spectrum. This requires a redefinition of how to conceptualize the role of political parties in civil society in contested states.

A collection of activists is exactly the type of group to be particularly sensitive to changes in a party's platform in a contested state. In Taiwan, pro-independence activists were keenly sensitive to changes within the DPP because they themselves were the ones most actively seeking to solve the ultimate question of contestation. Many Sunflower Movement activists could no longer view the DPP as either a pro-independence party or an organizationally clean party. The DPP's history of flip-flopping between pro-independence and pro–status quo caused activists to question what exactly the party wanted. Decades of corruption scandals also led activists to see the DPP as increasingly similar to the KMT in terms of shady political activity. Whether or not the DPP was in fact corrupt is beyond the scope of this discussion and largely irrelevant to the greater theoretical question of party formation. What mattered was activists' perceptions: that the DPP had declined because of growing corruption scandals. When pro-independence activists no longer find the established party as a viable party vehicle—in Taiwan's case, sensing a diminishment of the party that traditionally advocated for sovereignty—the likelihood that activists will take matters into their own hands increases.

The moderation of the mainstream pro-independence party—or at least activists' perception of its moderation—is a necessary condition for movement party formation in a contested state. Understanding how activists perceived the DPP in the lead-up to the Sunflower Movement is critical to contextualizing their motivation to form their own parties. It was the DPP's moderation that pushed activists away and eventually led to the formation of the TCU, which eventually birthed the NPP and the SDP. Moderation alone cannot explain movement party formation, but when it was combined with the climax of the domestic co-optation threat from China, conditions were highly conducive to movement party formation. All that was needed was the mechanism through which movement party formation was to occur.

FIVE

From Movement to Party

I, Freddy Lim, along with many other Taiwanese, want equality and dignity, which is that Taiwan and China are treated as two normal countries . . . You may want the ROC and PRC to exist, but you are for ROC independence. I'm for Taiwanese independence. —*Freddy Lim's first address to the Legislative Yuan as an elected member of the NPP*

There are two necessary conditions for movement parties to form in contested states: a dire level of domestic co-optation threat from the contesting state and a perception that the pro-independence party is no longer willing or able to advocate for the contested state's independence. This combination, of domestic and international dimensions of contestation, is what differentiates the necessary political contexts needed for movement party formation in contested states versus in non-contested states.

There is one last piece to the original puzzle. Once these necessary conditions are met, what is the mechanism through which movement party formation actually occurs? Existing theories fail to fully explain the case of Taiwan, and alternative explanations must be considered. Interview quotes, quotes of published sources, and thoughts from the founding members of these parties demonstrate how Chinese threats and dissatisfaction with the DPP were the primary mobilizing factors that inspired activists to take on the daunting task of movement party formation. But while it may seem obvious that the Sunflower movement was the mechanism through which party formation occurred, the microprocesses at work and the decisions made by movement party founders show that typical movement party formation theories do not fully explain the case of contested states like Taiwan. Contestation was at the forefront of Taiwan's party founders' motivations.

Alternative Explanations

What are the necessary conditions for new political parties to form out of social movements? This is an ongoing question in political science that has been the center of heated scholarly debates. One of the most prominent and often cited explanations within the party formation literature postulates that parties form when new issues arise or certain issues become inadequately represented by established parties.[1] Theories regarding political parties that form out of social movements, specifically movement parties, also emphasize the importance of *new and unrepresented political issues* or, as Herbert Kitschelt describes it, a "spatial" opening.[2] The explanation often goes as follows: if activists advocate for a new issue that is not represented by an established party already existing along a political spectrum, that "opening" within the political "space" creates a context for activists to form their own party in order to advocate for that issue in formal politics. This argument explains why green parties formed in some European countries but not in others.[3] Kitschelt specifically argues that existing parties that grow their platform to encompass new political realities are able to stop movement parties from forming because the existing parties take up that new political space. What would this explanation look like in Taiwan's context? It would require that activists from the Sunflower Movement were either advocating for a new or unrepresented issue or that whatever policy platform Sunflower activists advocated for was something that existing parties were not articulating or incorporating into their party platforms.

Another key alternative explanation for party formation is the *quality of the party system itself*. Are the barriers to entry and formation of a new party low or high? Barriers to entry include issues like costs, bureaucratic access, and the like.[4] For many democracies, political party formation and entry can be difficult because systems are designed to either dissuade parties from forming too often or to benefit the relative power of existing parties. This can be particularly true for formerly authoritarian countries like Taiwan, where the authoritarian power (the KMT) helped design the party system still in use.[5] For Taiwan, this explanation would require a party system that is designed to either make party formation bureaucratically difficult or too costly for social movement activists who are trying to enter formal politics.

A third important alternative explanation to address is the theory of *political opportunity structure*. This theory assesses the conditions under which social movements will mobilize or take action.[6] Perhaps one of the fundamental concepts for social movement mobilization, political opportunity structure posits that at certain points, political environments are either "open" or "closed" to social movement mobilization or political action. Different types of political systems can be relatively more open or more closed, depending on the regime. Democracies tend to be seen as more open, while authoritarian systems are more closed. But the regime is only part of the equation. More pertinent is the contemporary environment that movement activists exist within. Certain political moments or events can make the opportunity structure more open or more closed depending on the political context. Examples include realignments of political power during an election, conflict among elites, or the extent to which activists have access to resources or power. In a Taiwanese context, the theory posits that the political opportunity structure in 2014 that led to the Sunflower Movement would not only have to be open but also conducive for potential party formation in the aftermath of the movement.

Tracing the events and processes of how political activists formed both the NPP and the SDP through the Sunflower Movement highlights not just what created the conditions necessary for movement party formation, but also how the aforementioned alternative explanations fail to fully elucidate Taiwan's movement party formation process. Other secondary questions related to movement party formation after the Sunflower Movement are answered as well. For example, why did multiple parties form out of the movement instead of just one cohesive "Sunflower party?" Generally, intra-party politics and personal relations between social movement organization actors influence whether one or multiple parties will form. In Taiwan, even though everyone within the movement shared the same feeling of the China threat and dissatisfaction with the DPP, infighting and disagreements over tactics and organizational strategies existed such that no agreement was reachable. When such conflicts exist, multiple parties may form, even when all other political factors are held equal. In Taiwan's case, the NPP and the SDP formed separately not because of ideological differences or disagreements in political platforms, but over disputes in how to form and run their ideal type of movement party.

The Taiwan Citizen's Union

The story of the NPP and the SDP begins with Lin Yi-hsiung's departure from the DPP in 2006. Lin cited his inability to deal with the state of the party and its internal politics, but he had by no means left political life. Instead, he became a dedicated environmental activist and was still heavily invested in the future of Taiwan.

In 2013, despite his record-setting low approval ratings, President Ma Ying-jeou and the KMT were in full control of Taiwan's government. Even though discontent with the KMT within Taiwan's society was on the rise, pro-independence activists were hopeless about Taiwan's future. To them the DPP was an incompetent opposition party that had no chance of beating the KMT in the 2016 election, despite the KMT's growing relationship with the CCP. It cannot be overstated how bleak activists felt about Taiwan's future in 2013. Going into 2014, many were unsure what would happen to Taiwan were the KMT to win another presidential election or if the DPP would be able to meaningfully oppose it.

Lin was adamantly opposed to the KMT, but he was also tired of the DPP being the only pro-independence–leaning party. For a long time, activists had thought about the idea of creating another opposition party that was not connected to the DPP. Since the 2012 Anti–Media Monopoly Movement, individual social movement activists and leaders had loosely discussed the idea of creating their own political party but discussions never materialized into anything meaningful.[7] It was Lin, seeing the dangers of the KMT and incompetence of the DPP, who took it upon himself to seriously consider the idea of creating an alternative opposition party in the late summer of 2013, approximately six months before the Sunflower Movement.

Lin's first step was to create a group of like-minded pro–Taiwanese independence individuals, who together would work to foster a new opposition party. He invited NGOs groups, academics, activists, lawyers, and some Green Party politicians to his home for weekly meetings to openly discuss the idea of creating a new political party. No one agrees on when exactly the group became official, but sometime in late 2013 the Taiwan Citizens Union was formed.

What Was the TCU?

The TCU was not a political party, but it aspired to become one. Lin created the TCU specifically with the goal of building a new opposition political party that was progressive and pro-independence. Although the group's goal was clear, the TCU's primary task was to figure out how to take their ideas and materialize them into a real party. The TCU was a loosely knit organization and membership was not formal; the group did not publicly announce its existence until early 2014. At first, participation at the meetings was by invitation only, with Lin inviting only people he trusted. Eventually, other members brought in new participants as well. Some members came to every meeting, while others came only once or occasionally. No one agrees on an exact number, but somewhere between thirty and fifty people were at one time participating members of the TCU.

Different people involved in the TCU often had different agendas and goals. Although everyone knew that the eventual goal was to start some kind of new political party, participation was so inconsistent that the same topics would get discussed week after week, with no results. Eventually two people who participated regularly in the TCU meetings became the figureheads of the organization: Michael Lin and Lin Feng-cheng.

The most complete public list of TCU members comes from the group's first Facebook post in March 2014, though this list is incomplete. One of the most notable names missing from this list is that of Lin Yi-hsiung. Although Lin is the person every TCU member cites as responsible for bringing the group together, he did not actively engage with the direction or actions of the TCU. One reason for his distance was his personal desire to not be an active political entrepreneur in whatever the organization turned into. His goal was to help create a framework for the next generation, not to be an active member or organizer within it. Also, members of the TCU, including Lin, knew that connecting his name would overly politicize the group. Given his past connections with the DPP, he and the organization felt it better for him to play a less active role beyond initial organizer.

Almost every member noted during interviews that ideology was never an issue, because everyone within the group shared the same set of ideals: anti-KMT, pro-independence, pro-reform, and in favor of progressive social issues. As one member put it, "We did not have time to worry about the specifics of ideological issues . . . we knew we were on the same side. We were all pro-independence, we all hated the KMT, no one really aligned with the DPP; but the specifics about what some of us meant about 'pro-independence' or 'pro–social reform,' we did not have time to figure these things out back then. We had more urgent problems."[8]

The TCU, indeed, was full of problems. Everyone involved knew they wanted a new political party that could act as a meaningful alternative to the DPP, but no one could agree on how exactly they were going to do it. The TCU was plagued with conflicts over strategy, tactics, and clashing personalities.

The TCU and the Green Party

Was it really within the TCU's best interest to create a new political party? Or would it have been better for the organization to invest in reinvigorating a party that already existed? In Taiwan, two alternative pro-independence–leaning parties already existed: the Green Party Taiwan and the Taiwan Solidarity Union (TSU). The TSU was never considered a legitimate option in which to invest, however, because it was staffed and supported almost entirely by deep-green old guards from the 1990s. The TSU was largely unresponsive to the TCU when the new organization did reach out; it made no effort to work with its members and its members did not seem to particularly want to get involved.

No one in the TCU believed the TSU had the capacity to become something electorally viable. As one TCU member put it, "There was a serious generational gap between the TSU and every other activist, especially younger ones. We do not really have anything against them, we just knew it was impossible for us to work with them."[9] A founding member of the SDP echoed a similar sentiment: "If you want to join a long-standing political party in order to change it, it is an exhausting and time-consuming process. You need to first fight internally with the party to change it from within. Once the fighting is over, if you manage to make it your ideal party, you then have to convince voters that the party has changed . . . and the TSU would never accept young people telling them what to do."[10]

The Green Party, however, was for a time seriously considered as a viable party vehicle for channeling the TCU's resources. Despite a history of mediocre performance in elections, The Greens still typically received more votes than other non-DPP pro-independence parties and maintained some support across generations of pro-independence voters.[11] The Green Party leader at the time, Li Keng-cheng, was a regular at TCU meetings. Some members of the Green Party advocated for the whole party to merge with the TCU, while others wanted the TCU to act as a base of support for the Green Party. Both plans were problematic to Michael Lin and Lin Feng-cheng (who together are often referred to as the "Lin faction"), neither of whom wanted the TCU to turn into a lifeline for the Green Party. It was also well known within the TCU that both Lins had personality conflicts with Li Keng-cheng.

Most participants in the TCU at the time sided against the Green Party's desire to become the TCU's focus. Some thought the Green Party's preexisting reliance on environmental frames and its history of mediocre electoral performance would be too difficult to reform. Others claimed that the organizational structure of the Green Party was overly bureaucratized and dysfunctional. Many TCU members were worried that average citizens would not be inclined to change their preexisting notions of the Green Party. After a few months of heated clashes between the Green Party and the TCU, it was decided that a completely new political party would be the best option. After this initial dispute in late 2013, many Green Party members, including Li Keng-cheng, distanced themselves from the TCU.

During this initial clash, Fan Yun, the eventual founder of the SDP, was not yet a member. She was at the time on sabbatical from National Taiwan University to focus on writing a book but was introduced to the group through Lin Yi-hsiung, who knew her as an activist from the Wild Lily Movement in the 1990s. Around the time that Fan joined, the TCU registered as a formal NGO. The group stopped meeting at Lin Yi-hsiung's house and rented its own office space. Lin had hoped that Fan's participation would help give a boost of energy to the organization, and that Fan could become part of the organization's core leadership team. Meetings were held more regularly and seriously, yet party formation was still a distant dream for the organization. However, the meetings ended abruptly on March 18,

2014, when the organization's members headed to the Legislative Yuan to participate in the Sunflower Movement protest.

There are two critical takeaways from the TCU's initial formation and progression: that the spatial openings theory struggles to explain party formation and that contestation was central to the political agenda of everyone involved. Pro-independence, anti-KMT sentiment, anti-unification, and DPP dissatisfaction were central to everyone within the TCU as well as to the existing political parties with which the TCU considered working. Everyone largely agreed on *who* and *what* Taiwan ought to be: an independent country separate from China, without the KMT. It was these shared political values that brought all these people together in the first place. Contestation and related political questions were the unifying forces, but shared political ideals alone were not sufficient to unify the people. Varying approaches to tactics, strategy, and personalities got in the way of a singular, unified "Sunflower" party.

None of the TCU's grievances were new. Pro-independence, anti-KMT sentiment and dissatisfaction with the DPP had all been around for years. In fact, the TSU and the Green Party, the two preestablished political parties the TCU considered working with, had both already articulated these same political ideals. Contestation and its connected political questions had long defined Taiwanese politics. The TCU was not advocating for anything new, or anything that existing parties were not already advocating for. Rather, it was the quality of the existing political representation that was unacceptable. The TCU viewed the existing pro-independence parties as incapable, despite their decades of existence and experience. Party formation theories that rely on the idea of a spatial opening fail to explain the case of Taiwan, because there was no spatial opening: no new political issue or political space in need of filling. Instead, the same salient questions of Taiwan's contested status served as the ideological motivation for new party formation.

The theoretical argument of political space further falls apart when the Sunflower Movement itself is taken into consideration. Central to the Sunflower Movement's mobilization was anti-KMT sentiment, pro-independence advocacy combined with anti-CCP sentiment. These three political attitudes had been the cornerstone of pro-independence politics since democratization. Sunflower itself was not mobilized due to new political issues or to unrepresented issues. Rather, the movement was mobilized around the long-standing and salient political cleavage of independence versus unification. Unlike existing studies of movement party formation, which overstate the importance of a spatial opening, Taiwan's new movement parties did not need such a prerequisite.[12] Taiwan's new movement parties formed despite a lack of spatial opening.

The TCU during Sunflower

The formation of the TCU in the face of initial factionalization, heated arguments, and a steady decline in the organization's ability to successfully form a political party, all began before the Sunflower Movement. All efforts to create a new political party before Sunflower failed. No one in the TCU, however, expected or anticipated the Sunflower Movement to occur. The catalyst that caused the Sunflower Movement, the events that occurred on March 18, 2014, and the subsequent movement all developed separately from anything related to the TCU.

During the Sunflower Movement, the TCU as an organization tried to keep its distance even though almost every member of the TCU was an active participant. The purpose was strategic: the organization did not want to give the impression it was trying to take over or influence the movement. Since the Sunflower Movement used the frames of "youth-led" and "for the next generation," some of the older members of the TCU thought it might look too coercive to insert themselves into the movement as leaders. Instead, the TCU contributed by offering its offices for the movement's meetings and coordination. The TCU's office was conveniently located near the Legislative Yuan and was frequently used by Sunflower Movement leaders during the protests. Most activists, however, did not know of its location, since most Sunflower Movement activists did not even know of the TCU's existence.[13]

The most notable breakaway from the TCU's low-key activities during the Sunflower Movement was when Michael Lin posted a now infamous poem online in which he advocated for the need to "harvest the power of this movement into real political power."[14] His post was met with strong negative backlash, not only from movement activist, but from the leadership team itself. No one in the middle of the movement wanted to discuss political outcomes or party formation, especially in a way that used such opportunistic language. By the end of the movement, activists ultimately dismissed their negative reaction to Lin's idea. Since most Sunflower activists did not even know that it was Michael Lin who went on to establish the NPP, his negative reputation during the movement ultimately had little impact on the NPP's formation and growth.

Fan interacted more with Sunflower Movement leaders than did the Lin faction. Her participation with the TCU, like that of Huang Kuo-chang and others who were also key Sunflower Movement leaders, was separate from any responsibilities she had during the Sunflower. Part of the Sunflower Movement's leadership structure included over twenty NGO representatives, who were allowed a voice in the movement's decision-making process. Though Fan was not a key representative from an NGO, she was still able to be a proactive member of the movement and was privy to the decisions being made.

Factionalism within the TCU did not subside during the Sunflower Movement, but it did take a hiatus. During the Sunflower Movement, both Fan and the Lin faction began to actively recruit social movement activists and potential political entrepreneurs to be candidates for the political party they hoped to form. Neither faction established its own political party. Instead, these TCU leaders were feeling out whether they would be able to get support from certain activists or circles. It was during the Sunflower Movement, however, that the Lin faction first approached Freddy Lim about joining their efforts. Lim, although eventually present at the movement, was not part of its leadership circle. He was already famous in Taiwan, both for his history of activism with Amnesty International and as the lead singer of Cthonic, a death metal band famous for its pro-Taiwan independence politics. Although Lim himself played little to no role during the movement, he was the Lin faction's biggest recruitment goal at the time because of the sheer amount of influence he had among youth activists and youth culture. The Lin faction also reached out to Taichung activist Hung Tzu-yung, who had asked to join the Lin faction.[15] It is important to note that although the Lin faction approached Freddy Lim and Hung Tzu-yung during the Sunflower Movement, neither formally joined with the Lins until much later. Meanwhile, Fan began reaching out to members of some of the other

NGOs, including famous activists Miao Po-ya and Jennifer Lu. Both Miao and Lu were well-known feminist and LGBTQ+ activists who had a history of working with Fan. They too did not formally join the effort until after the movement ended in late 2014.

Movement as Mechanism

The Sunflower Movement served as the pathway for movement party formation. Movement party founders from both the NPP and the SDP repeatedly acknowledged during interviews that their party formation would not have happened without the Sunflower protests. As one TCU member put it, "It is likely that the SDP and NPP would have *tried* to form regardless of the Sunflower Movement. However, our success is entirely because of the Sunflower Movement." It was the movement that finally kick-started the creation of the TCU. Suddenly, the organization was able to reenvision its goal of creating a new political party.

The TCU was highly mobilized at the end of the Sunflower Movement. The protests showed the TCU members that they were not the only ones who felt Taiwan's democracy was under dire threat. Rather, this sentiment was growing throughout Taiwan, especially within youth activist circles. As one founder of the NPP put it, "2016 was the first election after the movement ended, and it was our first opportunity to harvest the power of Sunflower. It was a force the DPP never even considered. We could tell the youth activists were still too passive when it came to voting and still had such negative feelings towards the government. But we thought we had an opportunity to create a new platform that would get the youth to vote. Since so many young people still disliked the DPP after Sunflower, we thought creating a new party would get them to vote. More importantly, we could help win some districts to block the KMT from winning the Legislative Yuan. We ended up working with the DPP, but it was to protect Taiwan from the threat of China."[16]

There was also a qualitatively different feeling for activists after the Sunflower Movement than experienced in previous protests. A common sentiment among TCU members was that a different kind of enthusiasm to participate in formal politics was felt after the Sunflower Movement in a way that had not been felt before. Said one member, "One of the key ways our ability to create a party was successful was not just because the DPP could not represent the Sunflower Movement's goals, but also because activists actually had hopes and expectations for a new party. That kind of hope was not there during the Anti–Media Monopoly Movement but was there for Sunflower."[17]

Prior to the movement, the kind of party that the TCU wanted to form was only a vague idea. The TCU had struggled to maintain its organizational structure and already risked breakdown, but the Sunflower Movement breathed new life into it. Without the protests, the TCU likely would have sputtered out. But after the protests, the TCU felt there was meaningful demand from activists for the kind of party that they had always envisioned. The organization knew it could create the kind of political party that could meaningfully address the challenges they saw within Taiwan. The logistics of finally creating a new party, however, proved far more difficult.

The passionate inspiration felt within the TCU after the Sunflower Movement did not solve the organization's preexisting problems. Factional infighting, differences in goals and tactics, and personality clashes only intensified after the Sunflower Movement. Fan Yun, who joined the TCU only a couple of months prior to the Sunflower protests, became a regular fixture at TCU meetings after the protests ended. Tensions between Fan and the Lin faction, however, were apparent almost immediately. Although Fan was brought in with the intention of being part of the leadership of the TCU, her vision for a new movement party was seemingly opposite of the Lin faction's.

The TCU's meetings increased to weekly, sometimes daily, occurrences, but before the organization could form a new political party, it became stuck again. Members were faced with three fundamental disagreements: how to run the new party's election campaign, how to select candidates to run, and whether to cooperate with the DPP. To understand why these three disagreements existed and their relevance, it is necessary to understand who was disagreeing with whom. Following the Sunflower Movement, the TCU became dominated by two factions: one led by Fan Yun and Chen Shang-chich, a political science professor from National Chung Cheng University, and one led by the Lin faction. Not every TCU member was necessarily affiliated with one faction or the other, but the two factions were the dominant and divisive voices within the TCU.

Fan's camp held the following views on tactics: the new movement party should not spend excessive money on campaign advertising and should avoid overcrowding public spaces with political ads; the party should run the most clean and transparent campaign possible without relying on saturating society with their political messages. The candidates they nominate should not be the most famous activists, but rather the most qualified activists. Famous people, they argued, often make bad politicians. Instead, they should spend time investing in qualified social movement activists and training them to become capable politicians, even if those candidates did not win right away. Finally, their new political party should *not* cooperate with the DPP in any way, because doing so would put the DPP in a position of power and go against the new party's fundamental ideal of giving citizens a progressive alternative to the DPP itself.

The Lin faction held nearly the opposite views: Their vision of a new movement party focused on winning a first election; campaign spending on advertising was crucial and the party should use the same campaign tactics and strategies as other political parties in Taiwan, including public advertising, campaign cars, flyers, and various media outlets. The new party should reach out to famous or well-known individuals within activist circles as a means of attracting support for the party, specifically people like Freddy Lim and Huang Kuo-chang. The Lin faction argued that the party *should* cooperate with the DPP for the sake of at least blocking the KMT from winning.

Even beyond their fundamental disagreements in tactics, strategy, and party organization, plainly speaking the two factions within the TCU did not get along, personally or professionally. Both factions struggled for control over leadership and power within the group. The Lin faction constantly fought with Fan, whose actions they saw as ultimately counterproductive to starting a legitimate opposition party. The Lin faction claimed that Fan was overly idealistic, while Fan asserted that the Lin faction's alternative, pragmatic but well-rehearsed strategy would never lead to the desired changes. While not every member of the TCU picked a side, it was widely acknowledged by most members that clashing personalities led to the eventual breakdown of the organization. Lin Yi-hsiung, true to his nature, never sided with one faction or the other and instead tried his best to be the peacekeeper of the group, attempting to keep the organization together as long as possible.

Formation of the NPP and the SDP

The TCU lasted almost through the end of fall 2014. The two competing factions within the organization, however, had long before then all but given up on creating a unified party. Just months after the Sunflower Movement it became clear that the TCU was no longer needed as an organization, as the two factions had essentially split away from each other already. There are two versions of how the TCU officially dissolved. One is that after months of heated fighting, a meeting of the two factions was held at Lin Yi-hsiung's house, when the Lin faction formally left the TCU, "giving it to Fan Yun to run and manage."[18] Once the Lin faction was formally out of the TCU, both groups were free to start their own political parties as they saw fit. The other explanation is that there was no formal end to the TCU and the organization just faded away. Once the two factions stopped interacting, meetings naturally ended. One member of the NPP recalled: "In late 2014, it was time for the TCU to reregister with the government in order to maintain its status as an NGO. But . . . we had not met in such a long time; we had forgotten that the organization still even existed! It felt . . . awkward."[19]

The NPP formally registered as a party in January 2015 and the SDP did so in March 2015. However, the actual origins of these parties predate formal registration, beginning as early as the start of the Sunflower Movement. Since there was no official end to the TCU, it is difficult to say when the formation of the NPP and the SDP began, but it would be misleading to say these parties were fully formed by 2015. Key early members of the NPP and the SDP, such as Freddy Lim and Jennifer Lu, respectively, were already in places of leadership in their groups by around December 2014. Once formally acknowledged as members, the two began taking more active roles in forming their parties and recruiting members.[20]

Throughout the breakdown of the TCU, Lin Yi-hsiung never took a side. Even after the Lin faction left to form the NPP and Fan Yun's faction left to form the SDP, Lin Yi-hsiung encouraged both parties to maintain a professional attitude toward each other and to not fight publicly.[21] Even during the 2016 election he remained neutral and publicly endorsed candidates from both parties. He spent years as a goodwill advisor for both parties.

Alternative Explanation 1: Spatial Opening

For the spatial opening explanation to hold, a new or underrepresented political ideal or value must have emerged in Taiwan. However, Taiwanese independence and anti-KMT politics—the main political ideas held by both the NPP and the SDP—were not new. Pro-independence and anti-KMT politics were already established as key parts of Taiwan's political discourse. Not only were these political stances not new, but other political parties that advocated for these ideas were already formed and running in elections. Put simply, there was no spatial opening in Taiwan. Yet new movement parties formed anyway. If a spatial opening were a necessary condition for movement party formation, the NPP and the SDP would not have formed. Instead, the TCU would have invested its time and energy into helping one of the existing leftist parties, either the Green Party or the TSU, become electorally viable. The TCU opted to form a new party anyway and ended up with two, both of which exist within the exact same ideological space.

Spatial openings do not matter as much in contested states as social scientists might predict. This common wisdom explanation fails in the case of Taiwan because of its contested status. Political parties in contested states are not simply vehicles for electoral politics; they have a qualitatively deeper, more important meaning to voters. This type of organization can be the vehicle through which citizens have a means to try to change or resolve a contested state's status. When political identity is so deeply attached to a political party, especially when independence-unification politics define a contested state's political spectrum, the logic of why a party forms does not hold. So long as there is demand for independence or unification within Taiwan, parties pushing their own resolutions to this contested issue will continue to form. This reconceptualization of the importance of political space also helps explain why there are so many different pro-independence (and pro-unification) parties in Taiwan, despite them all existing within the same political space.

This is not to say that the idea of a spatial opening has no value. Instead, the amount of explanatory power the spatial opening argument presents in Taiwan's context is more limited than previous research would suggest. It does help us understand some aspects of party formation in other parts of the world. In Taiwan and under certain conditions, some parties may still form due to a spatial opening. For example, in recent years the issue of migrant worker rights has become increasingly salient in Taiwan and new political parties whose platforms focus on migrant worker issues have arisen. These parties are small and electorally unsuccessful, but they formed with the intention of advocating for an increasingly salient issue. An "opening," when understood purely to be related to a political cleavage, cannot explain how movement parties in Taiwan formed. Just because an existing party advocates for certain political issues does not mean additional parties will not form that articulate the same stances. Political representation itself is not enough to explain party formation. The quality of existing parties, their ability to perform electorally, their relation to activists, and activists' perceptions of the Chinese threat were more important in Taiwan's case than conditions of Taiwan's political structure.

Alternative Explanation 2: Political Opportunity Structure

Sociologist Ming-sho Ho argues this theory explains the mobilization and actions taken by activists during the Sunflower Movement, while also acknowledging there are limitations to the theory's explanatory power when it comes to political party formation.[22] As Ho notes, the inherent limitations to political opportunity structure as a theoretical framework is its tautological underpinnings. For some it is difficult to rely on the theory to describe a subjective opportunity within an objective structure.[23] Others have called for abandoning the theory and instead calling for a focus on considering political contexts instead of overly deterministic openings and closings within a structure.[24]

In Taiwan's context, political opportunity structure struggles to explain both party formation and the increase in mobilization after Ma Ying-jeou's tenure as president. The theory would assume that the political context following Ma's tenure was more conducive for social movement mobilization. Yet, politically speaking, the major protests during Ma's tenure, including the Wild Strawberry, Anti–Media Monopoly, and Sunflower Movements, were all rooted in the fear of threats to Taiwan's democracy. All three movements saw police crackdowns against protestors and threats made against activists by the opposition. This combination of Chinese threats and domestic repression made the cost of mobilization higher, which is counter to what political opportunity structure would expect. Ho argues that, for the Sunflower Movement in particular, the political context in which the KMT's elite were split, along with the timing of the passage of the Cross-Strait Service Trade Agreement, help explain why the Sunflower Movement itself mobilized. Even if we accept this theoretical explanation, however, it cannot explain why movement parties formed only in 2014 and not in 2012 or 2008, during the other major protests. Although the political opportunity structure theory may explain the mobilization around movements during Ma's era, it fails to explain party formation in 2014.

Alternative Explanation 3: Party System

Similar to political opportunity structure theory's inability to explain movement party formation in 2008 and 2012, this third alternative explanation, party system theory, cannot explain movement party formation in 2014. To understand why, it is first worth explaining how one creates a party in Taiwan and how Taiwan's elections work.[25] Within thirty days of a party's first meeting, members must submit an application to the Ministry of the Interior with at least one hundred signatures, the names of fifty official party members, a party name, a named leader, and a rough constitution of party rules. Once the government processes the application the new party is formed. It is an incredibly simple process with very low barriers to entry. It is so easy to start a political party in Taiwan that 378 registered parties exist, 81 of which are designated as "active."[26] Starting a political party in Taiwan is both easy and accomplished through an accessible process, with no major capital or political barriers to entry.

Even though it is easy to start a party in Taiwan, is Taiwan's electoral system conducive for new parties to enter the electoral arena and win seats, or does the structure favor a two-party system? Taiwan's major elections for president and Legislative Yuan use a mixed system of both first-past-the-post and proportional representation (PR). For the Legislative Yuan, the majority of seats are district seats and are competed over by the two main parties through first-past-the-post primaries. Elections typically favor the two parties and make it difficult for third parties that are new to politics to compete. In the case of the NPP, in 2016 the DPP cooperated with the new party and let it run candidates in some district elections against the KMT in the DPP's stead. When it comes to the thirty-four reserved PR seats in the Legislative Yuan, however, small parties do have a meaningful way to enter formal politics.

In major elections, Taiwanese vote three times: first for the president, then for their district representative, and then for whichever party they support most. It is this last vote that gives small parties a way into the Legislative Yuan. So long as a party gets at least 5 percent of the total proportional representation votes in a major election, it will gain at least two seats in the Legislative Yuan. When the NPP won 6.2 percent of the PR votes in 2016, it gave the party two additional seats in addition to the district races it won. Even though it does not lead to major representation, the PR vote allows small parties to find a way into formal politics in Taiwan's political system. So long as a small party can show that it has at least 5 percent of the voting population's support, the party is able to become part of Taiwan's formal political process. Unlike in the United States, which has no PR component to its electoral system, Taiwan is actually more welcoming to small parties that are seeking a foothold in the system.

What, then, does Taiwan's easy access to party formation and mixed electoral system say about the party system alternative explanation? The party system theory cannot explain why parties formed in 2014, because Taiwan's party system was the same in 2014 as it was every year starting in 2008.[27] Thus the choice to transform from a movement to a party cannot be explained by the electoral system or any changes to it. It was just as easy for activists to form political parties before 2014, but activists did not feel that their political situation was dire to the point of needing to enter formal politics. Instead, it was only in 2014, when activists perceived a serious threat from China and lacked faith in the DPP to counteract it, that they chose to take advantage of Taiwan's open party system.

Why Did Multiple Parties Form?

It is worth reflecting on one final point in the case of movement party formation in 2014. Instead of one cohesive Sunflower Movement party,

Taiwan saw the birth of many new political parties. Beyond the NPP and the SDP, other movement parties formed out of the Sunflower Movement, all of which shared the same pro-independence ideals but chose to form independently. Whether it was the Trees Party or the Free Taiwan Party, all the new movement parties overlapped ideologically with existing active political parties.[28] The formation of multiple parties was instead related to the political context of the social movement itself. The likelihood of multiple movement parties forming increases when interpersonal relations within a social movement organization break down.

While there was demand for a new political party from activists, there was *not* a demand for *multiple* new movement parties. Had these movement parties formed into one cohesive "Sunflower Movement party," their electoral odds would have been even stronger. Moreover, these new movement parties are virtually the same in terms of political ideology and platform. What makes the NPP and the SDP different is not their politics, but rather their strategies, tactics, and relations with existing political parties. In this case, the SDP and the NPP were founded based on very different approaches to running a political party and fielding candidates. The two parties also had very different relationships with the existing main opposition party, the DPP. The NPP was willing to work with the DPP, while the SDP was not. As one SDP member described these differences: "Variation in ideological stances within these parties would have been much more reasonable to deal with than to have such drastic differences in approach on how to run a party, especially during an election. If people cannot agree on how to run a party . . . that is way more difficult to manage than simply not agreeing on certain issues."[29] Finally, the two factions within the TCU that formed the two parties did not get along, personally or professionally. A simple counterfactual scenario helps further demonstrate this argument: if the two factions within the TCU got along and were friendly with each other, would two parties have still formed? Arguably, if the condition of bad interpersonal relations within the TCU was not present, we would have seen one party form instead of two.

The DPP's Perspective: A Robustness Check

One final source of data to consider is the DPP's perspective on post–Sunflower Movement party formation. Interviews of DPP legislators and leaders verified whether activists' perceptions of the party were known outside of activist circles and whether the DPP considered new movement parties to be politically meaningful.

It is not a surprise to learn that the DPP was aware of activists' dissatisfaction with the party and the subsequent growing demand for a new pro-independence political party, especially after the Sunflower Movement. One longtime DPP politician said: "To be frank, we were scared after the Sunflower Movement. Parties like the NPP and SDP were able to say things that we could not. They were able to mobilize groups of youngsters that we could not. We certainly considered the possibilities of what would happen if their movement grew—they most certainly could have replaced us."[30] Another DPP legislator echoed a similar sentiment: "Ever since the NPP was founded, I have been following public opinion polls closely. People under the age of thirty all want to support them, or some other third force party. This is scary. At the time I thought, for the DPP, one of the two big parties, how are we supposed to deal with a small party that youngsters support?"[31] Said another legislator, "I'm old colleagues with some of the NPP members. When the party was starting, they even reached out to me to ask if I wanted to join. I considered it," he said, laughing, since "it would have been nice to be in a party with a new reputation that had a fresh start."[32]

The DPP leaders were also keenly aware of the spatial differences between themselves and the NPP and the SDP. As one DPP politician put it, "We know we are pro–status quo. We've been this way for a while. We try to be practical about Taiwan's position, but I know we are no longer as pro-independence as many wished we were. These new parties were able to advocate for the kind of pro-Taiwan independence and local Taiwaneseness [*bentuhua*] that we could not. But it's not just about independence. If it were just about independence, there were plenty of other parties to pick from. Regardless of whether we were pro–status quo or pro-independence, they would not want to work with us."[33] Said one DPP city counselor: "The NPP and SDP are simply more to the left on Taiwan's independence spectrum than us. We are close enough that we can work together, especially against the KMT, but youngsters might want to support them more than us."[34]

The DPP well knew it would be unable to win over a meaningful cohort of activists and that perceptions of it among activists had soured, even though the KMT was far more detested in social movement circles. Although the DPP was poised to win the 2016 election because of the KMT's unpopularity, in part connected to the Sunflower Movement, the DPP itself did not unanimously win over the hearts and minds of activists. The desire and demand for a meaningful pro-independence political party without the political baggage of the DPP was not just in the heads of activists. But it was something the DPP knew to be a real and meaningful demand from civil society. Data from the DPP helps confirm not just the conditions of the China threat and activist dissatisfaction with the party, but that the post–Sunflower Movement parties were seen as a meaningful challenge to Taiwan's political system.

Two necessary conditions must be present for movement party formation in a contested state: a dire level of domestic co-optation threat from the contesting state and disillusionment with the established pro-sovereignty party by social activists. The Sunflower Movement itself served as the mechanism that triggered party formation form out of these ideal conditions and the typical factors used by social scientists to understand movement party formation either do not hold or lack the same level of explanatory power in contested states like Taiwan. When a state's fundamental political cleavage is defined by issues of who and where (and not typical left-right issues seen in most non-contested states), the political contexts for social movement mobilization and political party formation are different. Specifically, the typical understandings for movement party formation cannot fully explain the case of Taiwan's 2014 Sunflower Movement parties.

In 2014, there was no new or emerging political issue that existing parties were not already advocating for as part of their political platforms. Pro-independence politics was not new, and there was no lack of pro-independence parties. The political opportunity to form a new movement party in 2014 was both just as open and just as closed as before then. Regardless of the status of the political opportunity structure, movement parties still formed. Furthermore, Taiwan's party system is open and conducive to party formation at any time, and it is designed to give small parties a meaningful chance to win seats through a mixed electoral system. Political opening, political opportunity structure, and party system theories cannot explain movement party formation in Taiwan. Instead, international and domestic issues of contestation must be taken into account.

In 2014, domestic co-optation threat and apathy toward the DPP drove social movement actors to take matters into their own hands and create their own political parties. How they went from movement to party is an important piece of Taiwan's contested status puzzle. And, although the future of the NPP and the SDP after their formation in 2014 has been volatile, the parties' initial formation and impact on Taiwan's electoral system cannot be overstated.

SIX

Ukraine, a Contested State

Recognition alone is not a sufficient condition for a state to no longer be considered contested. Just because a state has de jure recognition does not mean its fundamental issues of contestation are resolved. Nor should the importance of recognition as a categorical variable be overstated, especially when it comes to conceptualizing who and what are the political dynamics of a contested state. When discussing Taiwan, this point may perhaps seem moot since Taiwan is not formally recognized. For those who support various kinds of pro-Taiwanese independence, recognition is still a fundamental, meaningful goal. But if the world collectively decided to recognize Taiwan, either as the Republic of China or as the Republic of Taiwan, its fundamental condition of contestation would not instantly resolve because contestation is a two-way street. So long as a contesting state claims a contested territory and the world acknowledges or recognizes those claims, the status of places like Taiwan will be nearly impossible to fully resolve. The underlying tensions of identity and relation to China will remain whether the world recognizes Taiwan as a state through formal means or not. Perhaps the best empirical case in point that demonstrates this conundrum is Ukraine.

In February 2022 the world watched with shock and horror as Russia invaded Ukraine. Once the war began, we saw with humbled eyes how the Ukrainian people responded to Russia with tenacity and resolve. In the initial six months of the war, perhaps the most common form of analysis for East Asia specialists was a comparative analysis between Ukraine and Taiwan. A steady stream of think pieces comparing Ukraine and Russia with China and Taiwan began to appear. After all, on the surface these places and conditions seem to share a similar dynamic: Russia claims Ukraine, China claims Taiwan.

While many of these pieces offered interesting insight on the contemporary relevance of Taiwan's and Ukraine's similar geopolitical situations, many of them only scratched the surface.[1] Indeed, the situations in Taiwan and Ukraine are important to compare. However, the reason they are comparable is not simply because of the recent Russian invasion or the deadly high tensions in both regions. Rather, it is because Ukraine, like Taiwan, is a contested state. Ukraine's situation, however, is not exactly like Taiwan's. While many were quick to compare the surface geopolitical realities between Ukraine and Taiwan and their fraught relations with Russia and China, respectively, the shared connection runs much deeper. Ukraine, like Taiwan, defines its politics through the same fundamental questions: Who are we? Where are we? What is our relationship to the contesting state that claims us? How does that existential relationship define our everyday politics?

The goal here is not to equate Ukrainian history and Taiwanese history as an identical same-case comparison. But there are meaningful parallels between Ukraine's and Taiwan's domestic development and their international relations with Russia and China. These parallels are meaningful not just in their shared characteristics but in how they explain Taiwan's and Ukraine's contested statuses from both domestic and international perspectives. Nevertheless, many readers who are familiar with Taiwanese and Ukrainian history will note key points where these two cases are not similar. Indeed, many such moments in history are not exactly the same, and the differences should be acknowledged and respected. These imperfect limitations are what makes comparative studies of Taiwan and Ukraine interesting. And, despite having so many shared characteristics and developments defined by contestation, Ukraine and Taiwan developed differently.

Historicizing Ukraine's Contested Status

Like Taiwan, Ukraine has at various points in its history enjoyed moments of sovereignty over its territory and been under the control of multiple empires and conquering countries. From the thirteenth to the seventeenth century, Ukraine was subject to control by Lithuania, Poland, Austria-Hungary, and Mongolia.[2] At different eras in time, different states fought over various parts of Ukraine. Ukraine, however, has always struggled to become a cohesive, sovereign state. Instead, it was historically often split and fought over by various Eastern European and Russian forces at different points in time. But, despite its constantly marginalized geographic position, a Ukrainian people who spoke a Ukrainian language has persisted, regardless of which state was governing the territory.[3]

Parallel to how the fundamental root of Taiwan's contestation story begins with China, the reason *why* Ukraine is contested today begins with Russia. Comparable to how China's borders shrank and grew with different dynasties, so too did the borders of Russia's empire. At different points in time Russia controlled parts of Central Asia and Eastern Europe and at other times did not. Both Imperial Russia and Soviet Russia were invested in spreading their borders and nationalizing all citizens within. The various state policies and processes of incorporating states and people into Russian and Soviet borders are referred to as Russification and Sovietization.[4]

The goal of both Russification and Sovietization later was to assimilate the various peripheral states surrounding Russia through coercive policies.[5] Such policies included mandating the use of the Russian language in formal settings (in schools and in business and government communications) and requiring Russian-centric education of children. The goal, as with any empire, was to spread a common identity and nationalism for people to identify with and rally around. Such a process, however, requires the marginalization and erasure of preexisting local identities and languages. Russia's policies gave it the ability to closely monitor and regulate how identity, language, culture, and politics were created, replicated, and practiced.[6] Simply put, the goal of Russification was to "transform" non-Russians into loyal Russian citizens.[7]

Russification and Sovietization, however, were not monolithic in nature. Instead, these measures varied widely across the empire and depended on the state in question. For example, some policies were more cultural and focused on promoting cultural nationalism and Russian identity, while others were political in nature and focused on spreading Marxist-Leninist norms.[8] Places like Central Asia faced much more aggressive assimilation policies that utilized settler-colonialist tactics. For example, through demographic transformation, mass migration, and relocation of Russian citizens into Kazakhstan, Soviet Russia was able to end the Kazakh people's nomadic practices.[9]

Ukraine, too, faced its own host of assimilationist policies over time. But, unlike the situations in the Baltics or Central Asia, Ukraine has had a particularly complex relationship with Russia because of its relative closeness.[10]

This closeness is not simply a matter of geographical proximity, but also one of cultural and linguistic ties. Ukrainian and Russian languages and Slavic cultural practices are distinct yet mutually comprehensible. Places like Armenia and Kazakhstan, despite being subject to Russification, do not hold the same nationalistic value to Russia that Ukraine does. Ukraine is, from the Russian government's perspective, part of Russia's national narrative and its historical origin myth. Russian narratives often portray Kyiv as being the geographical origin of Rus culture, making it, from Russia's perspective, politically, culturally, and ethnically tied deeply to Ukraine.[11]

Just as China employs the concept of "since ancient times" within its nation-building mythos, Russia employs a similar rhetorical tactic when imagining Ukraine.[12] Ukraine's history is long, complex, and full of various narratives. Its early history often begins when the earliest tribes that made up Russian and Ukrainian people descended from the East Slavic tribes of the Dnieper Basin.[13] One of the first states to form out of this group was at Kyivan Rus, today the capital of Ukraine. Later, another state known as Muscovite Russia was the predecessor to the Imperial Russian empire. From a Ukrainian perspective, the founding of Kyivan Rus began the process of Ukrainian nation-building that continues today. From Russia's perspective, Kyivan Rus is the clear historic and cultural connection between Ukraine and Russia.

During the Imperial Russian era, those who lived in Ukraine were referred to from Russia's perspective as "little Russians," as opposed to Russian nationals being "great Russians."[14] As early as the late 1700s, those who lived in today's Ukraine aspired for some version of self-determination. Despite being caught between various warring empires for centuries, by the early 1800s the eastern Ukraine territory was fully under Russian control, while western Ukraine was still considered part of Galicia. It was at this time that a budding sense of self-identity and a pro-Ukraine movement began to take hold. Literary magazines, novels, and intellectuals began to push for a stronger Ukrainian identity, more Ukrainian cultural products, and pride in being Ukrainian.[15]

By the mid-1800s the Russia-controlled parts of Ukraine began to sense this growing agitation. To counter the rising pro-Ukraine movement, Russia began to ban or otherwise severely limit Ukrainian literature and language from publication. In Galicia, the pro-Ukraine movement was also under attack from Polish elites who wanted to stop any sense of solidarity between eastern and western Ukraine. The two governments, however, were unable to stop this growing sense of Ukrainian identity and solidarity from forming. In Ukraine, writers instead began to publish pro-Ukrainian literature in Russian. In Galicia, Ukrainian leaders found avenues to connect with Ukrainian advocates in Russia.

Part of the challenge within Ukraine was the not-trivial number of elites who saw themselves as part of the Russian empire and who agreed with the idea that Ukraine was Little Russia.[16] One notable volume at the time argued that Ukrainians deserved a place of honor within the political and social echelons of the Russian empire, not necessarily as a separate Ukrainian nation or distinct identity. Others advocated for a federalist system in which Ukraine would have some autonomy within a larger Russia-Poland-Ukraine state. Part of the challenge in Galicia-controlled Ukraine were those who advocated for Ukrainian separation from Galicia but supported incorporation into Russia, instead of as an independent Ukrainian state. Others in both parts of Ukraine advocated for a sovereign Ukraine. Similar to how we see the modern political spectrum, there was early variation in how Ukrainians—even those who felt some degree of uniqueness—identified with independence, unification, and status quo politics.[17]

Sovereignty, however, was only part of the debate. The deeper, more existential question for Ukrainian intellectuals was over the fundamental question of identity. Such debates were not simply a matter of whether someone identified as Ukrainian or as Russian, but whether "Ukrainian" in and of itself is a legitimate, separate identity. Is Ukrainian identity something that can coexist with a Russian identity or is it something secondary to Russian identity? Is Ukrainian identity in and of itself entirely separate from Russian identity?

Like Taiwan, the questions Ukraine has been debating since the early 1900s are not just a matter of recognizing a Ukrainian state. Rather, it is a matter of fighting for the legitimacy of an identity that exists its own right, separate from the contesting state that claims otherwise. Ukraine exists as a contested state because for centuries those who have lived in Ukraine have been dealing with the fundamental questions of self-identity and relationship to the larger state that claims them. These fundamental political questions of sovereignty, identity, and connection to the state that claims Ukraine (Russia) have subsequently defined the political spectrum for and driven the actions of Ukrainians.

Perhaps the most common and contentious avenue through which debates over Ukrainian versus Russian identity, sovereignty, and contestation have taken place is language and language policy.[18] Debates over language have mirrored the debates about what Ukrainian identity is: Is Ukrainian a separate language or a dialect of Russian? Does it deserve to be seen and spoken with the same authority as Russian? Ukrainian independence activists have used language politics to advocate for Ukraine's legitimacy, but due to centuries of Russification, advocacy for the Ukrainian language has been a constant uphill battle.

As early as the late 1800s, the debate over Ukraine's contested status was focused on language politics.[19] Early Ukrainian advocates used the Ukrainian language to advocate for Ukraine but often ran into pushback from those who saw Ukrainian as secondary to Russian. When the Soviet Union annexed Ukraine formally into its territory, it doubled down on the ongoing Russification process begun by Imperial Russia. Just like the rest of the Soviet Union, Ukraine was coercively pushed into a whole new set of economic, political, and cultural practices. Along with doubling down on promoting Russian language policy, Ukrainian was further stigmatized by the Soviet government. Ukrainian was already seen as a lower-level language compared to Russian and Ukrainian speakers came to be seen as less-educated, uncivilized, and of a lower status than Russian speakers. When the Soviet state took power, it became dangerous to speak Ukrainian. There were instances of public figures being removed for speaking Ukrainian instead of Russian, and elites were rewarded for prioritizing Russian language over Ukrainian.

The challenge was that, at the time, many Ukrainians simply did not speak Russian and many in Ukraine struggled to adapt to Soviet top-down orders to transition into a more Russian-centric society. Many began using a Ukrainian-Russian hybrid language known as Surzhyk, but speaking such a language still carried a negative connotation.[20] Although speaking Ukrainian was not punished in as a severe way as speaking Taiwanese or Japanese was in Taiwan under martial law, linguistic policies still fundamentally shaped ethnic and nationalistic identities until the fall of the Soviet Union. The issue of linguistic politics and how it created political divisions within Ukraine followed the contested state through its formation in 1991.

It is worth recognizing that Ukraine is not the only contested state existing on Russia's borders.[21] It is on former Soviet and now Russian borders where many of today's contested states are found. Nagorno-Karabakh, Abkhazia, and South Ossetia share the same fundamental contested conditions as Taiwan and, to a degree, Ukraine.[22] Previous states like Yugoslavia eventually gave way to a number of contested states, including Kosovo and Serbia.[23] Although Ukraine is one of the former Soviet states that successfully became recognized when the Soviet Union fell, like many other formerly Sovietized states its newly drawn borders are contested. Just like the decolonial project in the Middle East and Africa in the mid-twentieth century, not everyone in Eastern Europe felt their new state's lines matched their imagined hopes. After decades of Soviet rule—and, for some, centuries of colonization—several newly formed states struggled with a sense of identity. Sovereignty, identity, and relations with Russia have all played an integral role in state formation from the late 1980s through today for most former Soviet states.[24]

What makes Ukraine different, however, is that it received recognition as a sovereign state.[25] From an international perspective, Ukraine achieved one of the goals that all aspiring states long for: recognition by not just powerful states, but international organizations, global businesses, and the world community at large. Recognition—one of the most critical elements to statehood—was bestowed upon Ukraine and gave the new country the international ability to establish itself as a sovereign state. However, despite enjoying sovereign recognition internationally, recognition did not solve Ukraine's domestic contested questions. Since becoming an independent state, Ukraine has not stop struggling with questions of identity and territory, continually navigating a complicated relationship with Russia, which has never fully relinquished its claims over large swaths of Ukraine's territory and people.

It is Russia's claim over Ukrainian territory that makes Ukraine further contested. Unlike other former Soviet states, Russia makes claims over Ukraine despite its de jure independent status. From Russia's perspective, Ukraine has historically been tied to its ethnicity, culture, and territory.

Unlike Poland or Kazakhstan, for which Russia does not make essentialist claims of ownership over Poles or Kazaks, it does do so over Ukrainians. Even though states like Poland or Kazakhstan were Russified and Sovietized into becoming Russian or Soviet citizens in the past, Russia's attachment to those states does not run so deep that it continues to make claims over them now that they have achieved independence. But Russia does continue to make such claims over Ukraine, regardless of its recognized status.

Russia's essentialist claims over Ukrainian identity and culture, and the fundamental impact these claims have on the political psyche of Ukrainian civil society, also make Ukraine qualitatively different from other post-Soviet states. Even though other states, such as Bosnia or Estonia, may define their political cleavage in part by their relationship with Russia, the same existential lines cannot be said of Ukraine.[26] Russia does not cast doubt that Bosnian or Polish people are of a unique ethnicity. Nor does Russia argue that these states' languages and identities are encompassed by Russian language and identity. But Russia does claim that Ukrainian as a language, ethnicity, culture, and identity are part of and subservient to Russia. While other former Soviet states may share Ukraine's political anxieties about relations with Russia, they do not do so at the same level of contestation.

Contemporary Contested Politics

In 1991, Russian-speaking and Ukrainian-speaking Ukrainians alike voted unanimously for independence, but this vote came in the context of having spent centuries caught between and within empires. Russification and Sovietization had deeply changed how Ukrainians saw themselves and their connection with Russia. Even though they were able to emphatically state they did not want to be part of the Russian Federation, how they felt about their future relationship with Russia, both politically and culturally, was still undetermined.[27] Ukrainian nationalists wanted to push back against the long-entrenched norms of seeing Russian as the more-elevated cultured language. Ukrainians with newfound statehood wanted to rejuvenate and celebrate Ukrainian language, culture, and heritage. Just like every other newly formed state, instilling a sense of pride and nationalism is a fundamental part of the state-building process.[28]

But not all Ukrainians were eager to embrace such strong feelings of Ukrainian nationalism.[29] In the early 1990s a not-insignificant number of those residing in eastern Ukraine did not identify strongly with Ukrainian nationalism.[30] Many Russian-speaking Ukrainians did not feel the need to drop what was their mother tongue for a new Ukrainian language they did not know or speak. Even if they were in favor of Ukrainian sovereignty, many Russian-speaking Ukrainians had to find a new space for themselves within a nationalized Ukrainian space. Debates within civil society began to revolve around what language government officials should use, what language should be spoken in professional versus home environments, and how children should be educated.[31] A spectrum began to ossify between Ukrainians who spoke Ukrainian, Russians who spoke Ukrainian, Ukrainians who spoke Russian, and Russians who spoke Russian, all of whom were negotiating the who and what of their newly formed Ukrainian state.[32]

The question of Ukrainian identity and how it has changed over time has been studied extensively by social scientists.[33] Just like how Taiwanese identity is perhaps the most fraught question in Taiwan, the same is true of Ukraine. More important, however, public opinion research shows that Ukrainian identity has been dynamic over the years, with increasing numbers of Ukrainians identifying as Ukrainian as time goes on.[34] As far back as the Soviet Union's collapse, political scientists have conducted dozens of waves of surveys asking people living in Ukraine regarding their identity, language preferences, and perceptions of Russia. Questions typically focus on what they feel their nationality is (Ukrainian, Russian, or both), what language they speak in various contexts (at home versus at work), and what they consider their homeland to be (Ukraine, the USSR, or Russia). Election specialists have also closely monitored which types of candidates (pro-Ukraine versus pro-Russia) are more electorally successful and where they succeed.

The divide between Ukrainians versus Russians living within Ukraine has been evident from the very beginning of Ukraine's independence. Early public opinion showed a clear divide in how people within Ukraine not only felt about themselves, but how they envisioned the future of Ukraine.[35] Specifically, the question about whether Ukraine was destined to become closer to Europe or closer to Russia became another key political cleavage and manifestation of contested identity and linked fate. Affiliation or desire to affiliate with the European Union (EU) versus integrating further with Russia continued to be a key part of debates over identity and the future of Ukraine as time went on.

Importantly, early surveys of Ukrainian citizens also identified how issues of identity and territory were influential on both public opinion and voting behavior. As early as 1992, even though Ukraine had just achieved independence, surveys showed a clear divide between how Ukraine-identifying Ukrainians versus Russia-identifying Ukrainians were voting and identifying with political parties.[36] Results showed one clear indicator for who was likely to identify as Ukrainian versus Russian and who was likely to vote for a pro-Ukraine versus a pro-Russian party: geography. Geographical region was such a strong indicator of identity and political ideology that the 1994 presidential election was nearly split between Leonid Kuchma, who campaigned on "fewer walls, more bridges" with Russia, and Leonid Kravchuk, who campaigned on Ukrainian sovereignty and statehood. All *oblasts* (Ukraine's equivalence of a province) on the eastern side of Ukraine voted for Kuchma, and all on the western side for Kravchuk. With a higher population in eastern Ukraine, Kuchma won, creating a political context for pro-Russian politicians, businesses, and civil societies to gain access to Ukraine's newly formed state.

From a counterfactual perspective, it is worth asking how we know these voting results are being driven by issues of identity and territory and not perhaps by economics or traditional left-right spectrum issues. As Paul Kubicek says in an early study that analyzed a combination of electoral and public opinion data from 1991, 1992, 1994, and 1998, voting behavior "cannot simply be explained primarily by orientation toward the market or reforms . . . instead, one would have to consider the importance of politics of symbols, culture, identity, and affection. . . . Thus, support for parties in Ukraine runs along the ethnic/territorial/cultural cleavages."[37] Kubicek may have not used the specific framing of contestation, but his data shows that contested issues of identity and territory were present as soon as an independent Ukrainian democracy began.

This emergence and solidification of contestation as the key political cleavage continued after the early 1990s. Ukrainian voters consistently based their political decisions on issues of contested identity and territory through the early 2000s.[38] Scholars on Ukraine's elections generally agree that, at least through 2014, elections in Ukraine ossified on this cleavage of contestation as the most salient political, cultural, and ideological division among voters. Some referred to this as the so-called Russia question or the pro-statehood/anti-statehood divide.[39] Demographic features like location and language consistently predicted political support for pro-Russia versus pro-Ukrainian parties. Even though geography continues to strongly predict political attitudes, certain events in Ukraine's history have managed to shake the hearts and minds of large swaths of eastern-residing Ukrainians, who were previously more likely to identify with Russia.

Like Taiwan, Ukraine's questions of identity and territory have not simply remained static since the 1990s. On the contrary, over the last three decades, how people identify, what language they choose to speak, and their affinity for the EU or Russia has changed. These changes are not random. Instead, they are often linked to critical junctures in Ukrainian-Russian relations.[40] Part of the fundamental challenge to contested states is that the contesting state is actively trying to find ways to pull the contested state back into its borders. Even though Ukraine had achieved independence in 1991, Russia has consistently tried to access Ukraine's democratic institutions, influence policy, and sway public opinion.[41] While often done through quiet means, at certain moments Russia's efforts to weaken Ukraine's sovereignty both domestically and internationally have caused questions of contestation to shift. In other words, every time Russia threatens or attacks Ukraine, it changes how Ukrainians identify with and feel toward Russia, Ukraine, and the EU.

Party Corruption and Domestic Co-optation Threat in Ukraine

Despite gaining formal recognition through critical international means, Ukraine continues to be contested because its fundamental political questions remain tied to issues of identity and territory. Moreover, the contesting state that claims Ukraine, Russia, has signaled as strongly as possible that it will not simply allow Ukraine to exist as a sovereign autonomous state and instead ought to be brought more closely into Russian control.

However, while Ukraine may look like a contested state, it is more important to acknowledge that it *acts* like a contested state. To reask a relevant question: Why do some threats from contesting states cause a mobilizing effect on the domestic politics of contested states and others do not? Does Ukrainian civil society react to Russian threats in a way similar to Taiwan's reactions to Chinese threats? Different types of threats from contesting states affect contested states differently. Specifically, domestic co-optation threat has the potential to lead to protest. When a contesting state is able to utilize a contested state's democratic institutions to push for unification, such actions have a mobilizing effect that rhetorical threats and military threats do not. While military threats and rhetorical threats can influence civil society's political behavior, if a contesting state is able to infiltrate the domestic politics of a contested state, a qualitatively different effect results, especially when that threat is sufficiently high. The fear of a contesting state taking over a contested state using its own institutions against the people causes people to mobilize in resistance to both the contesting state and to the domestic parties and politicians complicit in the parent-state's coercions.

One fundamental challenge for democracy in contested states like Ukraine and Taiwan is that the contesting states that claim them are autocratic governments. Thus, people and organizations that feel a sense of loyalty to their contesting state, whether it is pro-China groups in Taiwan or pro-Russia groups in Ukraine, both passively and actively endorse their authoritarian style of government. While not all contested-contesting state dynamics are questions of democracy versus autocracy, the divide adds another complicated layer between the two polities' dynamics. Even though pro-China and pro-Russia groups may advocate for and help build democratic institutions during moments of regime transition, there are incentives for these groups to create pathways for their contesting state to access and influence the newly formed democratic institutions. In Taiwan, this happened when civil society felt threatened by China's ability to influence its domestic democratic institutions. Ukraine has seen a similar effect, where pro-Russia loyalties have strong pro-autocracy implications.

Since the 1994 presidential election led to the election of pro-Russia-leaning Kuchma, Ukraine's democracy continued to grow but it opened clear access for pro-Russian influence. Ukraine continued to consolidate its democracy into the early 2000s, but there existed clear signs of weak institutions and rampant government corruption. Russian and Ukrainian oligarchs (wealthy individuals with business empires) held strong influence over politicians and Ukraine's economy, despite politicians paying lip service to the desire for trade diversity and stronger relations with the EU. Kuchma was reelected in 1999, but corruption within his administration became more obvious to civil society and international media as time went on.

The Orange Revolution

The months leading up to the 2004 election and the Orange Revolution were marked by deep corruption and even murder.[42] In 2000, Ukrainian journalist Georgiy Gongadze, who was known for reporting on corruption in government and anti-democratic practices by politicians, was kidnapped and murdered. A month after his murder, a cassette tape was leaked by former president Kuchma's bodyguard that connected Kuchma to Gongadze's murder. Although the president did not order the hit, he was caught on tape inferring that he wanted the journalist "dealt with." The scandal not only dropped Kuchma's approval rating to 9 percent, but it also colored how voters saw the candidate he endorsed for the next election, Viktor Yanukovych.[43]

When it came time for the 2004 presidential election, Kuchma was unable to run again due to Ukraine's two-term limit. Yanukovych, a pro-Russia leaning politician and Kuchma's prime minister since 2002, was set up to replace him. However, dissatisfaction with and distrust of the government, the quality of Ukrainian democracy, and the future of Ukraine were on the forefront of Ukrainian voters' minds. This was particularly true of Ukrainian voters in the west. Surveys show that in the lead-up to 2004, western Ukrainians were not only more likely to demonstrate a Ukrainian identity but were also more likely to participate in a wide variety of political activities, including protests. Western Ukrainians were also more likely to value a strong, independent civil society. Yanukovych's opponent, Viktor Yushchenko, was a pro-Ukraine opposition leader that had spent years pushing back against Kuchma's coalition.

Even before the election, Yushchenko was widely popular among western Ukrainians. The first presidential runoff eliminated all other smaller nominees and confirmed the Yushchenko versus Yanukovych showdown. In the campaign for the second runoff, politicking became almost deadly. Stories of voter intimidation and harassment by Yanukovych toward Yushchenko's supporters were widespread, and at one point Yushchenko was poisoned. Despite the assassination attempt, Yushchenko managed to make a full recovery and returned to the campaign trail. Tensions were extremely high as the time for the second vote came.

The second presidential runoff, however, is what pushed Ukraine into the Orange Revolution. Although the first runoff had the two candidates tied at about 40 percent each, predictions leading up to the second election put Yushchenko ahead of Yanukovych. When the results came out, however, Yanukovych was ahead of Yushchenko by 3 percent. Considering the context preceding the second presidential vote, it became emphatically clear the election had been neither free nor fair. Reports came out alleging electoral corruption and fraud. Protests broke out across Ukraine in opposition to corrupt political institutions that were degrading Ukraine's democracy. These largely peaceful protests became known as the Orange Revolution. Encouraged by Yushchenko, over 18 percent of Ukrainian citizens participated in the pro-Ukraine protests.[44] The protests were explicitly framed around pro-Ukrainian nationalism, anti-authoritarianism, and pro-democracy.

The Orange Revolution matters because it was one of the earliest mass protests mobilized against party corruption and domestic co-optation threat in a Ukrainian context. The electoral systems and bureaucracies that were designed to protect Ukrainian democracy were proved to be both ineffective and conducive to creating pathways for pro-Russian interests, which had a mobilizing effect within Ukrainian civil society. Although the protests were not explicitly anti-Russia, they were mobilized along fundamental lines of Ukraine's contestation.[45] Opposition to politicians who were seen as either sympathetic to Russia or against Ukraine's state-building project was fundamental to the protesters' motivations. It was not just about corrupt politicians—it was about corrupt politicians opposed to Ukrainian autonomy and state formation. In other words, it was opposition to potential domestic co-optation of Ukraine's democratic institutions. Although the Orange Revolution was perhaps less of a political revolution and more of a signal of democratic growth, it marked a turning point in which Ukrainian self-determination was brought back into the spotlight, despite the state having already achieved formal independence. It was also a critical antecedent to the 2014 Euromaidan protests, which involved many participants who were also active during the Orange Revolution.

Eventually the peaceful protests led to a second runoff vote that was closely monitored by both domestic and international election observers. This time Yushchenko emerged victorious, and he served as Ukraine's president for one term. Despite his pro-Ukraine leanings, he eventually faced his own share of corruption scandals. His popularity sank to the single digits, and in 2008 he did not run for reelection or endorse either of the candidates who were running. It is also worth noting that, during Yushchenko's presidency, a significant part of Ukrainian civil society still identified with Russia and felt that Ukraine ought to integrate closer with Russia. Despite the scandals surrounding his 2004 presidential run, Yanukovych ran again in 2010 and won against the opposition's Yulia Tymoshenko. In light of the 2004 election debacle, more election observers were stationed across Ukraine and eventually the election legitimate was declared legitimate despite distrust from the general public. One poll even showed that 82 percent of Ukrainians still expected vote rigging during the election.[46] Despite the controversies surrounding the race, Yanukovych began his presidency.

Euromaidan and Russian Threats

Even though Ukraine had elected a pro-Russia–leaning president, public opinion polls hinted that civil society was still moving in a pro-Ukrainian direction. The contradiction between Ukrainian citizens wanting to further institutionalize their recognized state-building project and the elected leadership of Ukraine wanting to push for the opposite created conditions that exacerbated Ukraine's contested status and led to one of the largest social protests in Ukraine's history: the Euromaidan protests, also known as the Maidan Uprising. In the lead-up to 2013, Ukrainian citizens were already increasingly identifying as Ukrainian.[47]

Even though Yanukovych had been seen as pro-Russia in the past, his pro-Russia leanings became increasingly less subtle once elected president.

His business and political ties with Russian oligarchs and political parties made it clear that he was not only invested in Russian interests, but that he was actively working against Ukrainian self-determination. To the Ukrainian opposition and civil society who did not identify with Russia, Yanukovych was a threat because he created a political context for Russian forces to infiltrate Ukrainian domestic institutions in ways that were overtly working against Ukrainian sovereignty and self-interest.

The prime example, which served as a critical catalyst for the Euromaidan protests, was a negotiated trade bill between Ukraine and the EU. For Ukrainians, closer ties with the EU were not simply about political affiliation or economic growth. They were more about symbolically establishing Ukraine as an autonomous, independent state that was fully separate from Russia. Affiliation with the EU was a key strategy used by pro-Ukraine citizens and politicians to resolve Ukraine's contested status.

Negotiations for a comprehensive trade agreement with the EU began in 2008, a process that had taken years to make a reality. It required Ukraine to pass and update laws that would drastically improve its human rights and labor laws. Originally, Yanukovych was complicit in pushing the Ukrainian parliament to pass the bill. In 2013 the Ukraine-European Union Association Agreement, a bill that was both symbolically and substantively critical for Ukraine's future, was written and ready to be passed.

But Russia, which had strong sway and control over Yanukovych, objected to the bill. In response to the bill's impending success, Russia began to embargo trade with Ukraine. Immediately, pro-Russia politicians began to change their minds about the trade bill and reversed their decision to support it. This led to pro-Russia parties calling to delay the bill's signing, saying that Ukraine ought to consider the ramifications to Ukrainian-Russian relations were the bill to pass. Eventually the Ukrainian government admitted that Russia had requested they delay the EU deal, with President Vladimir Putin saying outright that the deal was bad for Russia.[48] On November 13, 2013, after Russia's very overt intervention into Ukraine's economic and political future, Yanukovych suspended the signing of the bill and formally rejected the EU's offer, saying Ukraine would instead pursue a similar deal with Russia and the Eurasian Economic Union.[49]

Euromaidan Protests

Russia had successfully co-opted Ukraine's domestic democratic institutions to further integrate Ukraine into Russia's sphere of influence and away from the EU. To Ukrainian citizens, the clear infiltration of Russian interests into Ukrainian politics was so stark that civil society decided to take matters into its own hands. Beginning on the night of November 21, when the suspension of the EU deal was announced, thousands arrived in Kyiv to protest the pro-Russia turn of events and advocate for Ukraine to join the EU as planned.[50] Clashes with the police began three days later, with violence escalating through November 30, when police began using tear gas and other violent means to repress the protesters' activities. The police's escalation in repression tactics only served to grow the protests. More people joined the protests, and protesters themselves began using more violent tactics in response. Police brutality became a key frame for the protests, along with anti-Yanukovych politics. The movement continued to grow through the new year, leading to Yanukovych's government passing anti-protest laws, which only intensified the protest movement even further.[51]

From November 2013 through February 2014 the protests continued around Ukraine. The protesters framed their demands around Ukrainian autonomy and opposition to their president's co-optation by Russia.[52] Demands included direct lines of communication with the parties negotiating the EU trade deal, as well as banning Yanukovych from making geopolitical decisions on behalf of Ukraine. Opposition to Russia, as well as the historic memory of Ukraine's subservience to Russia, were expressed throughout the protests, both through chants and the direct action of smashing Lenin statues around Ukraine. The protests began as peaceful but quickly turned violent, both through the brutal methods used by riot police against journalists and protesters, and by protesters fighting back against the police. While there is debate about whether violence was inevitable during the Euromaidan protests, the events contrasted sharply with the peaceful nature of the Orange Revolution.[53] By January, Yanukovych and his pro-Russian parliament passed an anti-protest law that was meant to quell what were by then regularly violent protests. The laws were viewed as starkly anti-democratic and were feared to heavily restrict the rights to assembly and protest and freedom of the press. The law had the opposite effect: the protests continued to expand and became more violent and deadly.

After months of tenacious protests, an unrelenting parliament, intense clashes, and failed negotiations, the protests ended in late February 2014. An agreement was reached out of pressure from all sides to end what was becoming an increasingly bloody battlefield between protesters and riot police. The agreement also came with several political changes, including changing Ukraine's governing system to have a more equal balance of power. Most important, it called for an end to violence from all sides. More than one hundred people had been killed by the time protests ended. After the agreement was signed, in a climactic turn of events, Yanukovych fled Ukraine. Later it was learned that he fled to Russia, where he lives today. Soon after Yanukovych fled, he was formally impeached by the opposition politicians who remained in the Ukrainian parliament. In connection to Russia's annexation of Crimea, a 2019 court formally charged Yanukovych with treason. By the end of the Euromaidan Movement, protests had sparked in nearly every city in Ukraine, with hundreds of thousands of people having participated. The anti-protest laws were eventually repealed, and the trade deal with the EU was eventually signed by the government that came to power.

Euromaidan, like the Sunflower Movement, was not simply about a trade bill. Euromaidan was a protest movement that was attempting to resolve Ukraine's questions of contestation. It pushed back against not just Russian infiltration into Ukrainian institutions, but also against the fundamental idea that Ukraine ought to be politically, economically, and culturally tied with Russia. What started as a protest against a corrupt, pro-Russia government became a massive political statement on Ukrainian sovereignty and autonomy. Beyond the simple dichotomy of autocracy versus democracy, the protests signaled that Ukrainians had the right to advocate for an independent Ukraine that was not part of Russia, but an independent state able to thrive on its own merit.

Political Outcomes

When two necessary conditions are met—when perceptions of the existing pro-sovereignty party have become inept and people feel a dire sense of domestic co-optation threat—activists will form their own political parties and enter office. Was 2014 a conducive context for movement party formation in Ukraine? There was most certainly a critical level of domestic co-optation threat that mobilized Ukrainian civil society, but perceptions of pro-Ukrainian parties were not necessarily a central part of the Euromaidan protests. Although Tymoshenko lost to Yanukovych in 2010, it was not necessarily because Ukraine saw her as corrupt or the pro-Ukraine politicians as incapable. Arguably, there is no sufficient evidence to show that perceptions of pro-Ukraine parties were low in the same way the data shows perceptions of the DPP were low around the time of the Sunflower Movement in Taiwan.

Subsequently, there was no major movement party formation after Euromaidan, though over a dozen protest leaders did run for office, either as independents or as candidates for existing parties. One exception was the Right Sector, an alliance of far-rightist paramilitary groups that formed as a political party during Euromaidan. This political party's ideas were arguably less about Euromaidan's goals of Ukrainian sovereignty and more about a far-right political agenda.[54] Although some of the paramilitary groups had existed prior to the protests, their entrance into formal politics began after 2014 with the establishment of the Right Sector political party. Despite never passing the 5 percent threshold in national elections for proportional representation seats, the party did win one single member district seat in 2014 and has not won another seat since.[55] Unlike the movement parties that formed after the Sunflower Movement, this political party did not enjoy the type of popular support from civil society that the NPP and the SDP did.

Yanukovych's weakening of Ukrainian institutions and rejection of an EU bill in favor of a pro-Russia bill is another example of how domestic co-optation threat can lead to protests when issues of contestation and sovereignty are evoked. Political parties and actors working on behalf of pro-Russian forces attempted to use Ukrainian institutions to weaken Ukrainian sovereignty and push a pro-unification agenda. This type of domestic co-optation threat is similar to how the CSSTA bill was viewed, which sparked the Sunflower Movement in 2014. The example of Ukraine shows how different types of contesting state threats have different kinds of effects on civil society. Specifically, when threats are felt through domestic co-optation and the contesting state attempts to push for unification using established democratic institutions, it can cause a mobilizing effect leading to large-scale protest. Sometimes these protests lead to the formation of new movement parties, as shown in the case of Taiwan, but sometimes they do not. This type of threat may be a necessary condition, but alone it is an insufficient condition for movement party formation.

Military Threats and Mobilization

Euromaidan and the Orange Revolution demonstrate another example of how certain kinds of threats from a contesting state can cause mass mobilization.[56] What about other kinds of threats from contesting states? Did military threats have a similar kind of mobilizing effect on Ukrainians? As a brief comparison, we can consider the annexation of Crimea. A year after Euromaidan, Russia invaded and annexed Crimea from Ukraine. This major military threat to Ukrainian sovereignty was condemned by Ukrainians and the international community alike. The International Court of Justice deemed the annexation illegal and called for Russia to change course and return Crimea to Ukrainian control.[57] Yet domestically no mass mobilization or social movement arose to protest Russia on any scale compared to that of Euromaidan. While the annexation of Crimea may have had an effect on Ukrainian public opinion—despite the threat from Russia being far more direct through its use of military coercion—it did not have the same effect on civil society that the political context surrounding Euromaidan had generated.

Historically, regions like Crimea have been contested even within Ukraine. At different times in history Crimea was part of Ukraine and other times considered separate.[58] In 1954, then–Soviet leader Nikita Khrushchev "gifted" Crimea to Ukraine as a gesture of goodwill to celebrate three hundred years of Ukraine being a part of the Russian empire.[59] At the time, Khrushchev's gift appeared to be a purely symbolic act, because no territories within the Soviet Union enjoyed genuine independence. When the Soviet Union fell, the newly independent Ukraine still included Crimea within its borders, and until 2014 Crimea was part of Ukraine's sovereign territory.

A key feature of a contested state is not just whether it has recognized sovereignty over its territory, but also whether the contesting state claims its territory regardless of such recognition. In 2014 Russia, despite its cultural claims over Ukraine and its people, specifically targeted capture of Ukraine's eastern regions. Using a combination of military invasion and forced public referendums, Russia successfully annexed Crimea in 2014.

Russia's action did not happen randomly or in a vacuum. The dramatic territorial grab was connected to the 2014 Euromaidan protests.[60] After Russia saw its political channels into Ukrainian democracy ousted by a pro-Ukrainian sovereignty and anti-Russian protest movement, the authoritarian state needed to take bold action. From Russia's perspective, annexing Crimea served multiple purposes: it would be a punishment to Ukraine for the last half-year of anti-Russian protests; it would further reinforce Russia's claims over Ukraine and its lack of recognition of Ukrainian authority (since after the Euromaidan protests and the new Ukrainian government was elected, Russia did not recognize them as legitimate); and it demonstrated Russia's legitimacy and authority to its own people (some predicted the rise of the Euromaidan protest spirit could spill over into Russia).

Crimea and Ukraine's eastern oblasts were not randomly chosen for the incursion. As Ukraine's long-established demographic divide demonstrates, these parts of Ukraine are home to the most Russia-identifying Ukrainians: they predominantly speak Russian and are they are more sympathetic to Russia than other parts of Ukraine. Such statistics are not a justification or normative allowance for Russia's actions but rather show how Russia was able to legitimatize its moves. Russia framed its actions as "saving" or "protecting" Russian citizens from Ukraine, often co-opting such language as "wanting to protect people's right to self-determination."[61] Having a population that already identified more strongly with the contesting state made it particularly easy for Russia to justify its actions, regardless of whether Crimean citizens actually wanted unification with Russia.[62]

On February 27, Russian militias took over the parliamentary building in Crimea and flew a Russian flag over it. These Russian proxy forces installed a pro-Russian politician named Sergy Aksyonov as the new prime minister of Crimea. These actions and elections were not legal under Ukrainian law, but this fact was largely irrelevant to the new pro-Russian government.[63] Reports came out later that all dissent and pro-Ukrainian voices were intimidated or threatened into silence. Russia used both soft and hard power to justify its annexation of Crimea, with media narratives playing a strong role both inside and outside Eastern Europe. As Putin himself said, "In the hearts and minds of people, Crimea has always been an integral part of Russia."[64] Other media narratives portrayed the Crimean people as both not recognizing the post-Euromaidan government as legitimate and as *wanting* Russia to intervene and later annex its territory into the Russian Federation.

Russia's actions were motivated by the same issues of contested territory and identity that originally sparked the Euromaidan protests, only this time it was the contesting state responding to the contested state's push for greater sovereignty and autonomy.[65] This dynamic was not simply a matter of a larger state punishing a smaller state for acting in a way that it did not approve. Instead, it was about contested-contesting state dynamics; Russia was punishing a state that it saw as trying to break away from its own cultural and territorial integrity. Before the 2014 Euromaidan protests, Russia was able to accept Ukraine's de jure independence because it still had the ability to co-opt Ukraine's domestic institutions. After 2014, Ukraine was moving in a direction that Russia could no longer control. Russia utilized its claims over Ukrainian territory and identity to justify its coercive actions and seizure of Crimea. Russia's actions were in part trying to settle Ukraine's contested status through forced annexation. While not fully successful, Russia still managed to change the status quo of Ukraine forever, creating a context that Russia further took advantage of in the war of 2022.

Throughout Russia's annexation of Crimea, in both the military campaign and the soft power campaign, there was little to no protest as a response within Ukraine. Why did protests not break out when Russia annexed Crimea? Why did military threats—and military invasion—not spark the same type of mass protest that Russia's domestic co-optation of Ukrainian institutions did?

Military threats from a contesting state do not have a mobilizing effect in a way that common wisdom may ascribe to them. In Taiwan's context, this is because the frequency of military threats has become so regular that they are not taken seriously but also there is no meaningful avenue for protesting the contesting state's actions. In Ukraine's context, both explanations have these same merits and shortcomings. First, Russia was militarily threatening Ukraine with the same regularity or frequency that China has threatened

Taiwan. However, Russia's aggressive military actions have been seen across Eastern Europe since the fall of the Soviet Union. Threats of unification may not have been directly targeting Ukraine, but Russian military actions have become such a regular feature of Eastern European politics that they may register as normal, unexciting, and expected events for Ukrainian citizens. Without Russia regularly threatening Ukraine directly with military action, this explanation lacks the same power as in Taiwan's context.

Second, Ukrainians have no meaningful avenue for protesting Russian military action within Ukraine. Like Taiwan, protesting military actions in the contested state has no way of influencing or changing the contesting state's strategy. When it comes to domestic co-optation threat, though, there are specific actors within Ukraine's political context that citizens *can* protest and meanwhile push for meaningful change. Similar to how Taiwanese did not protest against military drills but did protest against a pro-China trade bill, Ukrainian citizens did not protest the Russian annexation of Crimea but did protest the pro-Russian government overtly pushing a pro-Russian political agenda that weakened Ukrainian sovereignty. Even though an action may directly alter the status quo of a contested-contesting state relationship, military threats alone do not mobilize protest in contested states.

This does not mean that military threats in Ukraine had no effect or went unnoticed. On the contrary, the annexation of Crimea has been shown to have critically affected Ukrainian civil society. Some studies show that, following the Crimean annexation, some Ukrainians who live in more Russia-leaning parts of Ukraine have become increasingly sympathetic to possessing a Ukrainian identity. Nevertheless, the looming invasion did not lead to mass protest domestically in the same way that was seen during the Orange Revolution or Euromaidan. But the lack of mass protest should not be interpreted to mean that civil society was apathetic, nor that people took no action, but rather that protest as a key tactic was not employed in the face of dire military threats.

A host of studies show that, following both Euromaidan and the annexation of Crimea, Ukraine saw an increase in the number of people who identified as Ukrainian, who preferred to speak Ukrainian, and who identified less and less with Russia. In other words, the potential effects of military threats are perhaps more embedded in the fabric of civil society. Military threats may not directly cause political action or inspire political participation, but they may change the hearts and minds of citizens of contested states in a direction that subtly pushes them farther away from their contesting state and closer to support of their home's independence.

Ukraine shares the same fundamental political context as Taiwan: its political spectrum is not defined by traditional left-right issues but instead by issues of contested territory and identity. These issues of Who are we? and Where are we? define everyday politics and how and why citizens relate to and participate in politics. Activists in Ukraine who feel threatened by Russia's domestic co-optation of Ukrainian democratic institutions have mobilize against these forces, but military threats and even invasion did not necessarily mobilize Ukrainian civil society to protest.

Even in today's context there was little mass-mobilization against Russian military aggression within Ukraine in the lead-up to the 2022 war. This point is in no way a criticism or critique of Ukrainian civil society, but rather an observation of how, despite decades of facing Russian antagonism, there was a perception of calm across Ukraine until the war began. Protests in support of Ukraine did begin to break out around the world in response to Russia's aggression, but these acts of international solidarity only came after the war began. This calls into question how contesting states mobilize the diasporic population of a contested state. Future research ought to examine not just this mobilizing effect on the diaspora, but the larger role that the diaspora plays in the politics of contested-contesting state dynamics.

While comparisons between Euromaidan and the Sunflower Movement are imperfect, they demonstrate how domestic co-optation threat mobilizes civil society in a contested state. Each movement began with something that on paper was seemingly benign: a trade bill. Yet in both places, it was not simply a trade bill, but a potential critical avenue for each place's respective contesting state to infiltrate the contested state's domestic institutions.

Looking at Taiwan and Ukraine in a comparative context reveals these two states have much to teach each other. While each state certainly exists in a unique political context, these unique features are not so differentiating as to be insignificant. On the contrary, contested states around the world share the same underlying political features and ought to be studied together. Taiwan and Ukraine are not unique in their contested status, but this similarity is a strength that social scientists ought to further explore in a comparative context, going beyond just security studies or geopolitical strategy. Questions of political participation, mobilization, and voting behavior are ripe for comparison in places like Taiwan and Ukraine.

Taiwan and Ukraine can be placed in conversation with each other in a way that goes beyond the many shallow headlines seen since the war in Ukraine began in 2022. The obvious comparisons of Ukraine struggling against Russia and Taiwan struggling against China are meaningful, but the deeper connection these two states have goes beyond a military struggle against a larger power. They share a connection of trying to establish not only who they are, but where they are and how their future will be shaped by their people and the state that claims them. What defines places like Taiwan and Ukraine is not inevitable conflict with a larger power, but the centuries of struggle trying to establish the who, what, and whereof their existence.

CONCLUSION

Since the dawn of the modern nation-state, some groups who sought self-determination gained statehood while others did not. But statehood is not a binary "have" or "have not." A third category has always existed. Contested states—those that exist in a gray zone of having statehood but are not recognized by other states—pose a unique set of challenges for social scientific theory. A contested state is not only state because it calls itself a state but because it actively functions with legitimacy and authority over its self-described boundaries. Among contested states, the who and the where are the fundamental political issues that define their domestic politics. But contestation is both a domestic and an international question. The contesting state that claims the contested state as its own both prevents the state from participating in the international order and seeks to unify it within the parent-state's borders. So long as the contesting state prevents the contested state from achieving full statehood, the contested state will continue to exist in a gray zone of de facto statehood.

Taiwan is a contested state, but what it means for Taiwan to be contested runs deeper than just a surface-level binary status of contested versus non-contested. It is not simply that Taiwan is unable to participate in the international order or that China claims that it belongs within its borders. Taiwan is contested because its fundamental political spectrum is defined by questions of identity and territorial integrity. Its domestic politics are defined not by typical left-right politics but by questions of who and where Taiwan is. Meanwhile, Taiwan exists under constant existential threat by a neighboring antagonistic power that claims it, the People's Republic of China. When a state like Taiwan exists under the constraints of contestation, many assumptions within the world of social science do not hold. Perhaps one of the most novel puzzles in contested states is that of social movements and political parties. The reason movements mobilize and form into political *movement parties* in contested states are different due to the contested context out of which they form.

It is these two contexts together, the international and the domestic, that define contestation. One goal of this project is to challenge the accepted conceptualization of what it means for a state to be contested. Quintessential studies of contested states cling to phrases like "unrecognized" or "unofficial" when describing these types of states. This framing is one of only international relations and it has a critical shortcoming: it fails to consider the underlying domestic political issues of contestation that drive domestic politics. Contestation is not just a question of international relations, but of domestic comparative politics too. To focus narrowly on international relations is to fundamentally miss what drives contested states to form and function in the way they do.

What can a focus on both domestic *and* international politics provide to social scientists? First, it allows an understanding of how domestic contestation affects contested states differently from non-contested states. Political participation—how parties form and how governments function and develop—are all connected to the underlying question of contestation. When a state is in constant negotiation with itself about whether it wants to become independent and recognized as a full state, whether to continue to exist within the gray zone status quo as a contested state, or whether to unify with the contesting state that claims it, the logic of the politics is fundamentally different from states with more traditional left-right political spectrums.

Studying domestic aspects of contestation also shows that recognition alone does not solve the question of contestation. As demonstrated with Taiwan and Ukraine, simply recognizing a contested state does not mean that questions of who a contested state is and where the contested state lies are settled. The world's recognition of the independent state of Ukraine did not stop Russia from attempting to coerce parts of it back into Russia's borders. If the world were to recognize Taiwan tomorrow as the independent state of Taiwan, it too would not instantly become a typical country like the United States or Germany. Rather, the People's Republic of China, the contesting state that claims Taiwan, would likely further increase its attempts to coercively unify Taiwan. Contestation becomes ingrained into the domestic politics of both contested state and contesting state; simple international recognition will not neutralize it.

Typically, we envision movement parties forming when new grassroots grievances arise or when the political context is suitable for social movement action. But these go-to explanations cannot account for why movement parties formed in Taiwan in 2014. Instead, we must consider contestation and the role it played in mobilizing the Sunflower Movement and pushing activists to enter formal politics. Activists felt their democratic institutions were being co-opted by China, and this threat pushed them to feel a sense of urgency. Activists anticipated that China, through the KMT, would put an end to Taiwan's democracy and replace it with China's authoritarianism. At the same time, activists felt that the DPP—the party that was perceived as the pro-independence party—was unable or unwilling to meaningfully protect the Taiwanese people or Taiwan's sovereignty on its own. This combination of fear over territory and identity together created conditions that pushed activists to create their own movement parties that could change Taiwan's future.

Epilogue: Taiwan Today

Readers at this point will have likely arrived at an important question: What about today's context? How does Taiwan's evolved role in the international order and increased military threats from China change any of the arguments made so far?

Indeed, Taiwan is a very different place today than it was when I began conducting fieldwork in 2015. Those differences hit me especially hard on August 2, 2022, the day I returned Taiwan to begin a job at National Chengchi University. I arrived in Taiwan two hours before Nancy Pelosi and her delegation from the United States landed at Taipei Songshan Airport. I spent the following three days in my government-mandated COVID-19 quarantine hotel, glued to my computer screen as the entire geopolitical world shifted around me.

I have argued that movement party formation in Taiwan has been caused by a high level of domestic co-optation threat and perceptions that the DPP is unable to advance Taiwan's cause. But those conditions have changed. Furthermore, what became of the NPP and the SDP since their foundings is a story separate from that of their contestation-driven origins. None of these domestic or international political changes negate the findings of this study. On the contrary, many of today's domestic contexts further strengthen the argument.

After Sunflower: The Highs and Lows of the NPP

In the wake of 2014, the NPP seemed to have captured lightning in a bottle. After less than a year of existence, the NPP went on to successfully win five seats in the Legislative Yuan. This was not an easy process, however. With their roots primarily in activism, many within the NPP struggled with designing and running a functioning political party. The NPP had to design and institutionalize a political party while simultaneously running its first batch of candidates. Thanks to strategic cooperation with the DPP, the NPP was able to win three district races that otherwise would have gone to the DPP. The NPP also received 6.1 percent of the party vote, giving it two additional seats. In just a matter of months the NPP had become the third most represented party in Taiwanese politics. For many in Taiwanese civil society, hope for a meaningful third party was becoming a realized dream.

The NPP had created good relations with the DPP and its activists were able to run a successful first election that demonstrated its potential to stay within Taiwan's political mainstream. The first two years of the party's life were relatively stable: it slowly grew, its members maintained a strong media presence, and its prospects were viewed optimistically in the lead-up to the 2018 local elections. Perhaps the only major challenge was a recall attempt against Huang Kuo-chang by an ultraconservative group in response to his support of marriage equality. The party was able to rally support, and he survived the recall campaign. Externally the party was perceived as being largely unified and steadily heading in a good direction but internally the reality was quite different.

If the NPP had an Achilles heel, it was institutional design.[1] Despite its seemingly strong exterior, the party was internally weak. When the NPP initially formed, members approved a bare-bones charter and set of rules and the TCU organizing committee that founded the party did not pay any particular attention to writing out a full-fledged party charter. The party was hyper-focused on performing well in the 2016 elections, and formalizing party rules was not a priority. This lack of prioritizing party organizational structure, however, ended up having long-term negative consequences.

It was not until 2019 that the party eventually fleshed out its charter and created more formalized rules, regulations, and agendas for the party to follow. Prior to 2019 much of the decisions in the party were made on an ad hoc basis or the result of factional infighting. Although there were basic rules, more complex issues such as funding, personnel, and internal decision-making were unclear. For example, questions arose over whether the party chair had more power than the central committee and whether the central committee could veto a decision made by the party chair. The latter issue came to light when the central committee tried to remove the former party chief's party secretary due to dissatisfactory performance. Huang and the executive committee heatedly clashed over who had the final decision, and in the end the executive committee, including Freddy Lim, simply backed down for the sake of avoiding further infighting.[2]

In a way that gives whiplash to those familiar with the story of the TCU, factions and factional infighting were a fundamental problem within the NPP. Even though the Lin faction within the TCU split from the organization for the sake of creating an organization of like-minded people to form a new political party, the issue of personality clashes still followed the group for years. The NPP's own factions formed in a drastic way that ultimately makes the TCU factional infighting seem relatively tame. Despite the NPP still being a small organization, there were four main factions within the party by 2019. The two biggest were Freddy Lim's and Huang Kuo-chang's. Despite their alliance dating back to the formation of the NPP, Lim and Huang did not get along and were not friends. Their professional relationship, despite being productive for years, declined as party infighting increased. Eventually these two key leaders could hardly stand to be in the same room together. As time went on, rumors began to spread about the party's internal instability, largely centered around Lim and Huang's relationship.

Rumors spread wildly around activist circles and organizations about what was happening to the NPP. Although gossip mills saw the story simply as Huang trying to commandeer the party for his own purposes, such gossip missed the more fundamental issue: the NPP's weak institutional design had led to the factional infighting. With few rules and regulations, many party decision-making processes were ad hoc or monopolized by party elites. The challenges culminated in the lead-up to the 2020 presidential election. As the party prepared for its second national election, rumors began to spread about whether the NPP would endorse President Tsai Ing-wen over KMT candidate Han Kuo-yu. Han, a deep-blue KMT politician, had taken Taiwan by storm and, in an unlikely turn of events, had become incredibly popular. Fear of a potential KMT win in the 2020 election echoed sentiments from 2016, and grassroots activists looked to the NPP to see how the party would respond to Han's popularity.

Lim wanted to endorse Tsai and maintain the healthy working relationship they had established with the DPP during the party's first presidential election. Huang did not. Huang felt that endorsing Tsai would just make the NPP look like a branch of the DPP. For Lim, any chance to lower the risk of the KMT winning the presidency was worth the risk, and endorsing Tsai was an obvious method. The NPP's lack of endorsement began to isolate not just Lim and his faction, as well as many of the NPP's rank-and-file voters who felt that Huang was acting more to punish Tsai and the DPP than to prevent the KMT from winning the election.

There was also the issue of whether to cooperate with Ko Wen-je, the former mayor of Taipei, who had founded his own new political party called the Taiwan People's Party. Ko was a former friend of the NPP and once shared a stage with Freddy Lim and Huang Kuo-chang, endorsing them and the NPP in the 2016 election. Ko first crashed onto Taiwan's political scene following the Sunflower Movement, in which he was an active participant and supporter. Because of his involvement with Sunflower and early endorsement of the NPP, he won over the support of grassroots activists, who perceived him to be, at the very least, pan-green leaning. Even the DPP supported Ko's mayoral run in 2014, forming a healthy relationship with him throughout his first term as mayor.[3] After Ko became mayor, though, his tone suddenly changed. He began endorsing far more pan-blue-leaning policies, including working closely with the Shanghai city government to grow sister-sister city relations and supporting the position of Two Sides of the Strait, One Family, a major deal-breaker for pro-independence activists. When it came time for Ko's reelection in 2018, the DPP did not endorse him and many of his initial supporters questioned their allegiance to him. When the DPP did not endorse Ko, it changed the relationship. Since then, Ko has taken an antagonistic stance toward the DPP. His relationship with the NPP also changed. Ko and Freddy Lim no longer saw eye-to-eye and their relationship soured. Huang Kuo-chang, however, became increasingly close with Ko and endorsed his antagonistic attitudes toward the DPP. Leading up to the 2020 election, Huang and Ko agreed that endorsing Tsai was not something they were willing to guarantee to their followers.

The spectacle over whether to endorse Tsai ended up becoming the straw that broke the camel's back for many NPP members and supporters. Most infamously, Freddy Lim and his entire faction left the party in August 2019. Beyond Lim, more and more of the original TCU founding members, including Michael Lin, left the NPP. Other members like Kawlo Iyun and Hsu Yung-ming were kicked out due to corruption scandals. The mass exodus did not end the NPP's troubles. After a series of scandals, including one corruption charge against former party chair Hsu Yung-ming, the party went through a rotating door of leadership. For the sake of finding solid ground to stand on, the party began bringing in a new cohort of candidates and leaders. Most of the major candidates on the NPP's party list or who ran for district elections joined the NPP for the 2020 election. In that election, the NPP lost every district race but managed to maintain its party-vote percentage, gaining enough votes to secure three politicians in the Legislative Yuan. Despite an extremely turbulent election cycle, the party managed to survive its second national election. From 2020 to2024 the NPP was a quiet party unable to regain its footing. In the 2024 election it did not even pass the 3 percent of the party vote mark and no longer had any formally elected officials in office. Today only one of the original TCU founding members is still in the NPP. The rest have left the party that they helped create.

Poor organizational design and a lack of institutionalization led to the NPP's decline. It was not that Taiwan suddenly became less pro-independence or that those who voted for the NPP in 2016 no longer valued pro-independence or progressive politics. Rather, the NPP's struggles show a critical yet underappreciated fact about movement parties: they are hard to grow and run. The activist community that began as the TCU and eventually formed the NPP had never actually run an organization, let alone a party, before founding the NPP. Within a year after forming, they suddenly had political success, needed funding, and the potential for a meaningful political future, but the people were still new to the world of politics. Mistakes were made around how the party was organized and run, and it was these errors that eventually led to the NPP's decline. The question of under what conditions movement parties succeed is beyond the scope of this book, but the case of the NPP offers some initial insights into what movement parties must prioritize when they form: institutionalization. Even if a new movement party like the NPP can capture activists' imaginations and capitalize on the ideal conditions necessary for forming a new movement party, it is all for naught if the subsequent organizational building is mismanaged.

The NPP's Decline Benefits the DPP

The cost the NPP paid for its early struggles was great, and the DPP ultimately benefited the most from the new movement party's struggles. Once Freddy Lim and his faction left the NPP, he remained independent and did not formally join another party, despite the DPP's best efforts to recruit him. Yet, because of his strong relationship with the DPP, Lim worked closely with the party throughout the 2020 election. His whole faction moved closer to the DPP, and a large swath of the NPP's base of support followed him from the NPP to the DPP. When it came time for the 2024 national election, most of Lim's former NPP faction had formally joined the DPP.

Huang Kuo-chang's popularity plummeted, and because of the dissatisfaction within his home district of Xizhi, where he faced low popularity numbers, he did not even contest his seat in 2020. With the KMT running unopposed in Xizhi, it fell to a young Sunflower activist who had previously worked in Freddy Lim's office, Lai Pin-yu, to rise to the challenge. Lai, whose father was a DPP politician, did not remain independent and joined the DPP to run in Xizhi. Her following as an activist and avid cosplayer from the Sunflower Movement skyrocketed her popularity, and in the end she won for the DPP one of the NPP's former seats. With lackluster results in 2020, Huang found himself out of the Legislative Yuan. The NPP as a party could sense the baggage he brought with him, given his unwillingness to work with the DPP and his suspiciously close relationship with Ko Wen-je, who had since founded a competing third party, the Taiwan People's Party (TPP).[4] Without his hold over the party, Huang Kuo-chang began to spend less and less time with the NPP. Although he formally remained a member until the end of 2023, for all practical purposes he was gone long before.

After the 2020 election, his relationship with Ko became more public and more obvious. Rumors swirled about Huang leaving the NPP and joining Ko's party, and Huang, indeed, did just that in the lead-up to the 2024 election. Huang went from founding and leading a pro-independence, anti-KMT party to joining a political party that endorsed closer relations with China and worked closely with the KMT. Today Huang is an elected member of Taiwan's Legislature, but under the TPP's banner, and he has since endorsed much of the KMT's policy agenda. It is perhaps one of the biggest distances along Taiwan's political spectrum a politician has ever jumped.

Lin Fei-fan, one of the key Sunflower Movement leaders and a longtime critic of the DPP, was expected to join the NPP. He shocked Taiwan by joining the DPP instead. Rumors of a falling out between Huang and Lin had surfaced once Huang decided to not endorse Tsai for president. Lin was not the only one who had grown disenfranchised by the NPP. Fellow leader Chen Wei-ting, who had worked in the NPP since its founding, quietly withdrew from the party as well. For the DPP, Lin Fei-fan, Lai Pin-yu, and Freddy Lim brought large swaths of the youth vote and the activist base they had lost to the NPP back into the fold. Undoubtedly the NPP's failures became the DPP's gains.

Why does it matter that the DPP won back this level of support from grassroots activists? Because today's conditions are dissimilar to those of 2014. There has been little to no mass mobilization by green-leaning activists in part because not only is the DPP in power, but relations between disenfranchised green-leaning activists and the DPP are more stable and functional than they were in 2014. Pro-independence activists and grassroots organizers are far more supportive of the DPP than they were in 2014, and this is reflected in their electoral preferences. Why exactly pro-independence activists find the DPP more palatable today is an important research question for the future. Given the decline of the NPP, the frustration and fatigue at the idea of starting yet another new movement party is a likely reason why activists would rather support the pro–status quo DPP today. That the almost romantic excitement when the NPP first saw its success in 2016 has evolved into its removal from formal politics in 2024 has left many activists jaded by the political party formation process and changed their perceptions of the DPP as more palatable than they may have thought ten years ago.

The NPP's eventual decline does not negate my argument. Movement parties still have the potential to be the most radically transformative players in formal politics, especially in contested states. The NPP possessed that potential in 2014. However, the NPP's mismanagement following activists' initial success, combined with the DPP's ability to co-opt and capitalize on the NPP's decline, emphasizes the importance of movement party relations. Central to the normalization of movement party relations was the NPP's struggle to institutionalize. By recruiting Sunflower leaders and former NPP members, the DPP simultaneously won back support from grassroots activists and hindered the NPP's ability to grow as quickly as it might have. Although the DPP's popularity across civil society has varied since its tenure began in 2016, many within the pro-independence activist cohort who participated in Sunflower now perceive the party as palatable. Without major contentious relations between activists and the DPP, Taiwan has seen minimal mobilization over the last eight years and, subsequently, no new movement party formation.[5]

A Fourth Taiwan Strait Crisis?

How to account for the NPP's decline? In 2020 it did not seem possible that something bigger than the return of the DPP could change Taiwan's domestic or international status quo. And yet, upon my return to Taiwan in 2022, I was greeted with an unexpected change in Cross-Strait politics. Nancy Pelosi arrived in Taiwan on August 2. Rumors of her trip had begun as early as April, but when the former Speaker of the House caught COVID-19, her planned delegation to the Asia Pacific was postponed.

Normally, US politicians who come to Taiwan do not announce their intentions to visit the ROC until they are already en route. This time, weeks before her trip was supposed to begin, someone within the State Department leaked to the *Financial Times* that Pelosi fully intended to visit Taiwan. By leaking her trip's information, the paper gave Beijing weeks to create a mountain out of what should have been a molehill over Pelosi's visit. Beijing declared any sort of trip by Pelosi to Taiwan would be seen as an act of provocation and unacceptable by China's standards.

Why would Beijing cause such a fuss? After all, US politicians visit Taiwan on unofficial delegations with regularity. Most of the time the PRC's Taiwan Affairs Office expresses discontent with the visit, but ultimately there are no major repercussions for such actions. Many supporters of Pelosi's visit even argued that there was precedent for her visit: Newt Gingrich had visited Taiwan in the 1990s when he was Speaker of the House.

But Nancy Pelosi is not Newt Gingrich, and cross-strait relations in 2022 are not what they were in the 1990s. Pelosi is a particular thorn in Beijing's side. She was outspoken in the 1990s during the Tiananmen Massacre and has since been a strong critic of China's human rights record. Her history of standing up to the PRC, combined with ever-growing tensions between the United States and China, made her trip unlike a typical US congressional delegation. This was something special.

Upon her arrival, thousands in Taipei gathered around Songshan Airport to see her plane land. For the next two days nothing else mattered in the world; only what Pelosi was doing in Taiwan. Beyond meeting with President Tsai, she also met with leaders from Taiwan Semiconductor Manufacturing Company TSMC and visited the Jingmei White Terror Memorial Park. During her address she lauded Tsai's leadership, acknowledged Tsai's historic role as a female president, and praised Taiwan's COVID-19 response. She made no mention of China and did not push US policy beyond any red lines. Forty-eight hours later, Pelosi was gone, and the world watched with bated breath to see how the PRC would react.

As expected, the PRC made a spectacle out of Pelosi's visit that was beyond imagination. After Pelosi left, the PRC announced it would spend the next week executing live-fire military drills around Taiwan. These exercises were the most dire and drastic military threats China had made to Taiwan since the 1996 Third Taiwan Strait Crisis. Experts even debated whether the August military drills were worthy of being titled the Fourth Taiwan Strait Crisis. China's military threats were far more dangerous than any used in decades, and their quantity outnumbered anything Taiwan had seen over the previous year. Even though military threats had been on a steady rise since 2018, the August 2022 threats took the PRC's intimidation tactics to a new level.

Outside of Taiwan, the world watched with bated breath at what appeared to be imminent war. News reports feared that war was coming, and suddenly people around the world worried that conflict in the Taiwan Strait was inevitable. International media reports about the drills led readers to believe that Taiwan was in hysterical panic over this potential conflict.

Domestically, no one paid much mind. Even though Taiwan was undergoing the scariest set of military threats from China in decades, daily life in Taiwan remained as normal and regular as it had always been. People still went to work, kids went out to play, Starbucks and night markets were just as busy as always. Taiwanese were by and large unfazed by the PRC's military drills. The response was like that of 1996: no mass mobilization, no protests in the streets, and no signs of political distress from civil society. Instead, Taiwan faced China's military threats with a sense of calm tenacity. It was clear that people in contested states feel threats differently than those in non-contested states; the facts to support this idea were being played out in real time. I had returned to Taiwan and stumbled into an era where military threats, something that most people in the world saw as scary and worthy of panic, were being treated as a benign, daily occurrence by people in Taiwan.

As one op-ed by a Taiwanese writer said in response to the threats, "Threats from China are nothing new. They have been a part of my life, my parents' lives, and their parents' lives for as long as almost anyone in my family can remember. . . . Our chilled out attitude in Taiwan can be misconstrued as complacency, but we are not oblivious to the threats before us. . . . If anything, I resent the seemingly performative panic that is expected of the people of Taiwan as we try our best to live our normal lives."[6]

The results of Pelosi's visit and subsequent military threats showed the world that civil society in contested states like Taiwan acts differently because of how accustomed they are to living under constant threat. In the same way that Taiwanese have remained unfazed by China's military threats for decades, the August 2022 threats were met with the same level of resilience. What some confuse with ignorance or ambivalence is instead normalcy. In contested states like Taiwan, where everyday life is constantly under military threat from the neighboring contesting state, military drills do not cause panic or distress. Instead, they are normal, everyday occurrences. Although the crisis of August 2022 was not identical to what was experienced in the Taiwan Strait in 1996, the outcomes were similar. Despite mass alarm outside of Taiwan, domestic life was largely unfazed.

Future Study of Movement Parties and Contested States

In this book I have attempted to combine two bodies of literature that are not typically put in conversation with each other: international relations of contested states and the domestic politics of social movement–political party relations. These two bodies of literature have much to teach each other, especially when it comes to understanding events in contested states like Taiwan. Scholars must look beyond just the international realm of politics. Contestation is not only an international phenomenon. Instead, it is also the defining feature of the contested state's domestic politics. To understand how contested states form, function, and grow, social scientists must take domestic politics into consideration.

Movement parties serve as a prime example of how domestic politics can affect the future direction of a contested state. After the Sunflower Movement and Taiwan's subsequent domestic political realignment, this contested state is now governed by a pro-sovereignty party that is pushing further way from China. For scholars of movement parties, cases like Taiwan offer a novel variation on a well-studied topic. Even though social scientists have many theories about social movement mobilization and political party formation, contested states challenge our preexisting notions. They present a rich cohort of cases that help us better understand not only some of the most important flashpoints in the world but also in a set of understudied and undertheorized parts of the world. My hope is to inspire other social scientists to reapproach contested states like Taiwan as not only important case studies, but important spaces for theory-building and testing, rather than simply one-off or unique cases.

To regional scholars, a critical takeaway of is the reimagining of Taiwan's role in the world. Taiwan scholars often see Taiwan as unique; a place to which no other country can compare because of its political development, constant existential crisis of threat from China, resultant complexity of domestic politics, and isolation from the international community. This is far too narrow of a way to conceptualize Taiwan as a case. Instead, Taiwan is one of many states that share these same anxieties, histories, complicated domestic politics, and isolation from the international order. By studying Taiwan comparatively with these other contested states, regional scholars can better learn about how Taiwan has developed or will develop in the future.

NOTES

Preface

Epigraph: In standard Chinese: 我們的行動在台灣與中國的關係之間, 我們做了新的定義. 我們告訴政府台灣的未來屬於全台灣二十三百萬台灣人民台灣的未來應該由我們自己決定."

1. Rowen, "Inside Taiwan's Sunflower Movement."

2. Rowen, "Inside Taiwan's Sunflower Movement."

3. Ho, "Occupy Congress in Taiwan."

4. Why was it called the "Sunflower Movement?" It is not entirely clear, but there are a few different theories. First is the historic use of flowers or plants as names for protests in Taiwan. Sunflower is in line with previous protests, including the Wild Strawberry Movement and the Wild Lily Movement. Another says that when protesters occupied the Legislative Yuan, sunflowers on the podium were handed out to activists. Still another says supportive florists donated sunflowers to the movement. Regardless of the origin of the name, the sunflower became the ubiquitous symbol of the protest.

5. Rowen, "Inside Taiwan's Sunflower Movement."

6. Ho, "Occupy Congress in Taiwan."

7. Ho, "Occupy Congress in Taiwan."

8. Rowen, "Inside Taiwan's Sunflower Movement."

9. For a full intricate retelling of every minor and major moment of the three-week long occupation, I highly recommend the archival "Daybreak Project" that documents all details of the Sunflower Movement, at https://daybreak.newbloommag.net.

10. Ho and Huang, "Movement Parties in Taiwan."

11. Nachman, "Misalignment between Social Movements and Political Parties."

Introduction

1. Personal interview, July 18, 2015.

2. Kitschelt, *The Logics of Party Formation.*

3. Hug, *Altering Party Systems.*

4. Meyer and Minkoff, "Conceptualizing Political Opportunity."

5. See the discussion in chapter 4, which fully unpacks and examines these alternative explanations.

6. Taiwan scholars may immediately think of the *tangwai* and the rise of the

DPP. Although certainly a valid example of a movement becoming a political party, and one discussed here, the DPP's rise occurred during Taiwan's authoritarian era, before democratization. It should not be considered a case among post-democratization movement parties because of the qualitatively different conditions under which the *tangwai* formed into a political party. Movement party formation in an authoritarian context is beyond the scope of this book.

7. Observers of Taiwan politics will already know the spoiler end to the story of the NPP, which is that it struggled to maintain its electoral power ten years after its formation. The question of under what conditions do movement parties succeed after electoral success is an important element of party organization, though separate from the question of party formation, and thus beyond the scope of this book. The question of movement party longevity is addressed in the conclusion, but a full study on the NPP's struggles following its electoral success can be found in Nachman, "Routine Problems."

8. Kitschelt, "Movement Parties."

9. McAdam and Tarrow, "Ballots and Barricades"; Della Porta et al., *Movement Parties against Austerity*; Anria, *When Movements Become Parties.*

10. Amenta et al., "The Political Consequences of Social Movements."

CHAPTER ONE *Conceptualizing Contestation*

1. Grant, "Defining Statehood."

2. Muschik, "Managing the World."

3. United Nations General Assembly, Declaration on the Granting of Independence to Colonial Countries and Peoples (1970), 121.

4. Crawford, *The Creation of States in International Law.*

5. Maoz, "Joining the Club of Nations."

6. Contested states, however, are not a new invention. Themes of contestation and the dynamics between a contested and a contesting state can be found throughout history. For example, in Ian Lustick's classic study of what he calls "unsettled states," the historic relationship between Ireland and Great Britain is the very same dynamic faced by contested states today. See Lustick, *Unsettled States, Disputed Lands.*

7. For more on the distinctions between de jure and de facto sovereignty, see Schultz, "What's in a Claim?"

8. Pegg, "De Facto States in the International System," 2.

9. Toomla, "Charting Informal Engagement between De Facto States."

10. Caspersen, *Unrecognized States*; Pegg, "De Facto States in the International System"; Toomla, "Charting Informal Engagement between De Facto States."

11. Here I use the name "contesting" state instead of "parent" state. Despite the extensive and seemingly unanimous use of "parent state" in the literature, some reflection on the term is overdue. "Parent" as a metaphor for the dynamic between a contested and a contesting state infers a biased power dynamic in favor the contesting state. If the contesting state is the parent, the contested state is the unruly "child state" causing trouble, not just for the contesting state but for all the other "adult" states. The phrase feels like an uncomfortable anthropomorphizing of states, one that privileges the parent state as having come first and, therefore, possessing the more legitimate claim. Although "contesting" state may be an imperfect substitute, it at least attempts to eliminate this bias.

12. Dobos, *Insurrection and Intervention.*

13. Caspersen, *Unrecognized States*, 40, with "parent" replaced with "contesting."

14. Some scholars use terms like "quasi-state," "state-within-state," or other similar-sounding names. For example, see Jackson, *Quasi-States.*

15. Caspersen, *Unrecognized States*, 346.

16. See Nicholson and Grant, "Theories of State Recognition"; Tomuschat, "Recognition of New States"; Crawford, *The Creation of States in International Law..*

17. This is part of the reason I do not engage with the legal definitions of statehood similar to other scholars, such as Crawford, *The Creation of States in International Law*. In the same vein as recognition, the international community's legal definition of a state cannot resolve the underlying question of contestation. To use the same comparison, if the world legally defined Taiwan as part of China, it would not end Taiwan's domestic goals of self-determination, and vice versa: if the world recognized Taiwan's legal independence, it would not end China's claims over Taiwan. Legal definitions, while important for many aspects of contestation and recognition—such as access to international organizations—are not fundamental to conceptualizing contested-contesting state dynamics.

18. Geldenhuys, *Contested States in World Politics.*

19. Achen and Wang, *The Taiwan Voter.*

20. Taiwan uses a hybrid electoral system that incorporates both single-member district first past the post voting and proportional representation voting. District representatives in Taiwan are elected by FPTP, but citizens also vote for a party in addition to a party's specific candidate. Additional seats in Taiwan's Legislative Yuan are proportionally divided based on the percentage of votes each party gets.

21. Hsieh and Niou, "Salient Issues in Taiwan's Electoral Politics"; Hsieh, "Ethnicity, National Identity, and Domestic Politics in Taiwan"; Sheng and Liao, "Issues, Political Cleavages, and Party Competition in Taiwan."

22. Sheng and Liao, "Issues, Political Cleavages, and Party Competition in Taiwan," 100.

23. Fell, *Party Politics in Taiwan*; Fell, *Taiwan's Green Parties*.

24. Fell, *Party Politics in Taiwan*; Fell, *Taiwan's Green Parties*.

25. Hsiao, Cheng, and Achen, "Political Left and Right in Taiwan."

CHAPTER TWO *How Taiwan Became Contested*

1. See Caspersen, *Unrecognized States*.

2. For example, see Xi Jinping, "Working Together to Realise Rejuvenation of the Chinese Nation and Advance China's Peaceful Reunification."

3. See Chang, *From Island Frontier to Imperial Colony*.

4. For comprehensive histories of this era, see Shepherd, *Statecraft and Political Economy on the Taiwan Frontier*; M. Brown, *Is Taiwan Chinese?*; Teng, *Taiwan's Imagined Geography*.

5. P. Friedman, "The Hegemony of the Local."

6. Simon, *Truly Human*, 37–38.

7. Vickers, "Three Faces of an Asian Hero."

8. Andrade, *Lost Colony*.

9. Wills, "The Seventeenth-Century Transformation."

10. M. Brown, *Is Taiwan Chinese?*, 40.

11. Teng, *Taiwan's Imagined Geography*, 34.

12. Teng, *Taiwan's Imagined Geography*, 35.

13. Leung, "The Quasi-War in East Asia."

14. Huang and Liu, "Discrimination and Incorporation of Taiwanese Indigenous Austronesian Peoples."

15. There was also the briefly lived Republic of Formosa, a group of former Qing officials claiming independence from both the Qing and the Japanese. Their rule did not last more than a matter of weeks in Taipei before fleeing down south to Tainan. From there the remaining officials were defeated in a matter of months. Although there was never any meaningful state created by the Republic of Formosa, today its flag is still seen as a popular symbol of Taiwanese Nationalism. See Lamley, "The 1895 Taiwan Republic."

16. Lee, "The International Legal Status of the Republic of China on Taiwan," 351; Hayton, "The South China Sea."

17. Chun, *Forget Chineseness*.

18. For a comprehensive history of the Japanese colonial era, see Ping-Hui, "Taiwan under Japanese Colonial Rule."

19. Heé, "Taiwan under Japanese Rule."

20. Barclay, *Colonial Development and Population in Taiwan*.

21. Hsiau, *Contemporary Taiwanese Cultural Nationalism*, 30.

22. Hsiau, *Contemporary Taiwanese Cultural Nationalism*, 31.
23. Hsiau, *Contemporary Taiwanese Cultural Nationalism*, 30.
24. Ching, *Becoming Japanese*.
25. Cited in Liao, "Tai-wan wen-tzu kai-ko yün-tung shih-lüe" (A brief history of the Taiwanese writing reform movement).
26. See Dawley, *Becoming Taiwanese*.
27. Wright, "Student Mobilization in Taiwan."
28. For a brief overview of the warlord era, see Roberts, "Warlordism in China."
29. For summaries and reflections on ROC-era China, see Wakeman and Edmonds, *Reappraising Republican China*.
30. Chong, *External Intervention and the Politics of State Formation*.
31. E. Snow, *Red Star over China*, 88–89.
32. L. Sullivan, "The Chinese Communist Party and the Status of Taiwan."
33. For more on the Taiwanese who served under Japan's Imperial Army, see Chen, "Imperial Army Betrayed."
34. The Cairo Declaration.
35. Conference for the Conclusion and Signature of the Treaty of Peace with Japan.
36. Chai, "The Future of Taiwan."
37. For more on varying opinions, see L. Sullivan, "The Chinese Communist Party and the Status of Taiwan."
38. The PRC representative to the UN, Wu Hsiu-chuan, said specifically, "When the Chinese Government accepted the surrender of the Japanese armed forces in Taiwan and established sovereignty over the island, Taiwan became not only de jure, but also de facto, an inalienable part of Chinese Territory." Jain, "The Legal Status of Formosa," 33.
39. As British foreign secretary Sir Anthony Eden said in 1955, "The Cairo Declaration . . . was a statement of intention that Formosa should be retroceded to China after the war. This retrocession has, in fact, never taken place because of the difficulties arising from the existence of two entities claiming to represent China. . . . Formosa and the Pescadores are therefore, in the view of Her Majesty's government, territory the de jure sovereignty over which is uncertain or undetermined." Jain, "The Legal Status of Formosa," 28. This issue was in part related to the UK's desire to secure convenience in Hong Kong. See Wolf, "To Secure a Convenience."
40. "Treaty of Peace Between the Republic of China and Japan (Treaty of Taipei) 1952, Signed at Taipei, April 28, 1952, Entered into force, August 5, 1952, by the exchange of the instruments of ratification at Taipei April 28, 1952, found at https://china.usc.edu/treaty-peace-between-republic-china-and-japan-treaty-taipei-1952.

41. Hsiau, *Contemporary Taiwanese Cultural Nationalism*, 26.

42. See Phillips, *Between Assimilation and Independence*; Louzon, "From Japanese Soldiers to Chinese Rebels."

43. Hsiau, *Contemporary Taiwanese Cultural Nationalism*, 54.

44. Lin, "Nostalgia for Japanese Colonialism."

45. Lai, "A Tragic Beginning," 56.

46. Smith, "Taiwan's 228 Incident and the Politics of Placing Blame."

47. The exact number is unknown, and estimates are highly politicized and vary by report. For more, see Rowen and Rowen, "Taiwan's Truth and Reconciliation Committee."

48. Looney, *Mobilizing for Development*.

49. See Yang, *The Great Exodus from China*.

50. Chang, *Modernism and the Nativist Resistance*.

51. M. Huang, "The Dilemmas of Becoming Chinese in Taiwan."

52. See Hsiau, *Contemporary Taiwanese Cultural Nationalism*, 98, 99.

53. Warner, "Nixon, Kissinger, and the Rapprochement with China."

54. For a full summary of the United States' Taiwan policy, see Sullivan and Nachman, "Taiwan."

55. Dumbaugh, "Taiwan's Political Status."

56. Liff and Lin, "The 'One China' Framework at 50."

57. See Looney, *Mobilizing for Development*.

58. Slater and Wong, *From Development to Democracy*.

59. The *tangwai*'s transition from movement to party is discussed in chapter 3. For a full story of the movement and its influence, see Rigger, *From Opposition to Power*.

60. Activists specifically did not want to be associated with the DPP because of the new party's then negative press. See Wright, *The Perils of Protest*, 111.

61. Nachman, "Student Movements."

62. As expert on the Wild Lily Movement Teresa Wright states, "[Though the Wild Lily Movement] was far more successful than its counterpart on the mainland, it is doubtful that the student demonstrations in Taiwan actually brought about a meaningful policy change." Wright, *The Perils of Protest*, 128.

63. While it is impossible to begin answering all such questions here, for attempts to deconstruct and address these varying questions see Chun, *Forget Chineseness*.

64. Achen and Wang, *The Taiwan Voter*.

65. A. Wang et al., "Strategic Ambiguity, Strategic Clarity, and Dual Clarity."

CHAPTER THREE *Mobilizing without the Missiles*

1. Personal interview, September 10, 2019.

2. Personal interview, July 10, 2018.

3. Personal interview, August 20, 2019.

4. Tilly, *From Mobilization to Revolution*, 133.

5. Greitens, *Dictators and Their Secret Police*.

6. Kitschelt et al., *Post-Communist Party Systems*.

7. Petersen, "Security Policy in the Post-Soviet Baltic States."

8. Noreen and Sjöstedt, "Estonian Identity Formations and Threat Framing in the Post–Cold War Era."

9. Callahan, "History, Identity, and Security."

10. E. Friedman, "China's Changing Taiwan Policy."

11. E. Friedman, "China's Changing Taiwan Policy."

12. Shirk, *China*.

13. Jacobs, *Democratizing Taiwan*, 186.

14. Hung and Hung, "How China's Cognitive Warfare Works."

15. Chong, Huang, and Wu, "'Stand Up Like a Taiwanese!'"

16. Chen et al., "The Multiverse of Taiwan's Future."

17. Snow et al., "Disrupting the 'Quotidian.'"

18. Amenta and Halfmann, "Opportunity Knocks."

19. Achen and Wang, *The Taiwan Voter*.

20. Rigger, *From Opposition to Power*.

21. Fell, *Party Politics in Taiwan*.

22. Jacobs, *Democratizing Taiwan*, 92.

23. *China News*, March 10, 1996, 1.

24. Jacobs, *Democratizing Taiwan*, 108.

25. *Ziyoushibao* 自由時報 (Liberty times), March 18, 1996, 2; *Zhongguo shibao* 中國時報 (China times), March 18, 1996, 9; and *Lianhebao* 聯合報 (United daily news), March 18, 1996, 7.

26. *Lianhebao* 聯合報 (United daily news), March 17, 1996, 1; *Ziyou shibao* 自由時報 (Liberty times), March 19, 1996, 20.

27. *Lianhebao* 聯合報 (United daily news), March 19, 1996, 13.

28. *Zhongguo shibao* 中國時報 (China times), March 19, 1996, 1.

29. *Ziyou shibao* 自由時報 (Liberty times), March 20, 1996, 13.

30. Jacobs, *Democratizing Taiwan*, 121.

31. Porch, "The Taiwan Strait Crisis of 1996."

32. Niou and Paolino, "The Rise of the Opposition Party in Taiwan."

33. The 1992 Consensus is one of the most controversial agreements between

China and Taiwan. The consensus supposedly states that each side of the strait acknowledges there is only one China. Former KMT politician Su Chi has since admitted that he made up such a consensus, but the truth of such a consensus matters little today. The CCP has stated repeatedly that recognition of the 1992 consensus is fundamental for any sort of peaceful talks between the PRC and the ROC. See D. Chen, "US–China Rivalry."

34. Shu-ling Ko, "DPP Bashes KMT Trip as 'Surrender,'" *Taipei Times*, March 29, 2005.

35. Jacobs, *Democratizing Taiwan*, 246.

36. Ralph Jennings, "Thousands Protest in Taiwan Against China Trade Deal," Reuters, June 26, 2010.

37. For a full summary of the movement, see Yuan, "Virtual Ecologies, Mobilization and Democratic Groups without Leaders."

38. Yuan, "Virtual Ecologies, Mobilization and Democratic Groups without Leaders."

39. Andrew Higgins, "Tycoon Prods Taiwan Closer to China," *Washington Post*, January 21, 2012, https://www.washingtonpost.com/world/asia_pacific/tycoon-prods-taiwan-closer-to-china/2012/01/20/gIQAhswmFQ_story.html.

40. Rawnsley and Feng, "Anti-Media-Monopoly Policies."

41. Ebsworth, "Not Wanting Want."

42. Ebsworth, "Not Wanting Want," 96.

43. Rawnsley and Feng, "Anti-Media-Monopoly Policies."

44. Original version appeared as "國民黨不倒,台灣不會好."

45. For a comprehensive review of these sentiments, see Nachman, "Misalignment between Social Movements and Political Parties."

46. Personal interview, July 30, 2019.

CHAPTER FOUR *Corruption in Contested States*

1. In standard Chinese, "我反對國民黨,但是不支持民進黨".

2. Ho, *Challenging Beijing's Mandate of Heaven*, 99–100.

3. Personal interview, July 15, 2016.

4. Personal interview, July 15, 2016.

5. Personal interview, July 28, 2015.

6. Personal interview, July 19, 2015.

7. Personal interview, July 28, 2015.

8. Personal interview, June 25, 2015.

9. Personal interview, July 18, 2015.

10. Malik and Singh, *Hindu Nationalists in India*.

11. Chhibber and Verma, *Ideology and Identity.*

12. Michels, *The Iron Law of Oligarchy.*

13. Heidenheimer and Johnston, *Political Corruption.*

14. Scott et al., "Handling Historical Comparisons Cross-Nationally," 123.

15. Gardiner, "Defining Corruption"; Fell, *Party Politics in Taiwan.*

16. In Taiwan, the standard Chinese phrase to refer to corruption in politics is 黑金 (*heijin*), literally translated as "black gold." Fell defines the term as "the involvement of gangsters in local politics, but it has also come to be used as a general term to describe political corruption" (57).

17. Fell, *Party Politics in Taiwan*, 56.

18. Falleti and Mahoney, "The Comparative Sequential Method."

19. Rigger, *From Opposition to Power.*

20. Rigger, *From Opposition to Power*, 18.

21. Cheng and Hsu, "Issue Structure, the DPP's Factionalism, and Party Realignment."

22. Rigger, *From Opposition to Power*, 23.

23. *Duli wanbao* (Independence evening post), September 13, 1990 (trans. JPRS-CAR-90-084:73), 5.

24. Cheng and Hsu, "Issue Structure, the DPP's Factionalism, and Party Realignment," 149.

25. Q. Huang, "The Democratic Progressive Party's Policies on Cross-Strait Relations."

26. Kuo, *Minjindang zhuanxing zhi tong* (The DPP's painful transformation).

27. For a full summary of the factional infighting that led to the New Tide faction's dominance, see Rigger, "Taiwan's Lee Teng-hui Complex," 266.

28. Fell, "Measuring and Explaining Party Change in Taiwan."

29. Hsiao et al., "Political Left and Right in Taiwan," 198.

30. Slater and Wong, "The Strength to Concede."

31. Rigger, "Taiwan's Lee Teng-hui Complex," 32.

32. Fell, "Measuring and Explaining Party Change in Taiwan."

33. Nachman and Hioe, "No, Taiwan's President Isn't 'Pro-Independence.'"

34. Yu, "Parties, Partisans, and Independents in Taiwan."

35. Fell, "Measuring and Explaining Party Change in Taiwan."

36. Fell, *Taiwan's Green Parties*, 61.

37. Niou and Paolino, "The Rise of the Opposition Party in Taiwan."

38. Li and Liu, "A Comparative Study of China's Policies."

39. Jacobs, *Democratizing Taiwan*, 147.

40. M. Cheng, "Constructing a New Political Spectacle."

41. See "美國務院新聲明 歡迎扁承諾四不" (New statement from the US

State Department welcomes Chen's four no's commitment), *Taiwan News*, May 16, 2006, https://news.tvbs.com.tw/local/362022.

42. Fell, *Party Politics in Taiwan*.

43. Cheng-feng Shih, "The DPP Outlook in Mayoral Races," *Taipei Times*, December 2, 2006, http://www.taipeitimes.com/News/editorials/archives/2006/12/03/2003338937.

44. Mark Mangier and Chou Pei-fen, "Wife of Taiwanese President Indicted," *LA Times*, November 4, 2006, https://www.latimes.com/archives/la-xpm-2006-nov-04-fg-taiwan4-story.html.

45. Chin, *Heijin*, 155, 181.

46. Keith Bradsher, "Protesters Fuel a Long-Shot Bid to Oust Taiwan's Leader," *New York Times*, September 28, 2006, https://www.nytimes.com/2006/09/28/world/asia/28taiwan.html.

47. Kathrin Hille, "Taiwan's Chen Gives Up Some Powers to Premier," *Financial Times*, June 1, 2006, https://www.ft.com/content/a8996c78-f129-11da-9338-0000779e2340.

48. Sullivan and Lowe, "Chen Shui-bian."

49. Fleischauer, "The 228 Incident."

50. See "Taiwan Scraps Unification Council," *BBC News*, February 27, 2006, http://news.bbc.co.uk/2/hi/asia-pacific/4753974.stm.

51. Hioe, "Lack of Clear Answers Regarding the Lin Family Massacre."

52. Rigger, *From Opposition to Power*, 57.

53. Rigger, *From Opposition to Power*, 77.

54. Lin's full speech is available at http://www.southnews.com.tw/polit/specil/polit_DDP/00/0033.htm.

55. Lin Yi-hsiung, "After Governing, the DPP Has Disappointed the People," *TVBS News*, October 1, 2006, https://news.tvbs.com.tw/health/349752.

56. Jewel Huang, "Former DPP Chairman Leaves Party," *Taipei Times*, January 25, 2006, http://www.taipeitimes.com/News/front/archives/2006/01/25/2003290603.

57. Personal interview, March 18, 2020.

58. Chris Wang, "Lin Starts Anti-Nuclear Hunger Strike," *Taipei Times*, April 24, 2014.

59. Personal interview, August 16, 2018.

60. Personal interview, July 30, 2018.

CHAPTER FIVE *From Movement to Party*

1. See Downs, "An Economic Theory of Political Action in a Democracy"; Kitschelt, *The Logics of Party Formation*; Kitschelt, "Movement Parties"; Hug, *Altering Party Systems*; Strom, "A Behavioral Theory of Competitive Political Parties."

2. Anria, *When Movements Become Parties*; Della Porta et al., *Movement Parties against Austerity*; Kitschelt, "Movement Parties"; Van Cott, *From Movements to Parties in Latin America*.

3. Kitschelt, *The Logics of Party Formation*.

4. See Olson, "Party Formation and Party System Consolidation"; Van Biezen and Rashkova, "Deterring New Party Entry?"; Tavits, "Party System Change."

5. Kitschelt et al., *Post-Communist Party Systems*.

6. Meyer and Minkoff, "Conceptualizing Political Opportunity"; della Porta, "Political Opportunity/Political Opportunity Structure"; Kriesi, *The Political Opportunity Structure of New Social Movements*.

7. Personal interview, January 8, 2018.

8. Personal interview, July 15, 2018.

9. Personal interview, July 8, 2018.

10. Personal interview, July 27, 2018.

11. For a full history of the Taiwan Green Party, its electoral record, and its advocacy for Taiwanese Independence, see Fell, *Taiwan's Green Parties*.

12. Della Porta et al., *Movement Parties against Austerity*; Kitschelt, *The Logics of Party Formation*.

13. This is based on dozens of interviews with Sunflower activists and NPP and SDP supporters, the majority of whom ironically did not know who or what the TCU was. Interviews with Sunflower Movement and TCU leaders also revealed that most activists would have no reason to know who the TCU was or what role they played in the formation of the NPP or the SDP.

14. See "公民組合」結社 黃國昌: 選舉與運動是兩碼事" (Huang Kuo-chang: Elections and movements are two different things), *Storm Magazine*, March 31, 2014, https://www.storm.mg/article/29408.

15. Hung was a former saleswoman turned activist after the mysterious death of her brother during disciplinary punishment while in the military.

16. Personal interview, September 11, 2019.

17. Personal interview, July 24, 2019.

18. Personal interview, July 8, 2018.

19. Personal interview, July 11, 2018,

20. It was originally Freddy Lim who thought of the name New Power Party (時代力量 in standard Chinese).

21. Personal interview, August 5, 2018,

22. Ho, "Occupy Congress in Taiwan."

23. Jasper, "Linking Arenas."

24. Amenta and Halfmann, "Opportunity Knocks."

25. For the full law of party formation, see Ministry of the Interior, "Political Parties Act," https://law.moj.gov.tw/LawClass/LawAll.aspx?pcode=D0020078.

26. A full list of previously registered and active parties in Taiwan can be found at https://party.moi.gov.tw.

27. In 2008 Taiwan reformed the Legislative Yuan from a single-non-transferable-vote system to the current mixed first-past-the-post-and-PR system. See Hsieh, "The Origins and Consequences of Electoral Reform in Taiwan."

28. Nachman, "Misalignment between Social Movements and Political Parties"; Fell, *Taiwan's Green Parties*.

29. Personal interview, June 21, 2018.

30. Personal interview, October 6, 2019.

31. Personal interview, June 28, 2019.

32. Personal interview, July 2, 2019.

33. Personal interview, June 26, 2019.

34. Personal interview, July 4, 2019.

CHAPTER SIX *Ukraine, a Contested State*

1. For an example of a good quality comparison, see Kharis Templeman, "Taiwan Is Not Ukraine: Stop Linking Their Fates Together," *War on the Rocks*, January 27, 2022, https://warontherocks.com/2022/01/taiwan-is-not-ukraine-stop-linking-their-fates-together/.

2. Shulman, "The Cultural Foundations of Ukrainian National Identity," 199.

3. Barrington, "Understanding Identity in Ukraine—and Elsewhere."

4. Staliūnas, "Making Russians."

5. Silver, "Social Mobilization and the Russification of Soviet Nationalities"; Thaden, *Russification in the Baltic Provinces and Finland*.

6. Staliūnas, "Making Russians."

7. Kassoff, "The Non-Russian Nationalities."

8. Shcherbak, "Nationalism in the USSR."

9. Hofmeister, "Civilization and Russification in Tsarist Central Asia."

10. Ukraine has also influenced Russian identity. Mikhail Molchanov writes: "Ukrainian-Russian relations cannot be disentangled from a history of intense interpenetration of Ukrainian and Russian cultures and national identities. Not only has the Ukrainian self-image been heavily Russified by the former empire, but the

latter also, in its own turn, became inadvertently Ukrainianized through the permanent influx of Ukrainian talent, cultural borrowing, and reflection on the common past" (Molchanov, "Political Culture and National Identity in Russian-Ukrainian Relations," 8).

11. Chernetsky, "Postcolonialism, Russia and Ukraine."

12. Odey and Bassey, "Ukrainian Foreign Policy toward Russia."

13. For a full summary of the contested histories between Ukraine and Russia, see Pelenski, "The Origins of the Official Muscovite Claims to the 'Kievan Inheritance'"; Pelenski, "The Contest for the 'Kievan Inheritance' in Russian-Ukrainian Relations."

14. Plokhy, *Unmaking Imperial Russia*, 28.

15. Luckyj, "Ukrainian Literature in the Twentieth Century."

16. Plokhy, *Unmaking Imperial Russia*, 21.

17. Some writers used the phrase "status quo" to describe the nature of the Ukraine-Russia dynamic and whether or not change in the status of Ukraine and Ukrainians was good or necessary. See Potulnytskyi, "The Image of Ukraine and the Ukrainians in Russian Political Thought," 17.

18. I am only scratching the surface of the vast body of studies of Ukrainian versus Russian language and language policy. For more, see Seals, "From Russification to Ukrainisation"; Kulyk, "Language Policy in Ukraine"; Maksimovtsova, "Language Policy in Education in Contemporary Ukraine"; Strikha, "Language and Language Policy in Ukraine."

19. Perhaps no better historical figure represents the movement for Ukrainian language and self-determination than Mykhailo Hrushevsky, whose writings on the struggle of the Ukrainian independence movement are fundamental to our contemporary understanding of Ukrainian culture and nationalism. See Plokhy, *Unmaking Imperial Russia*.

20. Bilaniuk, "A Typology of Surzhyk."

21. Unwin, "Contested Reconstruction of National Identities in Eastern Europe."

22. Askerov, "The Nagorno Karabakh Conflict"; Hewitt, "Abkhazia"; Toal and O'Loughlin, "Inside South Ossetia."

23. Bunce, "Peaceful versus Violent State Dismemberment."

24. Bassin and Kelly, *Soviet and Post-Soviet Identities*; Spehr and Kassenova, "Kazakhstan."

25. D'Anieri, "Ukrainian Foreign Policy from Independence to Inertia."

26. Berg and Ehin, *Identity and Foreign Policy*.

27. For a comprehensive breakdown of the Ukrainian-Russian identity spectrum, see Shulman, "The Cultural Foundations of Ukrainian National Identity."

28. Gellner, *Nations and Nationalism*.

29. Barrington and Herron, "One Ukraine or Many?"

30. Kubicek, "Regional Polarisation in Ukraine."

31. Seals, "From Russification to Ukrainisation"; Arel, "How Ukraine Has Become More Ukrainian."

32. Onuch and Hale, "Capturing Ethnicity."

33. See Veira-Ramos and Liubyva, "Ukrainian Identities in Transformation."

34. Onuch, Hale, and Sasse, "Studying Identity in Ukraine."

35. Kubicek, "Regional Polarisation in Ukraine."

36. Kubieck, "Regional Polarisation in Ukraine," 282.

37. Kubieck, "Regional Polarisation in Ukraine," 288.

38. Onuch and Hale, "Capturing Ethnicity."

39. Osipian and Osipian, "Regional Diversity and Divided Memories in Ukraine."

40. Kulyk, "Shedding Russianness, Recasting Ukrainianness."

41. Erlich and Garner, "Is Pro-Kremlin Disinformation Effective?"

42. Ukraine's presidential election system was conducted through a two-round majoritarian system: in the first round of voting all candidates except for the two who receives the most votes are eliminated; in the second round, with only two candidates, the person with the most votes is declared the winner.

43. For a comprehensive summary of the events and outcomes of the Orange Revolution, see Wilson, *Ukraine's Orange Revolution*.

44. Kuzio, "Nationalism, Identity and Civil Society in Ukraine."

45. Popova, "Why the Orange Revolution Was Short and Peaceful and Euromaidan Long and Violent."

46. Mark Rachkevych, "Election Watchers Worried by Lack of Independent Exit Poll: Survey Essential to Deterring Vote Fraud," *Kyiv Post*, December 11, 2009, https://www.kyivpost.com/article/content/ukraine politics/election-watchers-worried-by-lack-of-independent-e-54838.html.

47. Pop-Eleches and Robertson, "Identity and Political Preferences in Ukraine—Before and After the Euromaidan."

48. Al Jazeera, "Putin Fears Ukraine-EU Deal," November 27, 2013, https://www.aljazeera.com/news/2013/11/27/putin-says-ukraine-eu-deal-a-threat-to-russia.

49. Al Jazeera. "Ukraine Drops EU Plans, and Looks to Russia," November 21, 2013, https://www.aljazeera.com/news/2013/11/21/ukraine-drops-eu-plans-and-looks-to-russia.

50. Diuk, "Euromaidan."

51. For a comprehensive summary of the movement and its events, see Marples and Mills, *Ukraine's Euromaidan*.

52. Metzger et al., "Tweeting Identity?"

53. Popova, "Why the Orange Revolution Was Short."

54. Shekhovtsov and Umland, "The Maidan and Beyond."

55. Burlyuk, Shapovalova, and Zarembo, "Introduction to the Special Issue."

56. Pop-Eleches and Robertson, "Identity and Political Preferences in Ukraine."

57. UN, "General Assembly Adopts Resolution Calling upon States Not to Recognize Change in Status of Crimea Region," March 27, 2014.

58. Biersack and O'Lear, "The Geopolitics of Russia's Annexation of Crimea."

59. Rosemary Wardly, "300 Years of Embattled Crimea History in 6 Maps," *National Geographic*, March 5, 2014.

60. O'Loughlin and Toal, "The Crimea Conundrum."

61. Sasse and Lackner, "War and Identity."

62. Giuliano, "Who Supported Separatism in Donbas?"

63. Biersack and O'Lear, "The Geopolitics of Russia's Annexation of Crimea."

64. "Putin: 'Crimea Has Always Been an Integral Part of Russia,'" *Telegraph*, March 18, 2014, https://www.telegraph.co.uk/news/worldnews/europe/ukraine/10706182/Putin-Crimea-has-always-been-an-integral-part-of-Russia.html.

65. A gas pipeline deal with China and the need to control the Black Sea also factored into Russia's decision to annex Crimea. However, the legitimacy and justification of Russia's actions were couched in its contested claims over Ukraine. Economic motivation, however, should not be overstated in terms of the explanatory power behind Russia's actions. Similar to how the Sunflower Movement was not simply about economic trade, Russia's actions were not simply about a gas pipeline, even if the pipeline deal was a factor. See Biersack and O'Lear, "The Geopolitics of Russia's Annexation of Crimea."

Conclusion

1. For a full analysis of the NPP's institutionalization struggles, see Nachman, "Routine Problems."

2. Nachman, "Routine Problems."

3. Brian Hioe and Lev Nachman, "From Green to Blue: The Political History of Ko Wen-je," *Diplomat*, November 28, 2023, https://thediplomat.com/2023/11/from-green-to-blue-the-political-history-of-ko-wen-je.

4. It is worth noting that although the TPP is a small third party in Taiwan, it is qualitatively different from the NPP in a number of critical ways. First, it was not born out of a social movement. Wen-je Ko had grown his cult of personality following for years before eventually deciding to form a political party based on his own sense of identity. Ko is also not pro-independence and does not value

progressive politics like the NPP. Instead, Ko's party platform is vague, ambiguous, and claims to be above the question of Taiwan's contested status. In addition, the NPP is a new party in the sense that it started from scratch with no funding, resources, or established politicians. The TPP began political life with Ko already having accrued political, social, and economic capital. Members recruited by Ko, largely former KMT and New Party politicians, also came with their own established political networks. Although the TPP was a new party, those joining the party were not new to politics.

5. There are some examples of clashes between activists and the DPP. For example, the referendum over construction of an energy plant on the Datan algal reef in 2021 put environmental activists, who typically support the DPP, in a tough position when the DPP came out in favor of the plant. Although the moment was tense for movement party relations, it did not lead to mass protests or overt souring of relations between environmental activists and the DPP.

6. Clarissa Wei, "Opinion: Here's a Taiwan Chill Pill for Your Pelosi-Induced Anxiety," CNN, August 2, 2022, https://www.cnn.com/2022/08/02/opinions/taiwan-not-panicking-nancy-pelosi-wei/index.html.

BIBLIOGRAPHY

Achen, Christopher H., and T. Y. Wang, eds. *The Taiwan Voter*. Ann Arbor: University of Michigan Press, 2017.

Aliyev, Huseyn. "Post-Soviet Informality: Towards Theory-Building." *International Journal of Sociology and Social Policy* 35, no. 3–4 (2015): 182–98.

Amenta, Edwin, Neal Caren, Elizabeth Chiarello, and Yang Su. "The Political Consequences of Social Movements." *Annual Review of Sociology* 36 (2010): 287–307.

Amenta, Edwin, and Drew Halfmann. "Opportunity Knocks: The Trouble with Political Opportunity and What You Can Do about It." In *Contention in Context: Political Opportunities and the Emergence of Protest*, edited by Jeff Goodwin and James M. Jasper, 227–39. Redwood City, CA: Stanford University Press, 2011.

Andrade, Tonio. *Lost Colony: The Untold Story of China's First Great Victory over the West*. Princeton, NJ: Princeton University Press, 2011.

Anria, Santiago. *When Movements Become Parties: The Bolivian MAS in Comparative Perspective*. Cambridge: Cambridge University Press, 2018.

Arel, Dominique. "How Ukraine Has Become More Ukrainian." *Post-Soviet Affairs* 34, no. 2–3 (2018): 186–89.

Askerov, Ali. "The Nagorno Karabakh Conflict: The Beginning of the Soviet End." In *Post-Soviet Conflicts: The Thirty Years' Crisis*, edited by Ali Askerov, Stefan Brooks, and Lasha Tchantouridzé, 55–82. Lanham, MD: Rowman & Littlefield, 2020.

Barclay, George Watson. *Colonial Development and Population in Taiwan*. Princeton, NJ: Princeton University Press, 2015.

Barrington, Lowell W. "Understanding Identity in Ukraine—and Elsewhere." *Post-Soviet Affairs* 34, no. 2–3 (2018): 179–82.

Barrington, Lowell W., and Erik S. Herron. "One Ukraine or Many? Regionalism in Ukraine and Its Political Consequences." *Nationalities Papers* 32, no. 1 (2004): 53–86.

Bassin, Mark, and Catriona Kelly, eds. *Soviet and Post-Soviet Identities*. Cambridge: Cambridge University Press, 2012.

Berg, Eiki, and Piret Ehin, eds. *Identity and Foreign Policy: Baltic-Russian Relations and European Integration*. Abingdon-on-Thames: Routledge, 2016.

Biersack, John, and Shannon O'Lear. "The Geopolitics of Russia's Annexation of Crimea: Narratives, Identity, Silences, and Energy." *Eurasian Geography and Economics* 55, no. 3 (2014): 247–69.

Bilaniuk, Laada. "A Typology of Surzhyk: Mixed Ukrainian-Russian Language." *International Journal of Bilingualism* 8, no. 4 (2004): 409–25.

Brown, David. "Unproductive Military Posturing." *Comparative Connections* 6, no. 3 (October 2004).

Brown, Melissa J. *Is Taiwan Chinese? The Impact of Culture, Power, and Migration on Changing Identities*. Berkeley Series in Interdisciplinary Studies of China. Berkeley: University of California Press, 2004.

Bunce, Valerie. "Peaceful versus Violent State Dismemberment: A Comparison of the Soviet Union, Yugoslavia, and Czechoslovakia." *Politics and Society* 27, no. 2 (1999): 217–37.

Burlyuk, Olga, Natalia Shapovalova, and Kateryna Zarembo. "Introduction to the Special Issue: Civil Society in Ukraine: Building on Euromaidan Legacy." *Kyiv-Mohyla Law and Politics Journal* 3 (2017).

Callahan, William A. "History, Identity, and Security: Producing and Consuming Nationalism in China." *Critical Asian Studies* 38, no. 2 (2006): 179–208.

Caspersen, Nina. *Unrecognized States: The Struggle for Sovereignty in the Modern International System*. Hoboken, NJ: John Wiley & Sons, 2013.

Chai, Trong R. "The Future of Taiwan." *Asian Survey* 26, no. 12 (1986): 1309–23.

Chang, Lung-chih. *From Island Frontier to Imperial Colony: Qing and Japanese Sovereignty Debates and Territorial Projects in Taiwan, 1874–1906*. Cambridge, MA: Harvard University Press, 2003.

Chang, Sung-sheng Yvonne. *Modernism and the Nativist Resistance: Contemporary Chinese Fiction from Taiwan*. Durham, NC: Duke University Press, 1993.

Chen, Dean P. "US–China Rivalry and the Weakening of the KMT's '1992 Consensus' Policy: Second Image Reversed, Revisited." *Asian Survey* 56, no. 4 (2016): 754–78.

Chen, Fang-Yu, Austin Horng-En Wang, Charles K. S. Wu, and Yao-Yuan Yeh. "The Multiverse of Taiwan's Future: Reconsidering the Independence–Unification (Tondu) Attitudes." *Political Studies Review* 22, no. 4 (2023). DOI: 14789299231193572.

Chen, Yingzhen. "Imperial Army Betrayed." In *Perilous Memories: The Asia Pacific War(s)*, edited by T. Fujitani, Geoffrey M. White, and Lisa Yoneyama, 181–98. Durham, NC: Duke University Press, 2001.

Cheng, Maria. "Constructing a New Political Spectacle: Tactics of Chen Shui-bian's 2000 and 2004 Inaugural Speeches." *Discourse & Society* 17, no. 5 (2006): 583–608.

Cheng, Tun-jen, and Yung-ming Hsu. "Issue Structure, the DPP's Factionalism, and Party Realignment." In *Taiwan's Electoral Politics and Democratic Transition: Riding the Third Wave*, edited by Hung-Mao Tien, 137–73. Abingdon-on-Thames: Routledge, 1996.

Chernetsky, Vitaly. "Postcolonialism, Russia and Ukraine." *Ulbandus Review* 7 (2003): 32–62.
Chhibber, Pradeep K., and Rahul Verma. *Ideology and Identity: The Changing Party Systems of India*. Oxford: Oxford University Press, 2018.
Chin, Ko-lin. *Heijin: Organized Crime, Business, and Politics in Taiwan*. Armonk, NY: M. E. Sharpe, 2003.
Ching, Leo T. S. *Becoming Japanese: Colonial Taiwan and the Politics of Identity Formation*. Berkeley: University of California Press, 2001.
Chong, Ja Ian. *External Intervention and the Politics of State Formation: China, Indonesia, and Thailand, 1893–1952*. Cambridge: Cambridge University Press, 2012.
Chong, Ja Ian, David W. F. Huang, and Wen-Chin Wu. "'Stand Up Like a Taiwanese!': PRC Coercion and Public Preferences for Resistance." *Japanese Journal of Political Science* (2023): 1–22.
Chun, Allen. *Forget Chineseness: On the Geopolitics of Cultural Identification*. Albany: SUNY Press, 2018.
Cowell-Meyers, Kimberly B. "The Social Movement as Political Party: The Northern Ireland Women's Coalition and the Campaign for Inclusion." *Perspectives on Politics* 12, no. 1 (2014): 61–80.
Crawford, James R. *The Creation of States in International Law*. Oxford: Oxford University Press, 2010.
D'Anieri, Paul. "Ukrainian Foreign Policy from Independence to Inertia." *Communist and Post-Communist Studies* 45, no. 3–4 (2012): 447–56.
Dawley, E. N. *Becoming Taiwanese: Ethnogenesis in a Colonial City, 1880s to 1950s*. Cambridge, MA: Harvard University Press, 2019.
Della Porta, Donatella. "Political Opportunity/Political Opportunity Structure." In *The Wiley-Blackwell Encyclopedia of Social and Political Movements*, edited by David A. Snow, Donatella della Porta, Doug McAdam, and Bert Klandermans, 105–12. Hoboken, NJ: Wiley-Blackwell, 2013.
Della Porta, Donatella, Joseba Fernandez, Hara Kouki, and Lorenzo Mosca. *Movement Parties against Austerity*. Hoboken, NJ: John Wiley & Sons, 2017.
Democratic Progressive Party. Party Charter. https://www.dpp.org.tw/en/upload/download/Party_Constitution.pdf.
Deyermond, Ruth. "Security, History and the Boundaries of European Identity after Russia's Invasion of Ukraine." *New Perspectives* 30, no. 3 (2022): 230–35.
Diuk, Nadia. "Euromaidan: Ukraine's Self-Organizing Revolution." *World Affairs* 176 (2013): 9–17.
Dobos, Ned. *Insurrection and Intervention: The Two Faces of Sovereignty*. Cambridge: Cambridge University Press, 2011.
Downs, Anthony. "An Economic Theory of Political Action in a Democracy." *Journal of Political Economy* 65, no. 2 (1957): 135–50.

Dumbaugh, Kerry. "Taiwan's Political Status: Historical Background and Ongoing Implications." Washington, DC: Library of Congress Congressional Research Service, 2009.

Ebsworth, Rowena. "Not Wanting Want: The Anti-Media Monopoly Movement in Taiwan." In *Taiwan's Social Movements under Ma Ying-jeou*, edited by Dafydd Fell, 71–91. Abingdon-on-Thames: Routledge, 2017.

Elster, Jon, Claus Offe, Ulrich K. Preuss, Frank Boenker, Ulrike Goetting, and Friedbert W. Rueb. *Institutional Design in Post-Communist Societies: Rebuilding the Ship at Sea*. Cambridge: Cambridge University Press, 1998.

Erlich, Aaron, and Calvin Garner. "Is Pro-Kremlin Disinformation Effective? Evidence from Ukraine." *International Journal of Press/Politics* 28, no. 1 (2021). DOI: 19401612211045221.

Fabry, Mikulas. "The Contemporary Practice of State Recognition: Kosovo, South Ossetia, Abkhazia, and Their Aftermath." *Nationalities Papers* 40, no. 5 (2012): 661–76.

Falleti, Tulia G., and James Mahoney. "The Comparative Sequential Method." In *Advances in Comparative-Historical Analysis*, edited by James Mahoney and Kathleen Thelen, 211–39. Cambridge: Cambridge University Press, 2015.

Fell, Dafydd. "Measuring and Explaining Party Change in Taiwan: 1991–2004." *Journal of East Asian Studies* 5, no. 1 (2005): 105–33.

Fell, Dafydd. *Party Politics in Taiwan: Party Change and the Democratic Evolution of Taiwan, 1991–2004*. Abingdon-on-Thames: Routledge, 2006.

Fell, Dafydd. *Taiwan's Green Parties: Alternative Politics in Taiwan*. Abingdon-on-Thames: Routledge, 2021.

Fleischauer, Stefan. "The 228 Incident and the Taiwan Independence Movement's Construction of a Taiwanese Identity." *China Information* 21, no. 3 (November 2007): 373–401.

Friedman, Edward. "China's Changing Taiwan Policy." *American Journal of Chinese Studies* 14, no. 2 (2007): 119–34.

Friedman, P. Kerim. "The Hegemony of the Local: Taiwanese Multiculturalism and Indigenous Identity Politics." *boundary 2: An International Journal of Literature and Culture* 45, no. 3 (2018): 79–105.

Gardiner, John. "Defining Corruption." In *Political Corruption*, 3rd ed., edited by Michael Johnson, 25–40. Abingdon-on-Thames: Routledge, ebook 2017 (2002).

Geldenhuys, Deon. *Contested States in World Politics*. Basingstoke: Palgrave Macmillan, 2009.

Gellner, Ernest. *Nations and Nationalism*. Ithaca, NY: Cornell University Press, 2008.

Giuliano, Elise. "Who Supported Separatism in Donbas? Ethnicity and Popular

Opinion at the Start of the Ukraine Crisis." *Post-Soviet Affairs* 34, no. 2–3 (2018): 158–78.

Goble, Paul. "Russian National Identity and the Ukrainian Crisis." *Communist and Post-Communist Studies* 49, no. 1 (2016): 37–43.

Grant, Thomas D. "Defining Statehood: The Montevideo Convention and Its Discontents." *Columbia Journal of Transnational Law* 37 (1998): 403–59.

Greitens, Sheena Chestnut. *Dictators and Their Secret Police: Coercive Institutions and State Violence*. Cambridge Studies in Contentious Politics. Cambridge: Cambridge University Press, 2016.

Gunitsky, Seva. *Aftershocks: Great Powers and Domestic Reforms in the Twentieth Century*. Princeton Studies in International History and Politics 154. Princeton, NJ: Princeton University Press, 2017.

Harmel, Robert, and John D. Robertson. "Formation and Success of New Parties: A Cross-National Analysis." *International Political Science Review* 6, no. 4 (1985): 501–23.

Hayton, Bill. *The South China Sea: The Struggle for Power in Asia*. New Haven, CT: Yale University Press, 2014.

Heé, Nadin. "Taiwan under Japanese Rule, Showpiece of a Model Colony? Historiographical Tendencies in Narrating Colonialism." *History Compass* 12, no. 8 (2014): 632–41.

Heidenheimer, Arnold J., and Michael Johnston, eds. *Political Corruption: Concepts and Contexts*. Piscataway, NJ: Transaction, 2002.

Hewitt, B. George. "Abkhazia: A Problem of Identity and Ownership." *Central Asian Survey* 12, no. 3 (1993): 267–323.

Hioe, Brian. "Lack of Clear Answers Regarding the Lin Family Massacre Reflects the Dilemmas of Transitional Justice." *New Bloom*, February 23, 2020. https://newbloommag.net/2020/02/23/lin-family-massacre-transitional-justice/.

Ho, Ming-sho. *Challenging Beijing's Mandate of Heaven: Taiwan's Sunflower Movement and Hong Kong's Umbrella Movement*. Philadelphia: Temple University Press, 2019.

Ho, Ming-sho. "Occupy Congress in Taiwan: Political Opportunity, Threat, and the Sunflower Movement." *Journal of East Asian Studies* 15 (2015): 69–97.

Ho, Ming-sho, and Chun-Hao Huang. "Movement Parties in Taiwan, 1987–2016: A Political Opportunity Explanation." *Asian Survey* 57, no. 2 (2017): 343–67.

Hofmeister, Ulrich. "Civilization and Russification in Tsarist Central Asia, 1860–1917." *Journal of World History* 27 (2016): 411–42.

Hsiao, Yi-ching, Su-feng Cheng, and Christopher H. Achen. "Political Left and Right in Taiwan." In *The Taiwan Voter*, edited by Christopher H. Achen and T. Y. Wang, 198–222. Ann Arbor: University of Michigan Press, 2017.

Hsiau, A-chin. *Contemporary Taiwanese Cultural Nationalism*. Abingdon-on-Thames: Routledge, 2003.

Hsieh, John Fuh-sheng. "Ethnicity, National Identity, and Domestic Politics in Taiwan." *Journal of Asian and African Studies* 40, no. 1–2 (2005): 13–28.

Hsieh, John Fuh-sheng. "The Origins and Consequences of Electoral Reform in Taiwan." *Issues & Studies* 45, no. 2 (2009): 1–22.

Hsieh, John Fuh-sheng, and Emerson M. S. Niou. "Salient Issues in Taiwan's Electoral Politics." *Electoral Studies* 15, no. 2 (1996): 219–35.

Huang, Max Ko-wu. "The Dilemmas of Becoming Chinese in Taiwan." *China Review* 23, no. 2 (2023): 149–64.

Huang, Qingxian. "The Democratic Progressive Party's Policies on Cross-Strait Relations." *Strait Review* 304 (2016): 48–51.

Huang, Shu-Min, and Shao-Hua Liu. "Discrimination and Incorporation of Taiwanese Indigenous Austronesian Peoples." *Asian Ethnicity* 17, no. 2 (2016): 294–312.

Hug, Simon. *Altering Party Systems: Strategic Behavior and the Emergence of New Political Parties in Western Democracies*. Ann Arbor: University of Michigan Press, 2001.

Hung, Tzu-Chieh, and Tzu-Wei Hung. "How China's Cognitive Warfare Works: A Frontline Perspective of Taiwan's Anti-Disinformation Wars." *Journal of Global Security Studies* 7, no. 4 (December 2022): ogac016.

Jackson, Robert H. *Quasi-States: Sovereignty, International Relations and the Third World*. Cambridge Studies in International Relations. Cambridge: Cambridge University Press, 1993.

Jacobs, J. Bruce. *Democratizing Taiwan*. Leiden: Brill, 2012.

Jain, J. P. "The Legal Status of Formosa: A Study of British, Chinese and Indian Views." *American Journal of International Law* 57, no. 1 (1963): 25–43.

Jasper, James M. "Linking Arenas: Structuring Concepts in the Study of Politics and Protest." *Social Movement Studies* 20, no. 2 (2021): 243–257.

Kappeler, Andreas. "The Ambiguities of Russification." *Kritika: Explorations in Russian and Eurasian History* 5, no. 2 (2004): 291–97.

Kassoff, Allen. "The Non-Russian Nationalities." In *Prospects for Soviet Policy*, edited by Allen Kassoff, 143–98. New York: Praeger, 1968.

Kitschelt, Herbert. *The Logics of Party Formation: Ecological Politics in Belgium and West Germany*. Ithaca, NY: Cornell University Press, 2019 (1989).

Kitschelt, Herbert. "Movement Parties." In *Handbook of Party Politics*, edited by Richard S. Katz and William Crotty, 278–90. London: Sage, 2006.

Kitschelt, Herbert. "Social Movements, Political Parties, and Democratic Theory." *Annals of the American Academy of Political and Social Science* 528, no. 1 (1993): 13–29.

Kitschelt, Herbert, Zdenka Mansfeldova, Radoslaw Markowski, and Gabor Toka. *Post-Communist Party Systems: Competition, Representation, and Inter-Party Cooperation*. Cambridge: Cambridge University Press, 1999.

Kolossov, Vladimir, and John O'Loughlin. "Pseudo-States as Harbingers of a New Geopolitics: The Example of the Trans-Dniester Moldovan Republic (TMR)." *Geopolitics* 3, no. 1 (1998): 151–76.

Krauss, Ellis S., and Robert J. Pekkanen. *The Rise and Fall of Japan's LDP: Political Party Organizations as Historical Institutions*. Ithaca, NY: Cornell University Press, 2010.

Kriesi, Hanspeter. *The Political Opportunity Structure of New Social Movements: Its Impact on Their Mobilization*. Berlin: WZB, 1991.

Kubicek, Paul. "Regional Polarisation in Ukraine: Public Opinion, Voting and Legislative Behaviour." *Europe-Asia Studies* 52, no. 2 (2000): 273–94.

Kulyk, Volodymyr. "Language Policy in Ukraine: What People Want the State to Do." *East European Politics and Societies* 27, no. 2 (2013): 280–307.

Kulyk, Volodymyr. "Shedding Russianness, Recasting Ukrainianness: The Post-Euromaidan Dynamics of Ethnonational Identifications in Ukraine." *Post-Soviet Affairs* 34, no. 2–3 (2018): 119–38.

Kuo Cheng-liang, *Minjindang zhuanxing zhi tong* (The DPP's painful transformation). Taipei: Tianhsia, 1998.

Kuzio, Taras. "Nationalism, Identity and Civil Society in Ukraine: Understanding the Orange Revolution." *Communist and Post-Communist Studies* 43, no. 3 (2010): 285–96.

Lai, Myers. "A Tragic Beginning: The Taiwan Uprising of February 28, 1947." Redwood City, CA: Stanford University Press, 1991.

Lamley, Harry J. "The 1895 Taiwan Republic: A Significant Episode in Modern Chinese History." *Journal of Asian Studies* 27, no. 4 (1968): 739–62.

Lee, Tzu-wen. "The International Legal Status of the Republic of China on Taiwan." *UCLA Journal of International Law and Foreign Affairs* 1 (1996): 351–93.

Leung, Edwin Pak-Wah. "The Quasi-War in East Asia: Japan's Expedition to Taiwan and the Ryūkyū Controversy." *Modern Asian Studies* 17, no. 2 (1983): 257–81.

Li, Chengxi, and Xingren Liu. "A Comparative Study of China's Policies under the Chairs of Chen Shui-bian and Tsai Ing-wen of the Democratic Progressive Party." *Journal of Development and Prospects* 2 (2013): 21–46.

Liao, Yü-wen. "Tai-wan wen-tzu kai-ko yün-tung shih-lüe" (A brief history of the Taiwanese writing reform movement). In *Jih-chü hsia t'ai-wan hsin-wen-hsüeh ming-chi wu: wen-hsian tzu-liao hsüan-chi* (Taiwanese new literature under the Japanese rule, 5: Selected documents), edited by Li Nan-heng. Taipei: Ming-t'an, 1979.

Liff, Adam P., and Dalton Lin. "The 'One China' Framework at 50 (1972–2022):

The Myth of 'Consensus' and Its Evolving Policy Significance." *China Quarterly* 252 (2022): 1–24.

Lijphart, Arend, and Don Aitkin. *Electoral Systems and Party Systems: A Study of Twenty-Seven Democracies, 1945–1990*. Oxford: Oxford University Press, 1994.

Lin, James. "Nostalgia for Japanese Colonialism: Historical Memory and Postcolonialism in Contemporary Taiwan." *History Compass* 20, no. 11 (November 2022): e12751.

Lin, Tse-Min, Yun-Han Chu, and Melvin J. Hinich. "Conflict Displacement and Regime Transition in Taiwan: A Spatial Analysis." *World Politics* 48, no. 4 (July 1996): 453–81.

Lipset, Seymour Martin, and Stein Rokkan, eds. *Party Systems and Voter Alignments: Cross-National Perspectives*. New York: Free Press, 1967.

Long, Simon. "Taiwan's National Assembly Elections." *China Quarterly* 129 (1992): 216–28.

Looney, Kristen E. *Mobilizing for Development: The Modernization of Rural East Asia*. Ithaca, NY: Cornell University Press, 2020.

Louzon, V. "From Japanese Soldiers to Chinese Rebels: Colonial Hegemony, War Experience, and Spontaneous Remobilization during the 1947 Taiwanese Rebellion." *Journal of Asian Studies* 77, no. 1 (2018): 161–79.

Luckyj, George. "Ukrainian Literature in the Twentieth Century." In *Ukrainian Literature in the Twentieth Century: A Reader's Guide*. Toronto: University of Toronto Press, 1992.

Lustick, Ian. *Unsettled States, Disputed Lands: Britain and Ireland, France and Algeria, Israel and the West Bank–Gaza*. Ithaca, NY: Cornell University Press, 1993.

Ma, Ngok. "The Rise of 'Anti-China' Sentiments in Hong Kong and the 2012 Legislative Council Elections." *China Review* 15, no. 1 (2015): 39–66.

Maksimovtsova, Ksenia. "Language Policy in Education in Contemporary Ukraine: A Continuous Discussion of Contested National Identity." *Journal on Ethnopolitics and Minority Issues in Europe* 16 (2017): 1.

Malik, Yogendra K., and Vijay B. Singh. *Hindu Nationalists in India: The Rise of the Bharatiya Janata Party*. New Delhi: Vistaar, 1995.

Maoz, Zeev. "Joining the Club of Nations: Political Development and International Conflict, 1816–1976." *International Studies Quarterly* 33, no. 2 (1989): 199–231.

Marples, David R., and Frederick V. Mills, eds. *Ukraine's Euromaidan: Analyses of a Civil Revolution*. New York: Columbia University Press, 2014.

McAdam, Doug, and Sidney Tarrow. "Ballots and Barricades: On the Reciprocal Relationship between Elections and Social Movements." *Perspectives on Politics* 8, no. 2 (2010): 529–42.

McAllister, Ian. "Democratic Consolidation in Taiwan in Comparative Perspective." *Asian Journal of Comparative Politics* 1, no. 1 (2016): 44–61.

Metzger, Megan MacDuffee, Richard Bonneau, Jonathan Nagler, and Joshua A. Tucker. "Tweeting Identity? Ukrainian, Russian, and #euromaidan." *Journal of Comparative Economics* 44, no. 1 (2016): 16–40.

Meyer, David S., and Debra C. Minkoff. "Conceptualizing Political Opportunity." *Social Forces* 82, no. 4 (2004): 1457–92.

Michels, Robert. *The Iron Law of Oligarchy: A Sociological Study of the Oligarchical Tendencies of Modern Democracy*. Lancaster, PA: Wentworth, 2016.

Ministry of the Interior, Republic of China. The Website of Parties and National Political Associations. https://party.moi.gov.tw/PartyMain.aspx?n=16100&sms=13073&gs=P01.

Molchanov, Mikhail. "Political Culture and National Identity in Russian-Ukrainian Relations." Social Science Research Network, accessed November 21, 2022. https://papers.ssrn.com/sol3/papers.cfm?abstract_id=2874046.

Mosca, Lorenzo, and Mario Quaranta. "Voting for Movement Parties in Southern Europe: The Role of Protest and Digital Information." *South European Society and Politics* 22, no. 4 (December 2017): 427–46.

Muschik, Eva-Maria. "Managing the World: The United Nations, Decolonization, and the Strange Triumph of State Sovereignty in the 1950s and 1960s." *Journal of Global History* 13, no. 1 (2018): 121–44.

Musgrave, Paul. "International Hegemony Meets Domestic Politics: Why Liberals Can Be Pessimists." *Security Studies* 28, no. 3 (2019): 451–78.

Nachman, Lev. "From Sunflowers to Suits: How Spatial Openings Affect Movement Party Formation." In *Sunflowers and Umbrellas: Social Movements, Expressive Practices, and Political Culture in Taiwan and Hong Kong*, edited by Thomas Gold and Sebastian Veg, 200–227. Berkeley, CA: Institute of East Asian Studies, 2020.

Nachman, Lev. "Misalignment between Social Movements and Political Parties in Taiwan's 2016 Election: Not All Grass Roots Are Green." *Asian Survey* 58, no. 5 (2018): 874–97.

Nachman, Lev. "Routine Problems: Movement Party Institutionalization and the Case of Taiwan's New Power Party." *Studies in Comparative International Development* 58 (March 2023): 537–56.

Nachman, Lev. "Student Movements." In *Encyclopedia of Taiwan Studies Online*, edited by Hsin-Huang Michael Hsiao. Leiden: Brill, 2022.

Nachman, Lev, and Brian Hioe. "No, Taiwan's President Isn't 'Pro-Independence.'" *Diplomat* 23 (2020).

Nicholson, Rowan, and Thomas D. Grant. "Theories of State Recognition." In

Routledge Handbook of State Recognition, edited by John Doyle, Gëzim Visoka, and Edward Newman, 25–36. Abingdon-on-Thames: Routledge, 2019.

Niou, Emerson M. S. "Understanding Taiwan Independence and Its Policy Implications." *Asian Survey* 44, no. 4 (2004).

Niou, Emerson, and Philip Paolino. "The Rise of the Opposition Party in Taiwan: Explaining Chen Shui-bian's Victory in the 2000 Presidential Election." *Electoral Studies* 22, no. 4 (2003): 721–40.

Noreen, Erik, and Roxanna Sjöstedt. "Estonian Identity Formations and Threat Framing in the Post-Cold War Era." *Journal of Peace Research* 41, no. 6 (November 2004): 733–50.

Odey, Stephen Adi, and Samuel Akpan Bassey. "Ukrainian Foreign Policy toward Russia between 1991 and 2004: The Start of the Conflict." *Journal of Liberty and International Affairs* 8 (2022): 346–61.

O'Loughlin, John, and Gerard Toal. "The Crimea Conundrum: Legitimacy and Public Opinion after Annexation." *Eurasian Geography and Economics* 60, no. 1 (February 2019): 6–27.

Olson, David M. "Party Formation and Party System Consolidation in the New Democracies of Central Europe." *Political Studies* 46, no. 3 (1998): 432–64.

Onuch, Olga. "EuroMaidan Protests in Ukraine: Social Media versus Social Networks." *Problems of Post-Communism* 62, no. 4 (2015): 217–35.

Onuch, Olga, and Henry E. Hale. "Capturing Ethnicity: The Case of Ukraine." *Post-Soviet Affairs* 34, no. 2–3 (2018): 84–106.

Onuch, Olga, Henry E. Hale, and Gwendolyn Sasse. "Studying Identity in Ukraine." *Post-Soviet Affairs* 34, no. 2–3 (2018): 79–83.

Osipian, Ararat L., and Alexandr L. Osipian. "Regional Diversity and Divided Memories in Ukraine: Contested Past as Electoral Resource, 2004–2010." *East European Politics and Societies* 26, no. 3 (2012): 616–42.

Pegg, Scott. "De Facto States in the International System." Working paper no. 2. Vancouver: University of British Columbia Institute of International Relations, 1998.

Pelenski, Jaroslaw. "The Contest for the 'Kievan Inheritance' in Russian-Ukrainian Relations: The Origins and Early Ramifications." In *Ukraine and Russia in Their Historical Encounter*, edited by Peter J. Potichnyj, Marc Raeff, Jaroslaw Pelenski, and Gleb N. Zekulin, 3–19. Edmonton: Canadian Institute for Ukrainian Studies, 1992.

Pelenski, Jaroslaw. "The Origins of the Official Muscovite Claims to the 'Kievan Inheritance.'" *Harvard Ukrainian Studies* 1, no. 1 (1977): 29–52.

Petersen, Phillip. "Security Policy in the Post-Soviet Baltic States." *European Security* 1, no. 1 (1992): 13–49.

Phillips, Steven E. *Between Assimilation and Independence: The Taiwanese Encounter Nationalist China, 1945–1950*. Redwood City, CA: Stanford University Press, 2003.

Ping-Hui, Liao. "Taiwan under Japanese Colonial Rule, 1895–1945: History, Culture, Memory." In *Taiwan under Japanese Colonial Rule, 1895–1945*, edited by Ping-hui Liao and David Der-wei Wang, 1–16. New York: Columbia University Press, 2006.

Plokhy, Serhii. *Unmaking Imperial Russia: Mykhailo Hrushevsky and the Writing of Ukrainian History*. Toronto: University of Toronto Press, 2005.

Pop-Eleches, Grigore, and Graeme B. Robertson. "Identity and Political Preferences in Ukraine—Before and After the Euromaidan." *Post-Soviet Affairs* 34, no. 2–3 (2018): 107–18.

Popova, Maria. "Why the Orange Revolution Was Short and Peaceful and Euromaidan Long and Violent." *Problems of Post-Communism* 61, no. 6 (2014): 64–70.

Porch, Douglas. "The Taiwan Strait Crisis of 1996: Strategic Implications for the United States Navy." *Naval War College Review* 52, no. 3 (1999): 15–48.

Potulnytskyi, Volodymyr A. "The Image of Ukraine and the Ukrainians in Russian Political Thought (1860–1945)." *Acta Slavica Iaponica* 16 (1998): 1–29.

Rawnsley, Ming-Yeh T., and Chien-san Feng. "Anti-Media-Monopoly Policies and Further Democratisation in Taiwan." *Journal of Current Chinese Affairs* 43, no. 3 (2014): 105–28.

Rigger, Shelley. *From Opposition to Power: Taiwan's Democratic Progressive Party*. Boulder, CO: Lynne Rienner, 2001.

Rigger, Shelley. "Regional Perspectives and Domestic Imperatives: Maintaining the Status Quo: What It Means, and Why the Taiwanese Prefer it." *Cambridge Review of International Affairs* 14, no. 2 (2001): 103–14.

Rigger, Shelley. "Taiwan's Lee Teng-hui Complex." *Current History* 95, no. 602 (1996): 266–71.

Roberts, J. A. G. "Warlordism in China." *Review of African Political Economy* 16, no. 45–46 (1989): 26–33.

Rowen, Ian. "Inside Taiwan's Sunflower Movement: Twenty-Four Days in a Student Occupied Parliament, and the Future of the Region." *Journal of Asian Studies* 74 (2015): 5–21.

Rowen, Ian, and Jamie Rowen. "Taiwan's Truth and Reconciliation Committee: The Geopolitics of Transitional Justice in a Contested State." *International Journal of Transitional Justice* 11, no. 1 (2017): 92–112.

Ryabchuk, Anastasiya. "Right Revolution? Hopes and Perils of the Euromaidan Protests in Ukraine." *Debatte: Journal of Contemporary Central and Eastern Europe* 22, no. 1 (2014): 127–34.

Sasse, Gwendolyn, and Alice Lackner. "War and Identity: The Case of the Donbas in Ukraine." *Post-Soviet Affairs* 34, no. 2–3 (2018): 139–57.

Schultz, Kenneth A. "What's in a Claim? De Jure versus De Facto Borders in Interstate Territorial Disputes." *Journal of Conflict Resolution* 58, no. 6 (2014): 1059–84.

Scott, James C. "Handling Historical Comparisons Cross-Nationally." In *Political Corruption: Concepts and Contexts,* edited by Arnold J. Heidenheimer and Michael Johnston, 123–38. Piscataway, NJ: Transaction 2002.

Seals, Corinne. "From Russification to Ukrainisation: A Survey of Language Politics in Ukraine." *Undergraduate Journal on Slavic and East/Central European Studies* 2 (January 2009): 1–10.

Shcherbak, Andrey. "Nationalism in the USSR: A Historical and Comparative Perspective." *Nationalities Papers* 43, no. 6 (2015): 866–85.

Shekhovtsov, Anton, and Andreas Umland. "The Maidan and Beyond: Ukraine's Radical Right." *Journal of Democracy* 25, no. 3 (2014): 58–63.

Sheng, Shing-yuan, and Hsiao-chuan (Mandy) Liao. "Issues, Political Cleavages, and Party Competition in Taiwan." In *The Taiwan Voter*, edited by Christopher H. Achen and T. Y. Wang, 98–138. Ann Arbor: University of Michigan Press, 2017.

Shepherd, John Robert. *Statecraft and Political Economy on the Taiwan Frontier, 1600–1800*. Redwood City, CA: Stanford University Press, 1993.

Shevel, Oxana. "Towards New Horizons in the Study of Identities in Ukraine." *Post-Soviet Affairs* 34, no. 2–3 (2018): 183–85.

Shih, Fang-long. "The 'Red Tide' Anti-Corruption Protest: What Does It Mean for Democracy in Taiwan?." *Taiwan in Comparative Perspective* 1 (November 2007): 87–98.

Shirk, Susan L. *China: Fragile Superpower*. Oxford: Oxford University Press, 2007.

Shulman, Stephen. "The Cultural Foundations of Ukrainian National Identity." *Ethnic and Racial Studies* 22, no. 6 (1999): 1011–36.

Silver, Brian. "Social Mobilization and the Russification of Soviet Nationalities." *American Political Science Review* 68, no. 1 (1974): 45–66.

Simon, Scott E. *Truly Human: Indigeneity and Indigenous Resurgence on Formosa.* Toronto: University of Toronto Press, 2023.

Slater, Dan, and Joseph Wong. *From Development to Democracy: The Transformations of Modern Asia*. Princeton, NJ: Princeton University Press, 2022.

Slater, Dan, and Joseph Wong. "The Strength to Concede: Ruling Parties and Democratization in Developmental Asia." *Perspectives on Politics* 11, no. 3 (2013): 717–33.

Smith, Craig A. "Taiwan's 228 Incident and the Politics of Placing Blame." *Past Imperfect* 14 (2008).

Snow, David, Daniel Cress, Liam Downey, and Andrew Jones. "Disrupting the 'Quotidian': Reconceptualizing the Relationship between Breakdown and the Emergence of Collective Action." *Mobilization: An International Quarterly* 3, no. 1 (1998): 1–22.

Snow, Edgar. *Red Star over China*. New York: Random House, 1948.

Spehr, Scott, and Nargis Kassenova. "Kazakhstan: Constructing Identity in a Post-Soviet Society." *Asian Ethnicity* 13, no. 2 (2012): 135–51.

Staliūnas, Darius. *Making Russians: Meaning and Practice of Russification in Lithuania and Belarus after 1863: On the Boundary of Two Worlds: Identity, Freedom, and Moral Imagination in the Baltics*. Amsterdam: Rodopi, 2007.

Strikha, Maksym V. "Language and Language Policy in Ukraine." *Journal of Ukrainian Studies* 26, no. 1–2 (2001): 239.

Strom, Kaare. "A Behavioral Theory of Competitive Political Parties." *American Journal of Political Science* 34, no. 2 (May 1990): 565–98.

Sullivan, Jonathan, and Will Lowe. "Chen Shui-bian: On Independence." *China Quarterly* 203 (2010): 619–38.

Sullivan, Jonathan, and Lev Nachman. *Taiwan: A Contested Democracy Under Threat*. New York: Agenda, 2024.

Sullivan, Lawrence R. "The Chinese Communist Party and the Status of Taiwan, 1928–1943." *Pacific Affairs* 52, no. 3 (1979): 446–67.

Tavits, Margit. "Party System Change: Testing a Model of New Party Entry." *Party Politics* 12, no. 1 (2006): 99–119.

Teng, Emma Jinhua. *Taiwan's Imagined Geography: Chinese Colonial Travel Writing and Pictures, 1683–1895*. Cambridge, MA: Harvard University Press, 2004.

Thaden, Edward C., ed. *Russification in the Baltic Provinces and Finland, 1855–1914*. Princeton, NJ: Princeton University Press, 2014.

Tilly, Charles. *From Mobilization to Revolution*. Reading, MA: Addison-Wesley, 1978.

Toal, Gerard, and John O'Loughlin. "Inside South Ossetia: A Survey of Attitudes in a De Facto State." *Post-Soviet Affairs* 29, no. 2 (2013): 136–72.

Tomuschat, Christian. "Recognition of New States: The Case of Premature Recognition." In *Kosovo and International Law*, edited by Peter Hilpold, 31–45. Leiden: Brill Nijhoff, 2012.

Toomla, Raul. "Charting Informal Engagement between De Facto States: A Quantitative Analysis." *Space and Polity* 20, no. 3 (2016): 330–45.

Treaty of Taipei. Treaty of Peace between the Republic of China and Japan. Signed at Taipei, April 28, 1952, Entered into force, August 5, 1952. https://china.usc.edu/treaty-peace-between-republic-china-and-japan-treaty-taipei-1952.

Treisman, Daniel. "Crimea: Anatomy of a Decision." In *The New Autocracy:*

Information, Politics, and Policy in Putin's Russia, edited by Daniel Treisman, 277–95. Washington, DC: Brookings Institution Press, 2016.

Unwin, Tim. "Contested Reconstruction of National Identities in Eastern Europe: Landscape Implications." *Norsk Geografisk Tidsskrift–Norwegian Journal of Geography* 53, no. 2–3 (1999): 113–20.

US Department of State. The Cairo Declaration. November 26, 1943. History and Public Policy Program Digital Archive, Conferences at Cairo and Tehran, 1943, Foreign Relations of the United States Diplomatic Papers, 448–49. Washington, DC: State Department, 1961. https://digitalarchive.wilsoncenter.org/document/122101.

US Department of State. Conference for the Conclusion and Signature of the Treaty of Peace with Japan, San Francisco, California, September 4–8, 1951. Record of Proceedings. Washington, DC: State Department, 1951.

Van Biezen, Ingrid, and Ekaterina R. Rashkova. "Deterring New Party Entry? The Impact of State Regulation on the Permeability of Party Systems." *Party Politics* 20, no. 6 (2014): 890–903.

Van Cott, Donna Lee. *From Movements to Parties in Latin America*. Cambridge: Cambridge University Press, 2005.

Veira-Ramos, Alberto, and Tetiana Liubyva. "Ukrainian Identities in Transformation." In *Ukraine in Transformation: From Soviet Republic to European Society*, edited by Alberto Veira-Ramos, Tetiana Liubyva, and Evgenii Golovakha, 203–28. London: Palgrave Macmillan, 2020.

Vickers, Edward. "Three Faces of an Asian Hero: Commemorating Koxinga in Contemporary China, Taiwan, and Japan." In *Taiwan: Manipulation of Ideology and Struggle for Identity*, edited by Chris Shei, 157–82. Abingdon-on-Thames: Routledge, 2021.

Visoka, Gëzim. *Acting Like a State: Kosovo and the Everyday Making of Statehood*. Abingdon-on-Thames: Routledge, 2018.

Wakeman, Frederic, Jr., and Richard Louis Edmonds, eds. *Reappraising Republican China*. Oxford: Oxford University Press, 2000.

Wang, Austin Horng-En, Charles K. S. Wu, Yao-Yuan Yeh, and Fang-Yu Chen. "Strategic Ambiguity, Strategic Clarity, and Dual Clarity." *Foreign Policy Analysis* 20, no. 3 (2024).

Warner, Geoffrey. "Nixon, Kissinger and the Rapprochement with China, 1969–1972." *International Affairs* 83, no. 4 (2007): 763–81.

Wills, John E. "The Seventeenth-Century Transformation: Taiwan under the Dutch and the Cheng Regime." In *Taiwan: Manipulation of Ideology and Struggle for Identity*, edited by Chris Shei, 84–106. Abingdon-on-Thames: Routledge, 2020.

Wilson, Andrew. *Ukraine's Orange Revolution.* New Haven, CT: Yale University Press, 2005.

Wolf, David C. "'To Secure a Convenience': Britain Recognizes China–1950." *Journal of Contemporary History* 18, no. 2 (1983): 299–326.

Wright, Teresa. *The Perils of Protest: State Repression and Student Activism in China and Taiwan.* Honolulu: University of Hawaii Press, 2001.

Wright, Teresa. "Student Mobilization in Taiwan: Civil Society and Its Discontents." *Asian Survey* 39, no. 6 (1999): 986–1008.

Xi Jinping. "Working Together to Realise Rejuvenation of the Chinese Nation and Advance China's Peaceful Reunification." Speech at the Meeting Marking the 40th Anniversary of the Issuance of the Message to Compatriots in Taiwan, January 2, 2019. http://www.gwytb.gov.cn/wyly/201904/t20190412_12155687.htm.

Yang, Dominic Meng-Hsuan. *The Great Exodus from China: Trauma, Memory, and Identity in Modern Taiwan.* Cambridge: Cambridge University Press, 2020.

Yang, Dominic Meng-Hsuan, and Mau-Kuei Chang. "Understanding the Nuances of 'Waishengren': History and Agency." *China Perspectives* 83 (2010): 108–22.

Yu, Ching-hsin. "Parties, Partisans, and Independents in Taiwan." In *The Taiwan Voter*, edited by Christopher H. Achen and T. Y. Wang, 79–81. Ann Arbor: University of Michigan Press, 2017.

Yuan, Hsiao. "Virtual Ecologies, Mobilization and Democratic Groups without Leaders: Impacts of Internet Media on the Wild Strawberry Movement." In *Taiwan's Social Movements under Ma Ying-jeou*, edited by Dafydd Fell, 34–53. Abingdon-on-Thames: Routledge, 2017.

INDEX

TAIWAN AND THE WORLD

Good Wife, Wise Mother, by Fang Yu Hu

Taiwan Lives: A Social and Political History, by Niki J. P. Alsford

Contested Taiwan: Sovereignty, Social Movements, and Party Formation, by Lev Nachman

www.ingramcontent.com/pod-product-compliance
Lightning Source LLC
Chambersburg PA
CBHW031130270326
41929CB00011B/1569

* 9 7 8 0 2 9 5 7 5 3 9 2 8 *